TEACHER'S GUIDE

Connected Mathematics 2™

Shapes and Designs

Two-Dimensional Geometry

Glenda Lappan
James T. Fey
William M. Fitzgerald
Susan N. Friel
Elizabeth Difanis Phillips

PEARSON

Boston, Massachusetts · Glenview, Illinois · Shoreview, Minnesota · Upper Saddle River, New Jersey

Connected Mathematics™ was developed at Michigan State University with financial support from the Michigan State University Office of the Provost, Computing and Technology, and the College of Natural Science.

This material is based upon work supported by the National Science Foundation under Grant No. MDR 9150217 and Grant No. ESI 9986372. Opinions expressed are those of the authors and not necessarily those of the Foundation.

The Michigan State University authors and administration have agreed that all MSU royalties arising from this publication will be devoted to purposes supported by the Department of Mathematics and the MSU Mathematics Enrichment Fund.

Acknowledgments appear on page 117, which constitutes an extension of this copyright page. **Acknowledgments** for the student pages appear on student page 99, which constitutes an extension of this copyright page.

PEARSON

13-digit ISBN 978-0-13-366187-3
10-digit ISBN 0-13-366187-3
4 5 6 7 8 9 10 -V011- 14 13 12 11 10

Authors of Connected Mathematics

(from left to right) Glenda Lappan, Betty Phillips, Susan Friel, Bill Fitzgerald, Jim Fey

Glenda Lappan is a University Distinguished Professor in the Department of Mathematics at Michigan State University. Her research and development interests are in the connected areas of students' learning of mathematics and mathematics teachers' professional growth and change related to the development and enactment of K–12 curriculum materials.

James T. Fey is a Professor of Curriculum and Instruction and Mathematics at the University of Maryland. His consistent professional interest has been development and research focused on curriculum materials that engage middle and high school students in problem-based collaborative investigations of mathematical ideas and their applications.

William M. Fitzgerald (*Deceased*) was a Professor in the Department of Mathematics at Michigan State University. His early research was on the use of concrete materials in supporting student learning and led to the development of teaching materials for laboratory environments. Later he helped develop a teaching model to support student experimentation with mathematics.

Susan N. Friel is a Professor of Mathematics Education in the School of Education at the University of North Carolina at Chapel Hill. Her research interests focus on statistics education for middle-grade students and, more broadly, on teachers' professional development and growth in teaching mathematics K–8.

Elizabeth Difanis Phillips is a Senior Academic Specialist in the Mathematics Department of Michigan State University. She is interested in teaching and learning mathematics for both teachers and students. These interests have led to curriculum and professional development projects at the middle school and high school levels, as well as projects related to the teaching and learning of algebra across the grades.

CMP2 Development Staff

Teacher Collaborator in Residence

Yvonne Grant
Michigan State University

Administrative Assistant

Judith Martus Miller
Michigan State University

Production and Field Site Manager

Lisa Keller
Michigan State University

Technical and Editorial Support

Brin Keller, Peter Lappan, Jim Laser, Michael Masterson, Stacey Miceli

Assessment Team

June Bailey and **Debra Sobko** (Apollo Middle School, Rochester, New York), **George Bright** (University of North Carolina, Greensboro), **Gwen Ranzau Campbell** (Sunrise Park Middle School, White Bear Lake, Minnesota), **Holly DeRosia, Kathy Dole,** and **Teri Keusch** (Portland Middle School, Portland, Michigan), **Mary Beth Schmitt** (Traverse City East Junior High School, Traverse City, Michigan), **Genni Steele** (Central Middle School, White Bear Lake, Minnesota), **Jacqueline Stewart** (Okemos, Michigan), **Elizabeth Tye** (Magnolia Junior High School, Magnolia, Arkansas)

Development Assistants

At Lansing Community College *Undergraduate Assistant:* **James Brinegar**

At Michigan State University *Graduate Assistants:* **Dawn Berk, Emily Bouck, Bulent Buyukbozkirli, Kuo-Liang Chang, Christopher Danielson, Srinivasa Dharmavaram, Deb Johanning, Wesley Kretzschmar, Kelly Rivette, Sarah Sword, Tat Ming Sze, Marie Turini, Jeffrey Wanko;** *Undergraduate Assistants:* **Daniel Briggs, Jeffrey Chapin, Jade Corsé, Elisha Hardy, Alisha Harold, Elizabeth Keusch, Julia Letoutchaia, Karen Loeffler, Brian Oliver, Carl Oliver, Evonne Pedawi, Lauren Rebrovich**

At the University of Maryland *Graduate Assistants:* **Kim Harris Bethea, Kara Karch**

At the University of North Carolina (Chapel Hill) *Graduate Assistants:* **Mark Ellis, Trista Stearns;** *Undergraduate Assistant:* **Daniel Smith**

Advisory Board for CMP2

Thomas Banchoff
Professor of Mathematics
Brown University
Providence, Rhode Island

Anne Bartel
Mathematics Coordinator
Minneapolis Public Schools
Minneapolis, Minnesota

Hyman Bass
Professor of Mathematics
University of Michigan
Ann Arbor, Michigan

Joan Ferrini-Mundy
Associate Dean of the College of Natural Science; Professor
Michigan State University
East Lansing, Michigan

James Hiebert
Professor
University of Delaware
Newark, Delaware

Susan Hudson Hull
Charles A. Dana Center
University of Texas
Austin, Texas

Michele Luke
Mathematics Curriculum Coordinator
West Junior High
Minnetonka, Minnesota

Kay McClain
Assistant Professor of Mathematics Education
Vanderbilt University
Nashville, Tennessee

Edward Silver
Professor; Chair of Educational Studies
University of Michigan
Ann Arbor, Michigan

Judith Sowder
Professor Emerita
San Diego State University
San Diego, California

Lisa Usher
Mathematics Resource Teacher
California Academy of Mathematics and Science
San Pedro, California

Field Test Sites for CMP2

During the development of the revised edition of *Connected Mathematics* (CMP2), more than 100 classroom teachers have field-tested materials at 49 school sites in 12 states and the District of Columbia. This classroom testing occurred over three academic years (2001 through 2004), allowing careful study of the effectiveness of each of the 24 units that comprise the program. A special thanks to the students and teachers at these pilot schools.

Arkansas

Magnolia Public Schools
Kittena Bell*, Judith Trowell*; *Central Elementary School:* Maxine Broom, Betty Eddy, Tiffany Fallin, Bonnie Flurry, Carolyn Monk, Elizabeth Tye; *Magnolia Junior High School:* Monique Bryan, Ginger Cook, David Graham, Shelby Lamkin

Colorado

Boulder Public Schools
Nevin Platt Middle School: Judith Koenig

St. Vrain Valley School District, Longmont
Westview Middle School: Colleen Beyer, Kitty Canupp, Ellie Decker*, Peggy McCarthy, Tanya deNobrega, Cindy Payne, Ericka Pilon, Andrew Roberts

District of Columbia

Capitol Hill Day School: Ann Lawrence

Georgia

University of Georgia, Athens
Brad Findell

Madison Public Schools
Morgan County Middle School: Renee Burgdorf, Lynn Harris, Nancy Kurtz, Carolyn Stewart

Maine

Falmouth Public Schools
Falmouth Middle School: Donna Erikson, Joyce Hebert, Paula Hodgkins, Rick Hogan, David Legere, Cynthia Martin, Barbara Stiles, Shawn Towle*

Michigan

Portland Public Schools
Portland Middle School: Mark Braun, Holly DeRosia, Kathy Dole*, Angie Foote, Teri Keusch, Tammi Wardwell

Traverse City Area Public Schools
Bertha Vos Elementary: Kristin Sak; *Central Grade School:* Michelle Clark; Jody Meyers; *Eastern Elementary:* Karrie Tufts; *Interlochen Elementary:* Mary McGee-Cullen; *Long Lake Elementary:* Julie Faulkner*, Charlie Maxbauer, Katherine Sleder; *Norris Elementary:* Hope Slanaker; *Oak Park Elementary:* Jessica Steed; *Traverse Heights Elementary:* Jennifer Wolfert; *Westwoods Elementary:* Nancy Conn; *Old Mission Peninsula School:* Deb Larimer; *Traverse City East Junior High:* Ivanka Berkshire, Ruthanne Kladder, Jan Palkowski, Jane Peterson, Mary Beth Schmitt; *Traverse City West Junior High:* Dan Fouch*, Ray Fouch

Sturgis Public Schools
Sturgis Middle School: Ellen Eisele

Minnesota

Burnsville School District 191
Hidden Valley Elementary: Stephanie Cin, Jane McDevitt

Hopkins School District 270
Alice Smith Elementary: Sandra Cowing, Kathleen Gustafson, Martha Mason, Scott Stillman; *Eisenhower Elementary:* Chad Bellig, Patrick Berger, Nancy Glades, Kye Johnson, Shane Wasserman, Victoria Wilson; *Gatewood Elementary:* Sarah Ham, Julie Kloos, Janine Pung, Larry Wade; *Glen Lake Elementary:* Jacqueline Cramer, Kathy Hering, Cecelia Morris, Robb Trenda; *Katherine Curren Elementary:* Diane Bancroft, Sue DeWit, John Wilson; *L. H. Tanglen Elementary:* Kevin Athmann, Lisa Becker, Mary LaBelle, Kathy Rezac, Roberta Severson; *Meadowbrook Elementary:* Jan Gauger, Hildy Shank, Jessica Zimmerman; *North Junior High:* Laurel Hahn, Kristin Lee, Jodi Markuson, Bruce Mestemacher, Laurel Miller, Bonnie Rinker, Jeannine Salzer, Sarah Shafer, Cam Stottler; *West Junior High:* Alicia Beebe, Kristie Earl, Nobu Fujii, Pam Georgetti, Susan Gilbert, Regina Nelson Johnson, Debra Lindstrom, Michele Luke*, Jon Sorensen

Minneapolis School District 1
Ann Sullivan K–8 School: Bronwyn Collins; Anne Bartel* (Curriculum and Instruction Office)

Wayzata School District 284
Central Middle School: Sarajane Myers, Dan Nielsen, Tanya Ravnholdt

White Bear Lake School District 624
Central Middle School: Amy Jorgenson, Michelle Reich, Brenda Sammon

New York

New York City Public Schools
IS 89: Yelena Aynbinder, Chi-Man Ng, Nina Rapaport, Joel Spengler, Phyllis Tam*, Brent Wyso; *Wagner Middle School:* Jason Appel, Intissar Fernandez, Yee Gee Get, Richard Goldstein, Irving Marcus, Sue Norton, Bernadita Owens, Jennifer Rehn*, Kevin Yuhas

* indicates a Field Test Site Coordinator

Ohio

Talawanda School District, Oxford
Talawanda Middle School: Teresa Abrams, Larry Brock, Heather Brosey, Julie Churchman, Monna Even, Karen Fitch, Bob George, Amanda Klee, Pat Meade, Sandy Montgomery, Barbara Sherman, Lauren Steidl

Miami University
Jeffrey Wanko*

Springfield Public Schools
Rockway School: Jim Mamer

Pennsylvania

Pittsburgh Public Schools
Kenneth Labuskes, Marianne O'Connor, Mary Lynn Raith*; *Arthur J. Rooney Middle School:* David Hairston, Stamatina Mousetis, Alfredo Zangaro; *Frick International Studies Academy:* Suzanne Berry, Janet Falkowski, Constance Finseth, Romika Hodge, Frank Machi; *Reizenstein Middle School:* Jeff Baldwin, James Brautigam, Lorena Burnett, Glen Cobbett, Michael Jordan, Margaret Lazur, Tamar McPherson, Melissa Munnell, Holly Neely, Ingrid Reed, Dennis Reft

Texas

Austin Independent School District
Bedichek Middle School: Lisa Brown, Jennifer Glasscock, Vicki Massey

El Paso Independent School District
Cordova Middle School: Armando Aguirre, Anneliesa Durkes, Sylvia Guzman, Pat Holguin*, William Holguin, Nancy Nava, Laura Orozco, Michelle Peña, Roberta Rosen, Patsy Smith, Jeremy Wolf

Plano Independent School District
Patt Henry, James Wohlgehagen*; *Frankford Middle School:* Mandy Baker, Cheryl Butsch, Amy Dudley, Betsy Eshelman, Janet Greene, Cort Haynes, Kathy Letchworth, Kay Marshall, Kelly McCants, Amy Reck, Judy Scott, Syndy Snyder, Lisa Wang; *Wilson Middle School:* Darcie Bane, Amanda Bedenko, Whitney Evans, Tonelli Hatley, Sarah (Becky) Higgs, Kelly Johnston, Rebecca McElligott, Kay Neuse, Cheri Slocum, Kelli Straight

Washington

Evergreen School District
Shahala Middle School: Nicole Abrahamsen, Terry Coon*, Carey Doyle, Sheryl Drechsler, George Gemma, Gina Helland, Amy Hilario, Darla Lidyard, Sean McCarthy, Tilly Meyer, Willow Nuewelt, Todd Parsons, Brian Pederson, Stan Posey, Shawn Scott, Craig Sjoberg, Lynette Sundstrom, Charles Switzer, Luke Youngblood

Wisconsin

Beaver Dam Unified School District
Beaver Dam Middle School: Jim Braemer, Jeanne Frick, Jessica Greatens, Barbara Link, Dennis McCormick, Karen Michels, Nancy Nichols*, Nancy Palm, Shelly Stelsel, Susan Wiggins

---

* indicates a Field Test Site Coordinator

Reviews of CMP to Guide Development of CMP2

Before writing for CMP2 began or field tests were conducted, the first edition of *Connected Mathematics* was submitted to the mathematics faculties of school districts from many parts of the country and to 80 individual reviewers for extensive comments.

School District Survey Reviews of CMP

Arizona
Madison School District #38 (Phoenix)

Arkansas
Cabot School District, Little Rock School District, Magnolia School District

California
Los Angeles Unified School District

Colorado
St. Vrain Valley School District (Longmont)

Florida
Leon County Schools (Tallahassee)

Illinois
School District #21 (Wheeling)

Indiana
Joseph L. Block Junior High (East Chicago)

Kentucky
Fayette County Public Schools (Lexington)

Maine
Selection of Schools

Massachusetts
Selection of Schools

Michigan
Sparta Area Schools

Minnesota
Hopkins School District

Texas
Austin Independent School District, The El Paso Collaborative for Academic Excellence, Plano Independent School District

Wisconsin
Platteville Middle School

Individual Reviewers of CMP

Arkansas
Deborah Cramer; Robby Frizzell *(Taylor)*; Lowell Lynde *(University of Arkansas, Monticello)*; Leigh Manzer *(Norfork)*; Lynne Roberts *(Emerson High School, Emerson)*; Tony Timms *(Cabot Public Schools)*; Judith Trowell *(Arkansas Department of Higher Education)*

California
José Alcantar *(Gilroy)*; Eugenie Belcher *(Gilroy)*; Marian Pasternack *(Lowman M. S. T. Center, North Hollywood)*; Susana Pezoa *(San Jose)*; Todd Rabusin *(Hollister)*; Margaret Siegfried *(Ocala Middle School, San Jose)*; Polly Underwood *(Ocala Middle School, San Jose)*

Colorado
Janeane Golliher *(St. Vrain Valley School District, Longmont)*; Judith Koenig *(Nevin Platt Middle School, Boulder)*

Florida
Paige Loggins *(Swift Creek Middle School, Tallahassee)*

Illinois
Jan Robinson *(School District #21, Wheeling)*

Indiana
Frances Jackson *(Joseph L. Block Junior High, East Chicago)*

Kentucky
Natalee Feese *(Fayette County Public Schools, Lexington)*

Maine
Betsy Berry *(Maine Math & Science Alliance, Augusta)*

Maryland
Joseph Gagnon *(University of Maryland, College Park)*; Paula Maccini *(University of Maryland, College Park)*

Massachusetts
George Cobb *(Mt. Holyoke College, South Hadley)*; Cliff Kanold *(University of Massachusetts, Amherst)*

Michigan
Mary Bouck *(Farwell Area Schools)*; Carol Dorer *(Slauson Middle School, Ann Arbor)*; Carrie Heaney *(Forsythe Middle School, Ann Arbor)*; Ellen Hopkins *(Clague Middle School, Ann Arbor)*; Teri Keusch *(Portland Middle School, Portland)*; Valerie Mills *(Oakland Schools, Waterford)*; Mary Beth Schmitt *(Traverse City East Junior High, Traverse City)*; Jack Smith *(Michigan State University, East Lansing)*; Rebecca Spencer *(Sparta Middle School, Sparta)*; Ann Marie Nicoll Turner *(Tappan Middle School, Ann Arbor)*; Scott Turner *(Scarlett Middle School, Ann Arbor)*

Minnesota
Margarita Alvarez *(Olson Middle School, Minneapolis)*; Jane Amundson *(Nicollet Junior High, Burnsville)*; Anne Bartel *(Minneapolis Public Schools)*; Gwen Ranzau Campbell *(Sunrise Park Middle School, White Bear Lake)*; Stephanie Cin *(Hidden Valley Elementary, Burnsville)*; Joan Garfield *(University of Minnesota, Minneapolis)*; Gretchen Hall *(Richfield Middle School, Richfield)*; Jennifer Larson *(Olson Middle School, Minneapolis)*; Michele Luke *(West Junior High, Minnetonka)*; Jeni Meyer *(Richfield Junior High, Richfield)*; Judy Pfingsten *(Inver Grove Heights Middle School, Inver Grove Heights)*; Sarah Shafer *(North Junior High, Minnetonka)*; Genni Steele *(Central Middle School, White Bear Lake)*; Victoria Wilson *(Eisenhower Elementary, Hopkins)*; Paul Zorn *(St. Olaf College, Northfield)*

New York
Debra Altenau-Bartolino *(Greenwich Village Middle School, New York)*; Doug Clements *(University of Buffalo)*; Francis Curcio *(New York University, New York)*; Christine Dorosh *(Clinton School for Writers, Brooklyn)*; Jennifer Rehn *(East Side Middle School, New York)*; Phyllis Tam *(IS 89 Lab School, New York)*; Marie Turini *(Louis Armstrong Middle School, New York)*; Lucy West *(Community School District 2, New York)*; Monica Witt *(Simon Baruch Intermediate School 104, New York)*

Pennsylvania
Robert Aglietti *(Pittsburgh)*; Sharon Mihalich *(Freeport)*; Jennifer Plumb *(South Hills Middle School, Pittsburgh)*; Mary Lynn Raith *(Pittsburgh Public Schools)*

Texas
Michelle Bittick *(Austin Independent School District)*; Margaret Cregg *(Plano Independent School District)*; Sheila Cunningham *(Klein Independent School District)*; Judy Hill *(Austin Independent School District)*; Patricia Holguin *(El Paso Independent School District)*; Bonnie McNemar *(Arlington)*; Kay Neuse *(Plano Independent School District)*; Joyce Polanco *(Austin Independent School District)*; Marge Ramirez *(University of Texas at El Paso)*; Pat Rossman *(Baker Campus, Austin)*; Cindy Schimek *(Houston)*; Cynthia Schneider *(Charles A. Dana Center, University of Texas at Austin)*; Uri Treisman *(Charles A. Dana Center, University of Texas at Austin)*; Jacqueline Weilmuenster *(Grapevine-Colleyville Independent School District)*; LuAnn Weynand *(San Antonio)*; Carmen Whitman *(Austin Independent School District)*; James Wohlgehagen *(Plano Independent School District)*

Washington
Ramesh Gangolli *(University of Washington, Seattle)*

Wisconsin
Susan Lamon *(Marquette University, Hales Corner)*; Steve Reinhart *(retired, Chippewa Falls Middle School, Eau Claire)*

Table of Contents

Shapes and Designs

The Student Edition pages for the Unit Opener follow page 16.

Unit Introduction

Shapes and Designs

Two-Dimensional Geometry

Goals of the Unit

In *Shapes and Designs,* students will

- Understand some important properties of polygons and recognize polygonal shapes both in and out of the classroom
- Investigate the symmetries of a shape—rotation or reflection
- Estimate the measure of any angle using reference to a right angle and other benchmark angles
- Use an angle ruler for making more accurate angle measurements
- Explore parallel lines and angles created by lines intersecting parallel lines
- Find patterns that help determine angle sums of polygons
- Determine which polygons fit together to cover a flat surface and why
- Explain the property of triangles that makes them useful as a stable structure for building
- Find that the sum of two side lengths of a triangle is greater than the third side length
- Find that the sum of three side lengths of a quadrilateral is greater than the fourth side length
- Draw or sketch polygons with certain properties
- Reason about and solve problems involving shapes

Developing Students' Mathematical Habits

The overall goal of *Connected Mathematics* is to help students develop sound mathematical habits. As students work on the problems of this unit, they will be asking themselves important questions about situations involving shapes such as:

- *What kinds of shapes/polygons will cover a flat surface?*
- *What do these shapes have in common?*
- *How do simple polygons work together to make more complex shapes?*
- *How can angle measures be estimated?*
- *How much accuracy is needed in measuring angles?*

Overview

Shapes and Designs is the first unit in the geometry strand. It develops students' ability to recognize, display, analyze, measure, and reason about the shapes and visual patterns that are important features of our world. It builds on students' elementary school exposure to simple shapes, as they begin analyzing the properties that make certain shapes special. The unit focuses on polygons and on the side and angle relationships of regular and irregular polygons (circles and other curves are explored in later units).

In the Student Edition, the introduction develops the broad theme of the unit: out of all the shapes we use as basic components in buildings and art, some simple figures occur again and again because of properties that make them attractive and useful. The goal of *Shapes and Designs* is to have students discover and analyze many of the key properties of polygonal shapes that make them useful and attractive. As students become observant of the multitude of shapes that surround them and aware of the reasons that shapes are used for specific purposes, they will be amazed by the visual pleasure and practical insights their new knowledge provides. We suspect that teachers will share this eye-opening experience, finding new signs of beauty and structural significance in the things they see everyday.

The approach to geometry in this unit is somewhat unique. First, the primary focus of the unit is on recognition of properties of shapes that have important practical and aesthetic implications, not on simple classification and naming of figures. While some attention is given to naming familiar figures, each investigation focuses on particular key properties of figures and the importance of those properties in applications. For example, students are periodically asked to identify differences between squares, rectangles that are not squares, and parallelograms that are not rectangles. We use a few special names for types of quadrilaterals (square, rectangle, and parallelogram) and triangles (isosceles, equilateral, and scalene). We frequently ask students to find and describe places where they see polygons of particular types and to puzzle over why those particular shapes are used.

Summary of Investigations

Investigation 1

Bees and Polygons

Students sort polygons by common properties and develop rotation and reflection symmetries of a shape. Students also explore which shapes will tile a plane.

Investigation 2

Polygons and Angles

This investigation introduces three basic ways of thinking about angles (turn, wedge, or rays) and the ideas behind angle measurement. It gives students practice in estimating angle measurements based on a right angle. An angle ruler is introduced, allowing more precise measurements. Students look at the consequences of making measurement errors. They also explore the angles formed by a transversal and parallel lines. This will help students to better understand parallelograms.

Investigation 3

Polygon Properties and Tiling

Investigation 3 develops angle sums of polygons. Students begin by measuring the angles of regular polygons and looking for patterns among the angle sums. As the number of sides of a polygon increases by one, the sum increases by 180°. The teacher demonstrates the sum of the angles of a triangle and the sum of the angles of a quadrilateral.

In this investigation, geometric arguments are used to help students confirm their conjectures about angle sums. Students see that the sum of the angles of a polygon is based on the sum of the angles of a triangle. That is, a polygon is subdivided into triangles. Tiling is revisited and students use their knowledge about the measures of interior angles and angle sums of regular polygons to explain why some regular polygons tile and others do not.

Two other ideas are also explored: (1) in a polygon the exterior angle and its corresponding interior angle sum to 180° and (2) all the exterior angles of any polygon sum to 360°.

Investigation 4

Building Polygons

Investigation 4 looks at the condition on side lengths needed to form a triangle and then a quadrilateral. The last problem is a game using geoboards in which students change a quadrilateral by moving one or more vertices to form a new quadrilateral that fits a new set of criteria.

Mathematics Background

The development in *Shapes and Designs* is based on the van Hiele theory of geometry learning: we begin with recognition of shapes, then move to classification of shapes, and then to analysis of properties of those shapes. The overall development progresses from tactile and visual experiences to more general and abstract reasoning. We assume students have had prior exposure to the basic shapes and their names.

Polygons

There are several different, but equivalent, definitions of polygons. Each of them is a bit sophisticated. Students at this level need informal experiences with the concept of polygons before they see a more formal definition. At the beginning of this unit we say, "*A polygon is a collection of line segments put together in a special way*." Students look at two sets of shapes—polygons and non-polygons. After studying these two sets, and answering the question, "*What properties does a shape need to be a polygon?*," students develop a basic understanding of polygons that will continue to grow throughout the unit.

An important distinction to keep in mind in this unit and other geometric units, is that a polygon consists of only the line segments (or sides) that make up the polygon. These line segments enclose a region (of the plane). This region is sometimes called the **interior of the polygon** or **polygonal region**. The points in the interior are not part of the polygon, and the points on the sides of the polygon are not part of the interior. We can also talk about the exterior region of a polygon—this is the set of points that are neither on the polygon nor in the interior of the polygon. The distinctions that hold for polygons and polygonal regions also hold for any closed plane figure, including circles.

In another sixth grade unit, *Covering and Surrounding*, the primary focus is on **perimeter of the polygon** and **area of the polygonal region**. Technically, when we talk about area we should say area of the rectangular region or triangular region, etc., but it has become common practice to say area of a rectangle. It is understood that this is the area of the interior of the rectangle. The distinction is important to note so that students do not go away with unintentional misconceptions from the work or discussion in class. These ideas will be addressed more directly in the student materials of *Covering and Surrounding*.

Sorting Shapes

Before exploring tessellations, students spend a little time on developing understanding of polygons. Students use the Shapes Set (a set of plastic polygons) to sort the shapes into categories or subsets with specific properties that they have in common. Some may sort by regular and non-regular polygons. A regular polygon is a polygon whose side lengths are all equal and whose interior angle measures are all equal. Students look at specific quadrilaterals and form an intuitive understanding of parallelograms and non-parallelograms from their prior knowledge of squares and rectangles. They also sort triangles by the length of their sides—connecting with prior knowledge of scalene, isosceles, and equilateral triangles. Students use shapes to investigate which shapes will tile a surface. This is a beginning attempt to answer the question of why the bees use a hexagon as a shape of their honeycombs. For those shapes that do tile, students notice that the sides of the polygon must match and that the interior angles of a polygon must fit exactly around a point in the plane.

Symmetries of Shapes

Students explore the symmetries of shapes, such as reflection (or line) symmetry and rotation (or turn) symmetry. Reflection symmetry is also called mirror symmetry, since the half of the figure on one side of the line looks like it is being reflected in a mirror. Rotation symmetry is also called turn symmetry, because you can turn the figure around its center point and produce the same image.

Reflection Symmetry

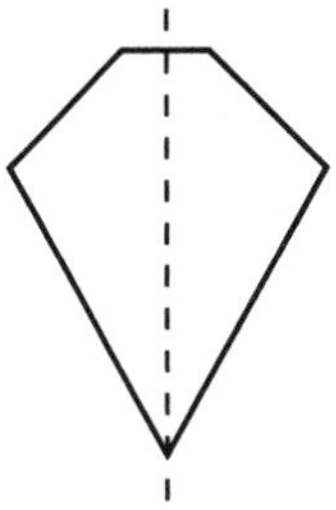

A polygon with reflection symmetry has two halves that are mirror images of each other. If the polygon is folded over the line of symmetry, the two halves of the polygon match exactly.

Rotation Symmetry

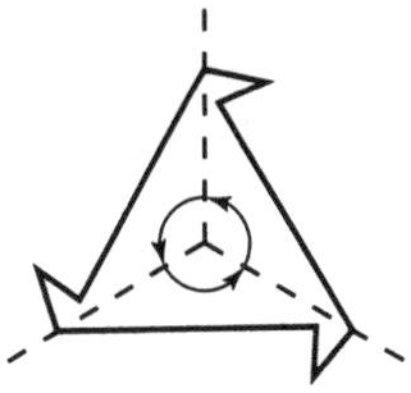

All shapes have "trivial" rotation symmetry in the sense that they can be rotated 360° and look the same as before the rotation. When we determine whether or not a shape "has" rotation symmetry we check for rotation symmetry for angles less than 360°. However the convention is that once we determine that a shape has rotation symmetry, when counting the rotation symmetries we include that "trivial" rotation as well.

For example, the shape at the right has two rotation symmetries: 180° and 360°. This convention works nicely because we can say that a square has four rotation symmetries, a regular pentagon has five rotation symmetries, and a regular hexagon has six rotation symmetries.

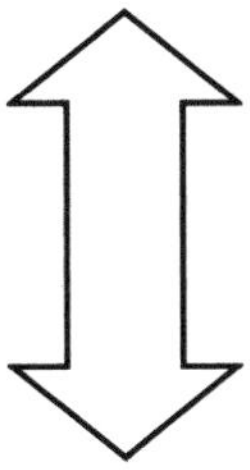

A polygon with rotation symmetry can be turned around its center point less than a full turn and still look the same at certain angles of rotation.

Throughout the unit students are encouraged to look for symmetries of a shape.

Tessellations

The first big question presented in *Shapes and Designs,* to motivate analysis of polygons, is the problem of tiling or tessellating a flat surface. The key is that, among the regular polygons (polygons with all edges the same length and all angles the same measure), only equilateral triangles, squares, and regular hexagons will tile a plane.

triangles

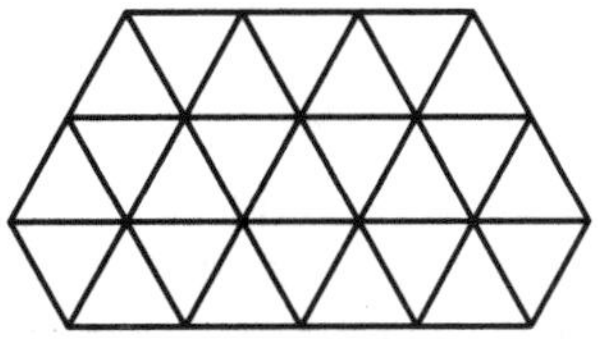

squares

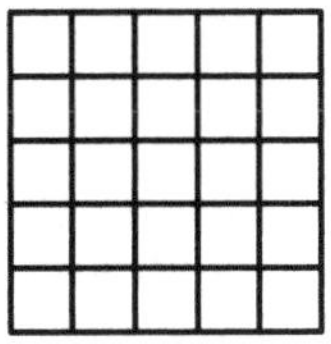

hexagons

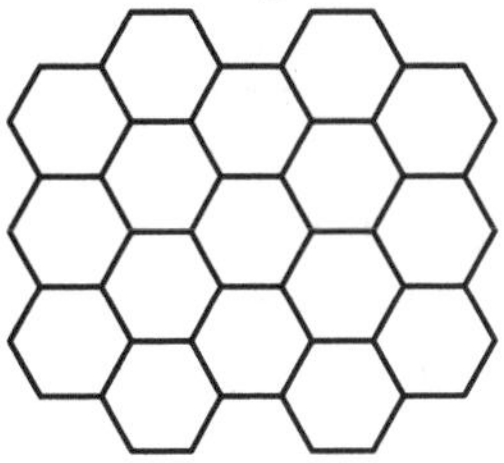

There are other combinations of figures that can be used to tile a plane. Three are given below:

squares and triangles

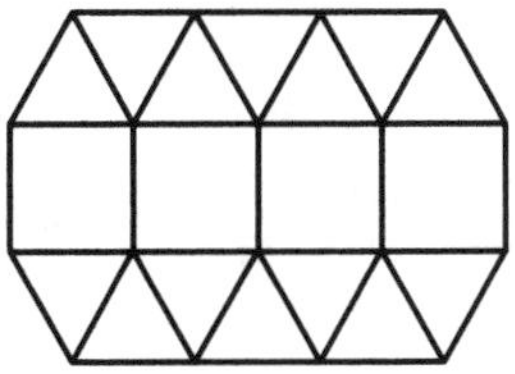

triangles and hexagons

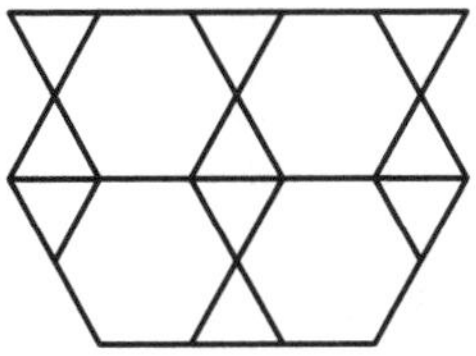

squares and octagons

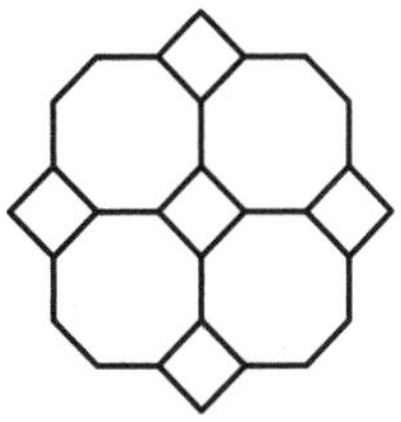

Some teachers use this opportunity to explain to students a short hand notation for describing the shapes and combinations of shapes used to tessellate. For example, to describe the tiling of squares one would write 4, 4, 4, 4 and for the triangles 3, 3, 3, 3, 3, 3. To describe the combination of shapes presented, you could write 4, 3, 3, 3, 4. The notation identifies the shape by its number of sides. It also tells the number of shapes, and the order in which the shapes surround a point. You could suggest that the class look for interesting tiling patterns in their homes or in school. Have them make a sketch of any designs they find.

For regular polygons to tile a plane, the angle measure of an interior angle must be a factor of 360. So an equilateral triangle (60° angles), a square (90° angles), and a regular hexagon (120° angles) are the only three regular polygons that can tile a plane. Copies of each of these will fit exactly around a point in a plane.

There are eight combinations of regular polygons that will tile so that each vertex has exactly the same pattern of polygons. These are sometimes called semi-regular or Archimedean tessellations. (note the numbers in parentheses refer to the polygon by side number—8 means a regular octagon, 6 means a regular hexagon, etc.—and the order they appear around a vertex of the tiling):

2 octagons and 1 square (8-8-4)
1 square, 1 hexagon, and 1 dodecagon (4-6-12)
4 triangles and 1 hexagon (3-3-3-3-6)
3 triangles and 2 squares (4-3-4-3-3)
1 triangle, 2 squares and 1 hexagon (4-3-4-6)
1 triangle and 2 dodecagons (3-12-12)
3 triangles and 2 squares (4-3-3-3-4)
2 triangles and 2 hexagons (3-6-3-6)

See page 72 for pictures of these arrangements.

Note that there are two arrangements with triangles and squares, but depending on the arrangement they produce different tile patterns, so order is important.

In addition, any triangle or quadrilateral will tile a plane as in these examples:

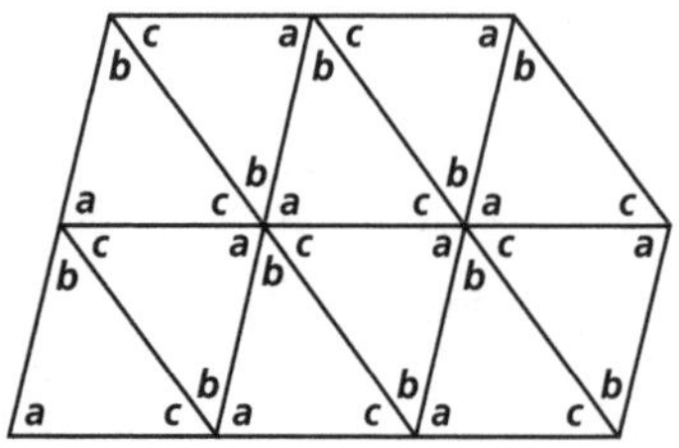

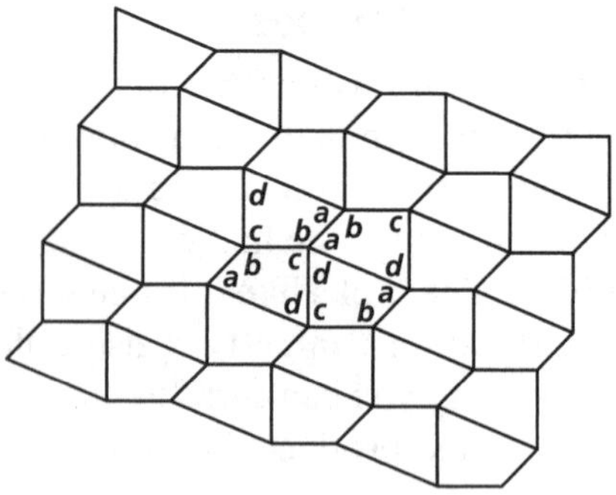

When one understands the important properties of simple polygons, one can create an abundance of aesthetically appealing tiling patterns, complete with artistic embellishments in the style of artist M. C. Escher. However, it is the discovery of what important properties of the figures make the tiling possible, not the tiling question itself, that is one of the foci of the unit.

Angle Measures

Students explore angles in depth. The shape of a polygon is linked to the measures of angles formed where its sides meet. (The sides or edges of an angle are also called rays. The vertex of an angle is the point where the two rays meet or intersect.)

Work is done to relate angles to right angles, focusing on developing students' estimation skills with angles. They use simple factors and multiples of 90° turns to develop estimations. That is, they use 30°, 45°, 60°, 90°, 120°, 180°, 270°, and 360° as benchmarks to estimate angle size. Skills dealing with these benchmarks are further developed in a game called Four-In-a-Row.

The need for more precision requires techniques for measuring angles. A new measuring tool, the goniometer or angle ruler, a tool used in the medical field for measuring angle of motion or the flexibility in body joints, such as knees is introduced.

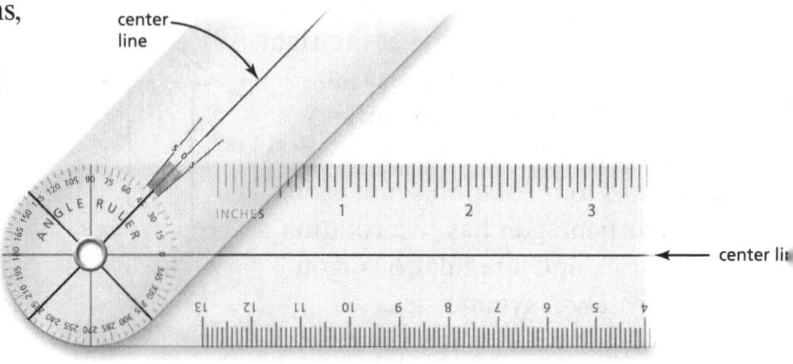

This diagram illustrates why another method for measuring angles with the angle ruler, called the gripping method, gives the same results as placing the rivet over the vertex of the angle being measured. The overlap of the sides of the ruler forms a rhombus as you separate them.

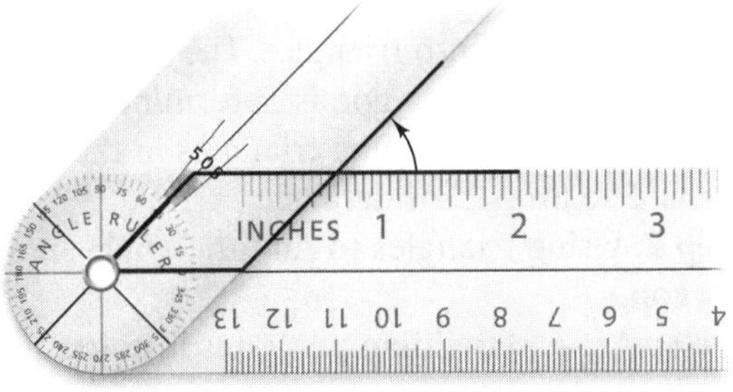

In a rhombus, opposite angles are equal. This means that the rhombus angle at the rivet and the opposite angle are equal. The angle opposite the rivet in the rhombus is also equal to the angle between the sides since they are vertical angles (i.e., angles formed by two intersecting lines). So, when you place a shape between the arms of the ruler, the angle at the rivet has the same measure as the angle between the arms.

We use students' intuitive knowledge of a right angle to define a one-degree angle as $\frac{1}{90}$ of a right angle (a 90° angle). Two important aspects of angles come into play in Problem 2.4 when students investigate the results of a measurement error that was made in the fatal flight of Amelia Earhart. The issue on the measure of an angle not being dependent of the lengths of the sides of the rays is a very important one. Students tend to have a hard time holding onto what is being measured when we measure an angle. Two things can cause confusion: the length of the rays and the distance between them. When we measure angles, we are measuring the "opening" or turn between the edges of the angle. The lengths of the two edges (rays) that form the angle do not affect the measure of the angle.

Angles of a Polygon

Consistent with formal mathematical definitions, we refer to *adjacent sides* and *adjacent angles* of a polygon.

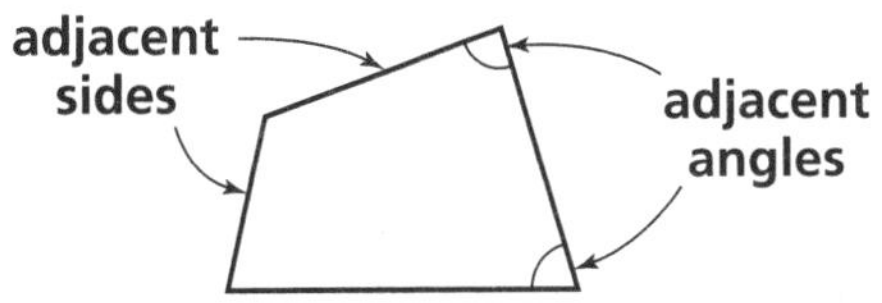

Some students may be familiar with another definition of adjacent angles for two angles that are not part of a polygon:

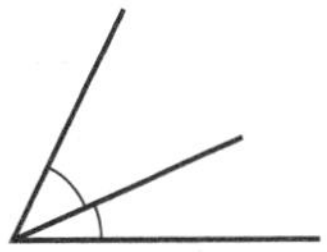

adjacent angles not in a polygon

With these students, you may prefer to use the alternate term *consecutive angles* when referring to adjacent angles in a polygon.

Angles and Parallel Lines

Students explore some interesting patterns among the angles created when a line cuts two or more parallel lines. Below is a pair of parallel lines that are cut by a third line. The line that intersects the parallel lines is called a transversal. As the transversal intersects the parallel lines, it creates several angles.

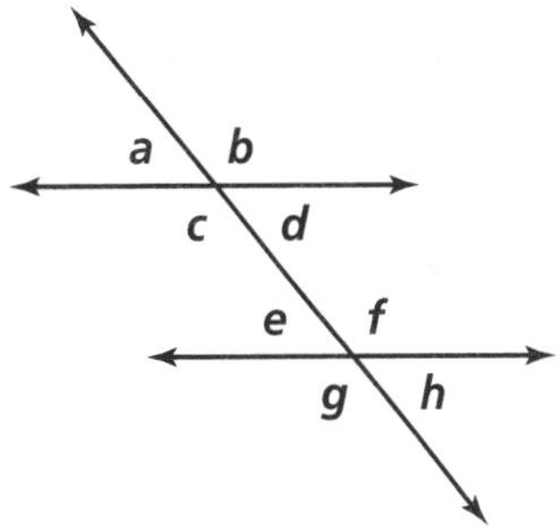

Angles a and e, angles b and f, angles c and g, and angles d and h are called corresponding angles. Angles d and e and angles c and f are alternate interior angles. Parallel lines cut by a transversal make equal corresponding angles and equal alternate interior angles. Two lines that intersect make two pairs of equal angles. In the diagram, angles b and c are equal, as are angles a

and d, e, and h, and f and g. These pairs of angles are called **vertical angles**. Angles b and d are **supplementary angles**. Their sum is 180°. At this point names are not stressed—only the relationship among angles. Students discover these relationships and others by looking at patterns.

Parallelograms are defined early in the unit as quadrilaterals with opposite sides of the same length and opposite angles of the same measure. A parallelogram can also be defined as a quadrilateral with opposite sides parallel. Parallel lines help explain these and other special features of parallelograms such as that the sum of the measures of two adjacent angles is 180°.

Students use these facts about angles formed by parallel lines and a transversal in an application problem to show that the sum of the angles of a triangle is 180°. In the picture below, if line l is parallel to line BC, then angles 1 and 4 are equal and angles 3 and 5 are equal. Since the sum of angles 1, 2, and 3 is 180, then by substitution the sum of angles 2, 4, and 5 is equal to 180°.

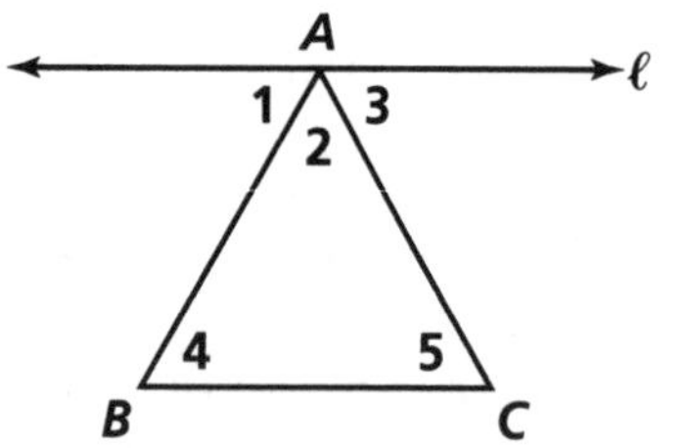

Note that the sum of the angles of a triangle and other polygons is first looked at experimentally, as discussed in the next section.

Sums of the Angles of Polygons

Step 1: Finding the angle sum of a triangle.

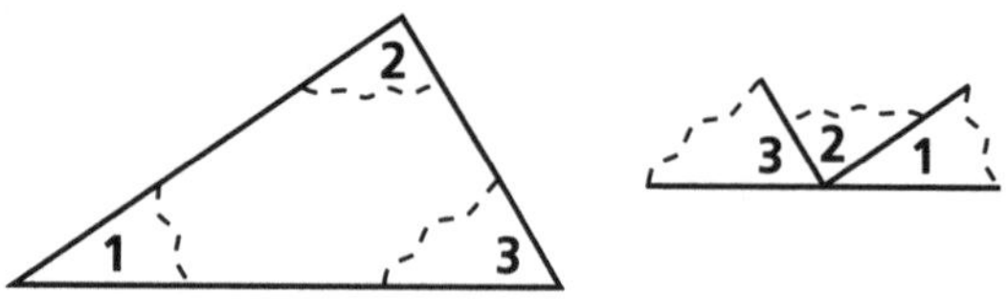

Students use their knowledge of 180° and 360° to experiment with the interior angles of a polygon. Students use three copies of a triangle. Each vertex in the triangle is numbered 1, 2, or 3. Students can arrange the three angles of the triangle around a point. The three angles form a 180° angle. This works for any triangle.

A similar experiment is conducted for any quadrilateral. The four angles of a quadrilateral will form a 360° angle or wrap around a point exactly once. A similar pattern holds for pentagons. The interior angles will form a 540° angle or wrap around a point one and one-half complete turns. For a hexagon it is 720° or two complete turns.

Also, to find the sum of the interior angles of a polygon with sides greater than three, the polygon can be subdivided into triangles. The sum of the interior angles of a polygon is determined by the number of non-overlapping triangles in the polygon. See Step 2 for details.

Step 2: Using triangles to find the angle sum of a polygon.

Method 1—subdividing polygons into triangles using diagonals

Some students will use the number of triangles to determine the sum of the angles for other polygons. For example, they may notice that by subdividing a polygon into triangles they will find that for pentagons there are three triangles and for hexagons there are four triangles. See a subdivided quadrilateral and pentagon below.

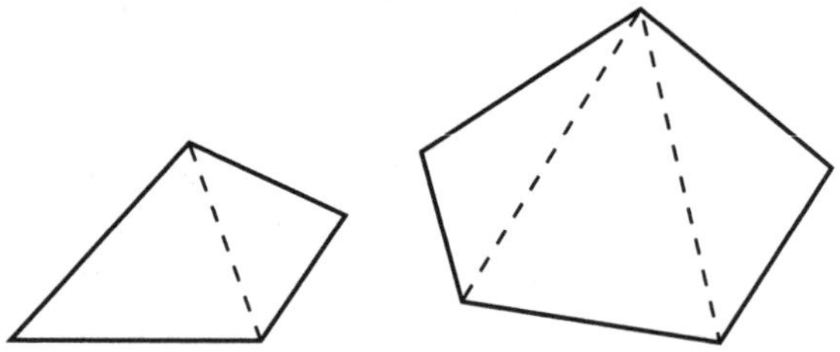

To reason about the angle sum in a polygon, you can triangulate the polygon: start at any vertex, and draw all the possible diagonals from that vertex. You can triangulate a square into two triangles, a pentagon into three triangles, a hexagon into four triangles, and so on. Each time the number of sides increases by one, the number of triangles increases by one, thus making a pattern: 3 sides give 1 triangle, 4 sides give 2 triangles, 5 sides give 3 triangles, 6 sides give 4 triangles, and so on.

We can use symbols to state a rule for this pattern. If we let N represent the number of sides in a polygon, then $(N - 2)$ represents the number of triangles we get by triangulating the polygon. If we multiply by 180° for each triangle, we have the formula: $(N - 2) \times 180° =$ the angle sum in an N-sided polygon. Note that this is true for both regular and irregular polygons.

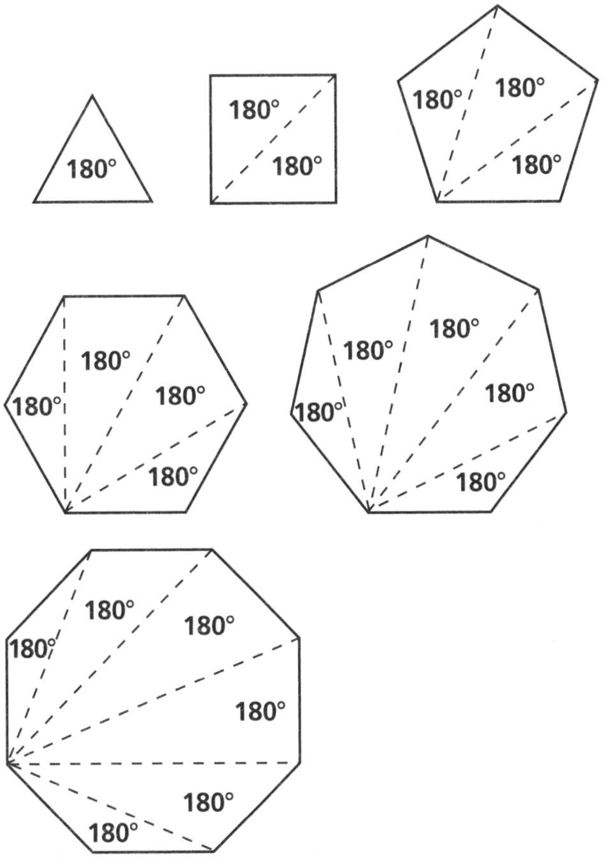

Method 2—subdividing polygons into triangles using a point in the interior of the polygon

Another method that students may use is to draw all the line segments from a point within a polygon to each vertex. This method subdivides the polygon into N triangles. In a quadrilateral, four triangles are formed. The number of triangles is the same as the number of vertices or sides of the quadrilateral. In the pentagon, five triangles are formed. Again, the number of triangles is equal to the number of sides or vertices of the pentagon.

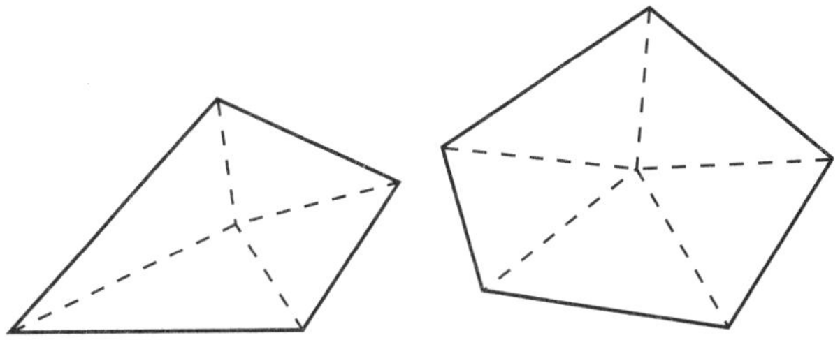

The sum of the angles of the four triangles in the quadrilateral is $180° \times 4$. But this sum includes 360° around the central point. Therefore, to find the sum of the interior angles of the quadrilateral, 360° must be subtracted from the sum of the angles of the four triangles. The sum of the interior angles of the quadrilateral is $180° \times (4) - 360° = 360°$.

The sum of the angles of the five triangles formed in a pentagon is $180° \times 5$. But this sum also includes 360° around the central point. So, to find the sum of the interior angles of a pentagon, 360° must be subtracted from the sum of the angles of the five triangles. The sum of the interior angles of the pentagon is $180° \times (5) - 360° = 540°$.

We notice that the sum of the interior angles of a quadrilateral or pentagon is 180° times the number of sides minus two. For the quadrilateral the sum is $180° (4 - 2)$ and for a pentagon the sum is $180° (5 - 2)$.

This method works for any polygon. For a polygon with N sides, the sum of its interior angles is: $180°(N) - 360° = 180°(N - 2)$.

The data from the methods above are arranged in a table, and students form the following generalizations. (Figure 1)

Figure 1

Regular Polygon	Number of Sides	Angle Sum	Measure of Interior Angle
Triangle	3	180	180 ÷ 3 = 60
Square	4	2(180) = 360	360 ÷ 4 = 90
Pentagon	5	3(180) = 540	540 ÷ 5 = 108
Hexagon	6	4(180) = 720	720 ÷ 6 = 120
Heptagon	7	5(180) = 900	900 ÷ 7 = 128.6
Octagon	8	6(180) = 1,080	1,080 ÷ 8 = 135
Nonagon	9	7(180) = 1,260	1,260 ÷ 9 = 140
Decagon	10	8(180) = 1,440	1,440 ÷ 10 = 144
N sides	*N*	(*N* −2)(180)	[(*N* −2)(180)] ÷ *N*

Interior Angles of Regular Polygons

If a polygon is regular, we can find the number of degrees in one of the angles by dividing the sum by the number of angles.

$\frac{(N - 2) \times 180°}{N}$ = the number of degrees in any angle of a regular N-sided polygon.

Students also notice that as the number of sides of a regular polygon increases, the measure for each interior angle also increases—it approaches 180°, which occurs as the shape of the polygon approaches that of a circle.

Exterior Angles of Regular Polygons

In a regular polygon of N sides the sum of the interior angles is $(N - 2)180°$. The measure of each angle is $\frac{(N - 2)180°}{N}$. So the measure of each corresponding exterior angle is

$180° - \frac{(N - 2)180°}{N}$.

The sum of N exterior angles

$$= N\left[180° - \frac{(N - 2)180°}{N}\right]$$
$$= 180°N - (N - 2)180°$$
$$= 180°N - 180°N + 360°$$
$$= 360°$$

Students arrive at this generalization by looking for patterns.

Exploring Side Lengths of Polygons

Students use polystrips to build triangles and quadrilaterals with given side lengths.

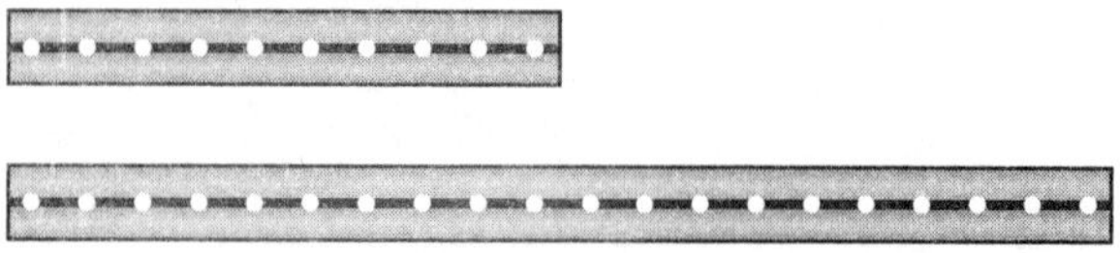

Students begin by considering the question of whether any three lengths will make a triangle. Students find that the sum of two side lengths of a triangle must be greater than the third side length. If the two side lengths equal the third side length, then the two smaller sides collapse or fit exactly on the third side and no triangle is formed. If the sum is smaller, then the two short sides collapse onto the third side, but do not fit exactly.

If a triangle is possible, then there is exactly one triangle that can be built. This explains the rigidity of triangles and the extensive use of triangular shapes in bracing in buildings: once three edges have been fitted together, they form a stable figure.

This side length result for triangles is called the **Triangle Inequality Theorem.** For example, if the side lengths are a, b, and c, then the sum of any two sides is greater than the third:

$a + b > c.$
$b + c > a.$
$c + a > b.$

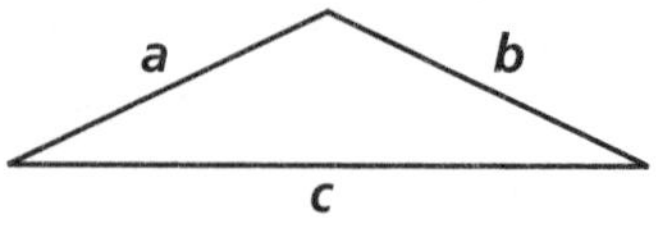

To make a quadrilateral, the sum of three side lengths must be greater than the fourth side length. If a quadrilateral can be built, different combinations of the side lengths will produce different-shaped quadrilaterals. Also by pushing on the vertex of a quadrilateral, the shape will change, thus producing different shapes with the same arrangement of side lengths.

A quadrilateral can be distorted into many other quadrilateral shapes, and can undergo a total collapse much more easily than a triangle. However, when a diagonal is inserted to form two triangles, the quadrilateral becomes rigid. Three examples of quadrilaterals that have corresponding sides with the same length are below.

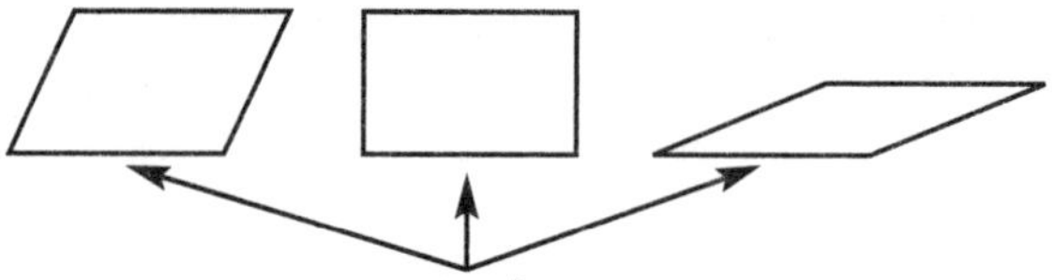

Content Connections to Other Units

Big Idea	Prior Work	Future Work
Understanding parts of polygons and how parts of polygons are related	Developing mathematical reasoning by analyzing integers and data (*Prime Time*); developing shape recognition skills (elementary school)	Studying properties of 3-D cube figures (*Ruins of Montarek ©2004*); exploring similarity of 2-D figures (*Stretching and Shrinking*); finding surface area and volume of 3-D figures (*Filling and Wrapping*)
Learning important properties of polygons that relate to the angles and sides of polygons	Developing classification skills through classifying integers (e.g., even, odd, abundant, deficient) and data (e.g., categorical or numerical) (*Prime Time*); developing shape recognition skills (elementary school)	Learning important properties of rectangles, triangles, and parallelograms (*Covering and Surrounding*); studying properties of 3-D cube figures (*Ruins of Montarek ©2004*); enlarging, shrinking, and distorting 2-D shapes (*Stretching and Shrinking*); learning properties of 3-D figures (*Filling and Wrapping*); learning and applying the Pythagorean Theorem (*Looking for Pythagoras*)
Creating tilings with polygons and determining the properties of shapes that can be used to tile a surface	Exploring how 2-D shapes fit together (elementary school)	Understanding area as the exact number of square units needed to cover a 2-D figure (*Covering and Surrounding*); subdividing figures into similar figures (*Stretching and Shrinking*); connecting tessellations to isometries (*Kaleidoscopes, Hubcaps, and Mirrors*)
Exploring symmetries in squares, rectangles, parallelograms, and equilateral triangles	Exploring symmetry informally by looking at shapes of data sets (*Data Distributions*)	Exploring symmetry informally by looking at shapes of data sets (*Data Distributions*) Identifying symmetry in 3-D cubic figures (*Ruins of Montarek ©2004*); connecting symmetry to isometries (*Kaleidoscopes, Hubcaps, and Mirrors*)
Developing understanding and techniques for measuring angles	Exploring measurement of line segments (elementary school)	Finding area and perimeter of 2-D figures (*Covering and Surrounding*)

Planning for the Unit

Pacing Suggestions and Materials

Investigations and Assessments	Pacing 45–50 min. classes	Materials for Students	Materials for Teachers
1 Bees and Polygons	4 days	Shapes Set (1 per group), poster paper, markers, Labsheet 1 ACE Exercises 3 and 4	Transparencies 1.1A–E, Transparencies 1.2A–C, pin, extra copy of Transparency 1.2A
Mathematical Reflections	$\frac{1}{2}$ day		
2 Polygons and Angles	7 days	Angle rulers (1 per student), rulers, Labsheets 2.2, 2.4, and 2.5, Shapes Sets (1 per group)	Transparencies 2.1, 2.2A, 2.2B, 2.3, 2.4, 2.5A, 2.5B, angle ruler, overhead Shapes Set (Transparency 1.1E)
Mathematical Reflections	$\frac{1}{2}$ day		
Assessment: Check Up	$\frac{1}{2}$ day		
3 Polygon Properties and Tiling	4 days	Angle rulers, construction paper, scissors, Shapes Sets (1 per group), Labsheet 3.2	Overhead Shapes Set (Transparency 1.1E), Transparencies 3.1A, 3.1B, and 3.2
Mathematical Reflections	$\frac{1}{2}$ day		
Assessment: Partner Quiz	1 day		
4 Building Polygons	4 days	Polystrips and fasteners (or Labsheet 4.1A), number cubes, rubber bands, geoboards, Labsheets 4.1B–4.3	Overhead geoboard or geoboard, rubber bands
Mathematical Reflections	$\frac{1}{2}$ day		
Looking Back and Looking Ahead	$\frac{1}{2}$ day		
Assessment: Unit Project	Optional	Magazines, newspapers, envelopes	
Assessment: Self Assessment	Take Home		
Assessment: Unit Test	1 day		

Total Time **24 days**

For detailed pacing for Problems within each Investigation, see the Suggested Pacing at the beginning of each investigation.

For pacing with block scheduling, see next page.

Materials to Use in All Investigations	
Blank transparencies and transparency markers (optional), student notebooks, Shapes Set, rulers	Blank transparencies and transparency markers (optional)

Pacing for Block Scheduling (90-minute class periods)

Investigation	Suggested Pacing	Investigation	Suggested Pacing
Investigation 1	**$2\frac{1}{2}$ days**	**Investigation 3**	**$2\frac{1}{2}$ days**
Problem 1.1	$\frac{1}{2}$ day	Problem 3.1	$\frac{1}{2}$ day
Problem 1.2	1 day	Problem 3.2	$\frac{1}{2}$ day
Problem 1.3	$\frac{1}{2}$ day	Problem 3.3	$\frac{1}{2}$ day
Math Reflections	$\frac{1}{2}$ day	Problem 3.4	$\frac{1}{2}$ day
Investigation 2	**4 days**	Math Reflections	$\frac{1}{2}$ day
Problem 2.1	$\frac{1}{2}$ day	**Investigation 4**	**$2\frac{1}{2}$ days**
Problem 2.2	$\frac{1}{2}$ day	Problem 4.1	1 day
Problem 2.3	1 day	Problem 4.2	$\frac{1}{2}$ day
Problem 2.4	$\frac{1}{2}$ day	Problem 4.3	$\frac{1}{2}$ day
Problem 2.5	1 day	Math Reflections	$\frac{1}{2}$ day
Math Reflections	$\frac{1}{2}$ day		

Vocabulary

Essential Terms Developed in This Unit		Useful Terms Referenced in This Unit		Terms Developed in Previous Units
angle	quadrilateral	acute angle	obtuse angle	benchmark
angle sum	ray (half line)	angle ruler	perpendicular lines	conjecture
degree	rectangle	central angle	plane	denominator
equilateral triangle	reflection symmetry	decagon	property	equivalent fractions
hexagon	regular polygon	diagonal	reflections	factors
isosceles triangle	right angle	dodecagon	rhombus	fraction
line of symmetry	rotation symmetry	exterior angle	rotations	prime factorization
line segment	scalene triangle	heptagon	straight angle	
octagon	square	interior angle	tiling	
parallel lines	symmetry	irregular polygon	trapezoid	
parallelogram	transversal	line symmetry	turn symmetry	
pentagon	triangle	midpoint		
polygon	vertex (vertices)	nonagon		

Program Resources

Go Online
PHSchool.com
For: Multiple-Choice Skills Practice
Web Code: amk–5500

Components

Use the chart below to quickly see which components are available for each Investigation.

Investigation	Labsheets	Additional Practice	Transparencies		Formal Assessment		Assessment Options	
			Problem	Summary	Check Up	Partner Quiz	Multiple-Choice	Question Bank
1	Shapes Set	✔	1.1A–E, 1.2A–C				✔	✔
2	Shapes Set 2.2, 2.4, 2.5	✔	1.1E, 2.1, 2.2A, 2.2B, 2.3, 2.4, 2.5A, 2.5B		✔		✔	✔
3	Shapes Set, 3.2	✔	1.1E, 3.1A, 3.1B, 3.2			✔	✔	✔
4	Shapes Set, 4.1, 4.2, 4.3	✔					✔	✔
Unit Project								
For the Unit		*ExamView* CD-ROM, Web site	LBLA		Unit Test, Notebook Check, Self Assessment		Multiple-Choice Items, Question Bank, *ExamView* CD-ROM	

Also Available for Use With This Unit

- Parent Guide: take-home letter for the unit
- Implementing CMP
- Spanish Assessment Resources
- Additional online and technology resources

Technology

The Use of Calculators

Connected Mathematics was developed with the belief that calculators should be available and that students should learn when their use is appropriate. For this reason, we do not designate specific problems as "calculator problems." The calculations in *Shapes and Designs* involve only simple arithmetic, so nonscientific calculators are adequate.

Student Activity CD-ROM

Includes interactive activities to enhance the learning in the Problems within Investigations.

PHSchool.com

For Students Multiple-choice practice with instant feedback, updated data sources, and data sets for Tinkerplots data software.

For Teachers Professional development, curriculum support, downloadable forms, and more.

See also www.math.msu.edu/cmp for more resources for both teachers and students.

ExamView® CD-ROM

Create multiple versions of practice sheets and tests for course objectives and standardized tests. Includes dynamic questions, online testing, student reports, and all test items in Spanish, plus all the Assessment Resources and Additional Practice questions.

TeacherExpress™ CD-ROM

Includes a lesson planning tool, the Teacher's Guide pages, and all the teaching resources.

LessonLab Online Courses

LessonLab offers comprehensive, facilitated professional development designed to help teachers implement CMP and improve student achievement. To learn more, please visit PHSchool.com/cmp2.

Assessment Summary

Ongoing Informal Assessment

Embedded in the Student Unit

Problems Use students' work from the Problems to informally check student understanding.

ACE exercises Use ACE exercises for homework assignments to assess student understanding.

Mathematical Reflections Have students summarize their learning at the end of each Investigation.

Looking Back and Looking Ahead At the end of the unit, use the first two sections to allow students to show what they know about the unit.

Additional Resources

Teacher's Guide Use the Check for Understanding feature of some Summaries and the probing questions that appear in the *Launch, Explore,* or *Summarize* sections of all Investigations to check student understanding.

Summary Transparencies Use these transparencies to focus class attention on a summary check for understanding.

Self Assessment

Notebook Check Students use this tool to organize and check their notebooks before giving them to their teacher. Located in *Assessment Resources*.

Self Assessment At the end of the unit, students reflect on and provide examples of what they learned. Located in *Assessment Resources*.

Formal Assessment

Choose the assessment materials that are appropriate for your students.

Assessment	For Use After	Focus	Student Work
Check Up	Invest. 2	Skills	Individual
Partner Quiz	Invest. 3	Rich problems	Pair
Unit Test	The Unit	Skills, rich problems	Individual
Unit Project	The Unit	Rich problems	Individual

Additional Resources

Multiple-Choice Items Use these items for homework, review, a quiz, or add them to the Unit Test.

Question Bank Choose from these questions for homework, review, or replacements for Quiz, Check Up, or Unit Test questions.

Additional Practice Choose practice exercises for each investigation for homework, review, or formal assessments.

***ExamView* Test Generator** Create practice sheets, review quizzes, and tests with this dynamic software. Give online tests and receive student progress reports. *(All test items are also available in Spanish.)*

Spanish Assessment Resources

Includes Partner Quizzes, Check Ups, Unit Test, Multiple-Choice Items, Question Bank, Notebook Check, and Self Assessment. Plus, the *ExamView* Test Generator has all test items in Spanish.

Correlation to Standardized Tests

Investigation	NAEP	Terra Nova		ITBS	SAT10	Local Test
		CAT6	CTBS			
1 Bees and Polygons	G1b, G1c, G1d, G2a, G2d	✔	✔	✔	✔	
2 Polygons and Angles	M1c, M1g, M2e, G3g, A2c		✔		✔	
3 Polygon Properties and Tilings	G1d, G2d, G3c, G3f, A1a		✔	✔		
4 Building Polygons	G1d		✔	✔		

NAEP National Assessment of Educational Progress
CAT6/Terra Nova California Achievement Test, 6th Ed.
CTBS/Terra Nova Comprehensive Test of Basic Skills
ITBS Iowa Test of Basic Skills, Form M
SAT10 Stanford Achievement Test, 10th Ed.

Launching the Unit

Introducing Your Students to *Shapes and Designs*

One way to introduce *Shapes and Designs* is to ask your students to brainstorm about the shapes that they see in everyday life and the properties they have. Tell your students that, in *Shapes and Designs,* they will study different types of shapes.

Using the Unit Opener

When students have had a chance to brainstorm about shapes they see in everyday life, explain that there are important and interesting reasons why different shapes are used in art and in architecture. Refer students to the questions posed on the opening page of the student edition. You may want to have a class discussion about these questions, but do not worry about finding the "correct" answers at this time. Each question is posed again in the investigations, at the time when the students have learned the mathematical concepts required to answer it. Ask your students to keep these questions in mind as they work through the investigations and to think about how they might use the ideas they are learning to help them determine the answers.

After you discuss the questions, introduce students to the unit project.

Introducing the Unit Project

An optional assessment item for *Shapes and Designs* is the unit project *What I Know About Shapes and Designs.* Here students are asked to begin collecting drawings, photos, and magazine clippings of shapes being used in the world around them. Throughout the unit, students are reminded to use the concepts they are learning to write more information about the characteristics of specific shapes: triangles, squares, rectangles, parallelograms, quadrilaterals, pentagons, hexagons, and octagons. At the end of the unit, students are asked to create projects that show all they have learned about shapes and designs.

It is recommended that you introduce the project prior to Investigation 1. Students could start a special "shapes section" in their notebook to record what they are learning about shapes. They will need to keep track of:

a. Characteristics and properties of the following shapes: triangle, square, quadrilateral, rectangle, pentagon, parallelogram, hexagon, and octagon.

b. Relationships among these shapes.

c. Examples of places where these shapes can be found, shown by, for example, a collection of drawings and magazine and newspaper cuttings of specific shapes.

Students should add to their "shapes section" throughout the unit. You may wish to provide some time in class for them to record their information about characteristics and relationships. Remind students to use their vocabulary words as they write. You may want them to share their entries with a partner or group. A periodic sharing of examples during class may also help encourage students to see shapes around them. Encourage them to add to their own entries after hearing the ideas of others.

Remind students that they need to collect their examples, part (c), on their own. You may wish to invite artists, architects, engineers, or others who work with shapes and designs to speak to your class. You might ask your media specialist to help you locate books about particular shapes to keep on display in your classroom during the unit.

See the unit project section starting on page 99 of this Teacher's Guide for a rubric and samples of student projects. Each sample is followed by a teacher's comments about assessing the project.

Using the Mathematical Highlights

The Mathematical Highlights page provides information to students and to parents and other family members. It gives students a preview of the mathematics and some of the overarching questions they should ask themselves while studying *Shapes and Designs*. As they work through the unit, students can refer back to the Mathematical Highlights page to review what they have learned and to preview what is still to come. This page also tells students' families what mathematical ideas and activities will be covered as the class works through *Shapes and Designs.*

Connected Mathematics 2™

Shapes and Designs

Two-Dimensional Geometry

Glenda Lappan
James T. Fey
William M. Fitzgerald
Susan N. Friel
Elizabeth Difanis Phillips

PEARSON

Boston, Massachusetts · Glenview, Illinois · Shoreview, Minnesota · Upper Saddle River, New Jersey

STUDENT PAGE

STUDENT PAGE

Notes ______________________________

Shapes and Designs

Two-Dimensional Geometry

What property of a hexagon makes it a good shape for the cells of a honeycomb?

Why do some shapes occur more often than other shapes in art, rug, and quilt designs?

Why are braces on towers, roofs, and bridges in the shape of triangles and not rectangles or pentagons?

Notes

The world is filled with shapes and designs. Your clothes, your home, the games you play, and the tools you work with are built on frames of geometric shapes and decorated with an endless variety of designs. If you look closely, you can even find shapes and designs in the animals and plants around you.

Builders and designers can imagine many different shapes and patterns. Frank O. Gehry used unique shapes in the design of the Massachusetts Institute of Technology's Stata Center shown below. But there are some simple shapes (triangles, rectangles, circles, and squares) that they use again and again. In this unit, you will discover properties of geometric figures that make them attractive for designs and useful for structures.

STUDENT PAGE

Notes ______________________________

Mathematical Highlights

Two-Dimensional Geometry

In *Shapes and Designs*, you will explore important properties of polygons.

You will learn how to

- Identify some important properties of polygons
- Recognize polygonal shapes both in and out of the classroom
- Investigate reflection and rotation symmetries of a shape
- Estimate the measures of angles by comparing them to a right angle or other benchmark angles
- Use an angle ruler to measure an angle
- Explore properties of parallel lines
- Find patterns that help you determine the sum of the interior angle measures of any polygon
- Find which polygons fit together to cover a flat surface and understand why they fit together
- Explain which properties of triangles make them a stable building unit
- Find that the sum of two side lengths of a triangle is greater than the third side length
- Find that the sum of three side lengths of a quadrilateral is greater than the fourth side length
- Draw or sketch polygons with certain properties
- Reason about and solve problems involving shapes

As you work on problems in this unit, ask yourself questions about situations that involve shapes.

What kinds of shapes/polygons will cover a flat surface?

What do these shapes have in common?

How do simple polygons work together to make more complex shapes?

What kinds of polygons are used in buildings and art?

How can angle measures be estimated?

How much accuracy is needed in measuring angles?

STUDENT PAGE

Notes

Unit Project

What I Know About Shapes and Designs

As you work in this unit, you will be asked to think about the characteristics of different shapes. You will determine how unusual a shape can be and still be a triangle, quadrilateral, pentagon, or hexagon. You will also be asked to think about the relationships among these shapes. It is these characteristics of shapes and the relationships among them that affect the designs you see in your world.

One of the ways you will be asked to demonstrate your understanding of the mathematics in this unit is through a final project. At the end of this unit, you will use what you have learned to create a project. Your project could be a book, a poster, a report, a mobile, a movie, or a slide show.

Notes

You can start preparing your project now. Make a special "shapes section" in your notebook, where you can collect information about

- The characteristics of triangles, squares, rectangles, parallelograms, quadrilaterals, pentagons, hexagons, and octagons
- The relationships among these shapes
- Examples of places where these shapes can be found in the world

After each investigation, record all the new information you have learned about shapes. Use as many of the new vocabulary words as you can. As you work through this unit, look for examples of the shapes being used in many ways. Cut out examples from magazines and newspapers. Draw pictures of shapes you see around you. You could use an envelope for collecting and storing your examples.

Use the information you have collected, plus what you learned from this unit, to prepare your final project. Your project should include the following:

- All the facts you know about the relations among the sides of polygons. Consider properties of all polygons and properties of special polygons, such as squares, rectangles, and other parallelograms.
- All the facts you know about the relations among angles of polygons. Again, consider properties of all polygons and properties of special polygons.

Notes

Investigation 1 Bees and Polygons

Mathematical and Problem-Solving Goals

- Sort shapes according to some special properties and describe these properties
- Introduce students to rotation and reflection symmetries of figures
- Decide what shapes will tile a surface and what common properties these shapes may have.

Summary of Problems

Problem 1.1 Sorting Shapes

Students sort shapes (polygons) according to some special properties they observe and describe these properties.

Problem 1.2 Symmetries of Shapes

Students are introduced to rotation and reflection symmetries of a figure.

Problem 1.3 Tiling a Beehive

Students decide which shapes will tile a surface and what common properties these shapes may have.

INVESTIGATION 1

	Suggested Pacing	Materials for Students	Materials for Teachers	ACE Assignments
All	$4\frac{1}{2}$ days	Calculators, Shapes Set (1 per group), and student notebooks	Transparency 1.1A and 1.1E, transparency markers	
1.1	1 day	Markers and poster paper, Labsheet 1ACE Exercises 3 and 4	Transparencies 1.1B–D	1–5, 17–25
1.2	2 days		Transparency 1.2A (two copies), Transparencies 1.2B and 1.2C, pin	6–11, 26–27, 29–33
1.3	1 day		Transparency 1.1B	12–16, 28, 34–36
MR	$\frac{1}{2}$ day			

1.1 Sorting Shapes

Goal

- Sort shapes according to some special properties and describe these properties

Students may sort triangles by side lengths: for example, triangles with no equal side lengths (scalene), two equal side lengths (isosceles), or three equal side lengths (equilateral). Students may sort quadrilaterals by the categories of no side lengths equal, two side lengths equal, or opposite side lengths equal.

Mathematics Background

For background on polygons, see page 4.

Launch 1.1

To launch this Investigation, tell the story of the bees. Show a picture of the honeycomb (Transparency 1.1B).

Suggested Questions Ask:

- *Why do you think bees use this shape?*

Tell the class that the cells in a honeycomb are polygons with six sides. Discuss the shapes in the piece of art before the Getting Ready.

To help students develop understanding of polygonal shapes, you might want to review the concepts of line and line segment.

Put up Transparency 1.1C on polygons (Getting Ready). Explain to students that some of these are polygons and some are non-polygons. Let students discuss the questions on the transparency.

Suggested Questions Some questions you may want to ask students include:

- *A polygon is a collection of line segments put together in a special way. What properties does the set of polygons have in common?*
- *Sketch an example of another polygon. Explain why your shape is a polygon.*
- *Sketch an example of a figure that is not a polygon. Explain why your shape is not a polygon.*
- *How would you define a "polygon"?* (Collect student's responses and record them on a chart paper or the board. Then refine the definition. Informal: A polygon is a closed shape made of line segments that do not cross.)

Explain to students that polygons are named after the number of sides they have. Put up the list of the names of the polygons on Transparency 1.1D. Have students look back to the polygons on Transparency 1.1C and name them. Be sure students understand the terms *sides* and *vertices* (*vertex*).

Put some of the shapes from the Shapes Sets on the overhead. Ask students to pick a shape and think about its properties. Call on a student and have the student describe the shape without naming it. Let the rest of the class guess the name of the shape the student is describing.

Now challenge the students to sort the shapes by common properties. Remind them to write down the common properties for each set.

Problem 1.1 will give you some sense of the knowledge that students bring to the *Shapes and Designs* unit.

Groups of 2–4 students can be used for this problem.

Explore 1.1

As you move around the room, look for more clues about students' prior knowledge of shapes. Students can put the results of grouping polygons, including pictures and descriptors, on poster paper. You may want to place them around the room.

Summarize 1.1

Gather some interesting ways the class sorted the polygons for Question A. In Question B, if the students sorted by equal side lengths for the set of triangles, you can give them the names for these triangles—scalene (no side lengths equal), isosceles (two side lengths equal), and equilateral (three side lengths equal). In Question C, you can also name some of the subsets by lengths of sides. From this discussion, the names for squares, rectangles, and parallelograms emerge. It is not necessary to overemphasize vocabulary at this point.

Angle measure is covered formally in Investigation 2. For now, encourage students to examine the square corners of squares and rectangles. Relate the square corners to right angles and discuss how all right angles have equal measures.

Suggested Questions You might ask students to describe squares and rectangles.

- *How are they the same?* (They each have four sides and four right angles.)
- *How are they different?* (To be a square, all sides and all angles must be equal. Rectangles just have to have opposite sides equal and all angles equal.)
- *What about the Shape L in the Shape Set? Is it a rectangle? Why or why not?* (It is not a rectangle since it does not have four right angles.)

The intention is to review squares and rectangles and to get an informal definition of parallelograms on the table. At this point, parallelograms are defined as quadrilaterals with opposite sides with the same length and opposite angles of the same measure. Parallelograms also have opposite sides that are parallel. This fact will be discussed in the next investigation.

Suggested Questions Next ask students the following:

- *Is a rectangle a parallelogram? Why or why not?* (Yes, since it is a quadrilateral with opposite sides equal and opposite angles of the same measure.)
- *Is a square a rectangle? Why or why not?* (Yes. A square is a special type of rectangle where not only are opposite sides equal, but all sides are equal to each other.)

Note that squares are rectangles and rectangles are parallelograms. Hold up a quadrilateral from the Shapes Set that is not a parallelogram (O, Q, R, S, or U) and ask if it is a parallelogram. Have students explain their reasoning. Note that Shapes O, S, and R each have exactly one pair of opposite sides parallel. They are called trapezoids. Some textbooks define trapezoids as having *exactly* one pair of opposite sides parallel, while others define trapezoids as having *at least* one pair of opposite sides parallel. The first definition is an *exclusive* definition, since it excludes many shapes from being defined as trapezoid. The second definition is an *inclusive* definition since it includes more shapes. There are many mathematical reasons why the inclusive definition is used more frequently these days. With this definition, a square, rectangle, parallelogram, and rhombus are also trapezoids. Thus, there are many other shapes in the Shapes Set that are also classified as trapezoids. We are using the inclusive definition. Trapezoids are not essential to the development of the ideas in this unit. They are in some ACE questions and some students find them interesting.

You may want to draw a quadrilateral that has no parallel sides or use Shape Q or U. However, other than squares, rectangles, and parallelograms, it is not necessary to dwell on names, and informal definitions of these quadrilaterals will suffice.

You could end this problem by having the class make a Venn diagram to sort the polygons. Venn diagrams were discussed in the *Prime Time* unit.

1.1 Sorting Shapes

At a Glance

PACING 1 day

Mathematical Goal

- Sort shapes according to some special properties and describe these properties

Launch

Tell the story of bees. Show a picture of the honeycomb (Transparency 1.1B).

- *Why do you think bees use this shape?*

Put up Transparency 1.1C of polygons versus non-polygons.

- *What properties do the set of polygons have in common?*
- *Sketch an example of another polygon. Explain why your shape is a polygon.*
- *Sketch an example of a figure that is not a polygon. Explain why your shape is not a polygon.*
- *How would you define a "polygon"?*

Put up Transparency 1.1D; have students try to name some of the polygons in the Shapes Set (Transparency 1.1A) and on Transparency 1.1C.

Groups of 2–4 students can be used for this problem.

Materials
- Transparencies 1.1A–D
- Transparency markers
- Overhead Shapes Set (Transparency 1.1E)

Vocabulary
- polygon
- vertex (vertices)
- line segment

Explore

As you move around the room, look for more clues about students' prior knowledge of shapes. Students can put the results of grouping polygons, including pictures and descriptions, on poster paper.

Materials
- Shapes Set (1 per group)
- Markers and poster paper

Summarize

Gather some interesting ways the class sorted the polygons for Question A.

In Question B, if the students sorted by equal side lengths for the set of triangles, you can give them the names for these triangles.

In Question C, you can also name some of the subsets by lengths of sides. From this discussion, the names of squares, rectangles, and parallelograms emerge.

Angle measure is covered formally in Investigation 2. For now, encourage students to examine the square corners of squares and rectangles. Relate the square corners to right angles and discuss how all right angles have equal measures.

During this discussion on squares and rectangles, ask:

- *How are they the same?*
- *How are they different?*

Materials
- Student notebooks

Vocabulary
- equilateral triangle
- isosceles triangle
- scalene triangle
- rectangle
- square
- parallelogram

continued on next page

Summarize
continued

- *What about the Shape L of the Shape Set (a parallelogram)? Is it a rectangle? Why or why not?*

At this point, parallelograms are defined as quadrilaterals with opposite sides with the same length and opposite angles of the same measure. Next ask the students the following:

- *Is a rectangle a parallelogram? Why or why not?*
- *Is a square a rectangle? Why or why not?*

Hold up a quadrilateral from the Shapes Set that is not a parallelogram (O, Q, R, S, or U).

- *Is this shape a parallelogram? Explain.*

Other than squares, rectangles, and parallelograms, students are not expected to know the names for other quadrilaterals.

ACE Assignment Guide for Problem 1.1

Differentiated Instruction
Solutions for All Learners

Core 1–5 (You may want students to use Labsheet 1ACE Exercises 3 and 4.)
Other *Connections* 17–25

Adapted For suggestions about adapting ACE exercises, see the CMP *Special Needs Handbook*.
Connecting to Prior Units 17–25: *Bits and Pieces I*

Answers to Problem 1.1

A. The shapes can be sorted a number of ways, for example, by comparing the number of sides, the number of angles, the lengths of sides, or the measures of the angles. For example, for the lengths of sides category, we get the following groups:

- Group one: All sides equal: A–F, K, V
- Group two: Exactly two sides equal: P and R
- Group three: Exactly two pairs of equal sides: G, H, J, L, M, N, Q (some students may also include Shape B, the square)
- Group four: No sides equal: I, O, S, T, U

B. Possible answer: The triangles are sorted by side length:

- Group one: A (3 sides the same length)
- Group two: P (2 sides the same length)
- Group three: I and T (no sides the same length)

C. Possible answer: The quadrilaterals can be sorted by side length:

- Group one: All sides the same length: B, K, and V
- Group two: All sides are not the same length, but two pairs of sides are equal: G, H, J, L, M, N, Q
- Group three: No sides the same length: O, S, U

D. They are quadrilaterals with only one pair of opposite sides parallel. Shape U would not belong to this group because it does not have any parallel sides. Note: Students may not use the term *parallel*; they may describe the slant of the lines. Parallel lines will be introduced in the next investigation.

1.2 Symmetries of Shapes

Goal

- Introduce students to rotation and reflection symmetries of figures

Mathematics Background

For background on rotation symmetry, see page 5.

Launch 1.2

Show Transparency 1.2A of two polygons on the overhead. Describe and demonstrate reflection and rotation symmetry by flipping and rotating the two shapes or have students come up and demonstrate the symmetries.

Make a second copy of the two polygons on a different transparency. Place this transparency on top of the original and then rotate or reflect it to show how it lands in its original position. Point out the role of the line of reflection, the role of the center of rotation, and the angle of rotation. Note that students will learn more about angles in the next investigation.

Put up a parallelogram on the overhead and ask if it has symmetries. A non-rectangular parallelogram has no reflection but does have rotation symmetry (180° and 360°). Hold up a regular polygon, such as a square, or an equilateral triangle, and ask for symmetries. Regular polygons have both reflection and rotation symmetries. Students will formally be introduced to regular polygons in Problem 1.3.

Suggested Questions Challenge the class to explore the symmetries of the polygons listed in the Getting Ready for Problem 1.2 (Transparency 1.2B) using the following questions. Alternatively the Getting Ready can be used at the end of the summary.

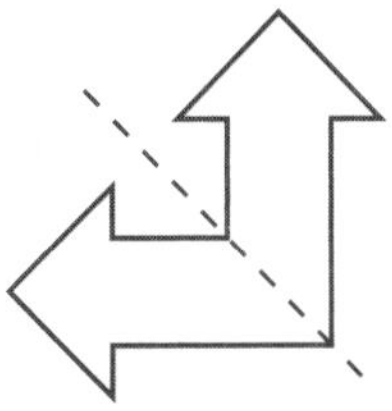

- *Which of the following shapes have reflection symmetry?* (The heart and the fourth and fifth shapes from the left. Also the double-headed right angle arrow has reflection symmetry but is harder to see. The line of reflection is shown above.)
- *Which of the following shapes have rotation symmetry?* (Every shape except the double-headed right angle arrow and the heart has rotation symmetry.)

In this problem, students will go on to first explore the symmetries of triangles, then quadrilaterals, and then other polygons.

Students can work in groups of 2–4 on this problem. They may want to divide up the work in the group and then share later as a whole group.

Explore 1.2

Students will explore the symmetries of triangles, then quadrilaterals, and then other polygons. Ask groups to:

- *Describe the relationship between the two shapes that a line of reflection creates in the original figure.* (The two shapes are congruent. Corresponding sides have equal lengths and corresponding angles have equal measures.)

At this point, students may say the shapes are identical.

Summarize 1.2

Have a few groups share their findings. The triangles are interesting. Triangles with three sides of equal length (equilateral) have three lines of symmetry and three angles of rotation. Triangles with two sides of equal length (isosceles) have one line of reflection and no rotation symmetry. A triangle with no sides of equal length (scalene) has no symmetries.

Students may have difficulty describing rotation or turn symmetries. You can demonstrate at the overhead projector using a copy of Shape A from the Shapes Set on Transparency 1.2C. Hold the triangle down by putting a pin through its center.

Suggested Questions Ask students:

- *If I put a pin in the equilateral triangle to hold the center in place, how can I turn the triangle so that it looks the same as at its starting position?*

Help the students to see that you can turn the triangle a third of a full turn, as shown below.

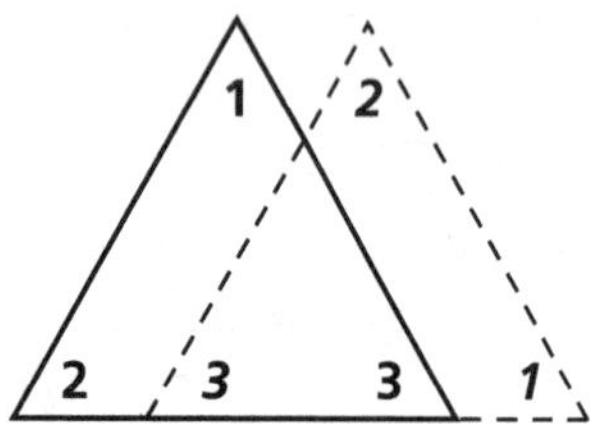

- *I can turn the triangle one third of a full turn, so that vertex 1 is at position 3, vertex 2 is at position 1, and vertex 3 is at position 2. The triangle looks like its starting position. How can we tell what angle of turn this is?*

Some students may say that in an equilateral triangle, three of the rotations described above equal a full turn or 360° turn. Since $360 \div 3 = 120$, one third of a full 360° turn is 120°. Angles are discussed in the next investigation and are not something that students must master at this time. After students have noticed the 120° turn, ask:

- *Can I turn the triangle some more to find another turn symmetry?*

Help students to see that you can turn the triangle another third of a full turn. This is a 240° turn from its original position. You can also turn the triangle completely around, so vertex 1 is at the top, which is a 360° turn.

Finally, some groups may have found the pattern for the symmetries of regular polygons. A regular polygon with N sides has N lines of reflection and N angles of rotation.

1.2 Symmetries of Shapes

At a Glance

PACING 2 days

Mathematical Goal

- Introduce students to rotation and reflection symmetries of figures

Launch

Use Transparency 1.2A of two polygons to demonstrate reflection and rotation symmetry by flipping and rotating the shapes. Make a second copy of the two polygons on a different transparency. Place this transparency on top of the original and then rotate or reflect it to show how it lands in its original position. Point out the role of the line of reflection and the role of the center of rotation. Put up a parallelogram on the overhead:

- *Does this parallelogram have any symmetries?*

Hold up a regular polygon, such as a square or an equilateral triangle:

- *What types of symmetries do these shapes have?*

Regular polygons have both reflection and rotation symmetries. The Getting Ready for Problem 1.2 can be used to give students a chance to practice describing symmetries. Students will be formally introduced to regular polygons in Problem 1.3.

Students can work in groups of 2–4 on this problem.

Materials

- Transparencies 1.2A and 1.2B
- Additional copy of Transparency 1.2A
- Overhead Shapes Set (Transparency 1.1E)

Vocabulary

- reflection symmetry
- line of symmetry
- rotation symmetry

Explore

Students will explore the symmetries of triangles, then quadrilaterals, and then other polygons. Ask groups to:

- *Describe the relationship between the two shapes that a line of reflection creates in the original figure.*

At this point, students may say the shapes are identical.

Materials

- Shapes Set (1 per group)

Summarize

Have a few groups share their findings. Students may have difficulty describing rotation or turn symmetries. Demonstrate at the overhead projector using a copy of Shape A from the Shapes Set cut from a transparency. Hold the triangle down by putting a pin through its center. Ask:

- *If I put a pin in the equilateral triangle to hold the center in place, how can I turn the triangle so that it looks the same as at its starting position?*

Explain how to turn the triangle:

- *How can we tell what angle of turn this is?*

Angles are discussed in the next investigation and are not something that students must master.

Materials

- Student notebooks
- Transparency 1.2C
- Pin

continued on next page

Summarize *continued*

After students have noticed the 120° turn, ask:

- *Can I turn the triangle some more to find another turn symmetry?*

Some students may see the pattern that regular polygons with N sides have N rotation symmetries and N reflection symmetries.

ACE Assignment Guide for Problem 1.2

Differentiated Instruction
Solutions for All Learners

Core 6–9

Other *Applications* 10, 11; *Connections* 26, 27; *Extensions* 29–33; unassigned choices from previous problems

Adapted For suggestions about adapting Exercise 6 and other ACE exercises, see the CMP *Special Needs Handbook*.

Connecting to Prior Units 26, 27: *Bits and Pieces I*

Answers to Problem 1.2

A. 1. Shape A has three lines of symmetry, which are drawn from the midpoint of each side to the opposite vertex. Shape P has one line of symmetry, which is drawn from the non-congruent side to the opposite vertex.

Shape A:

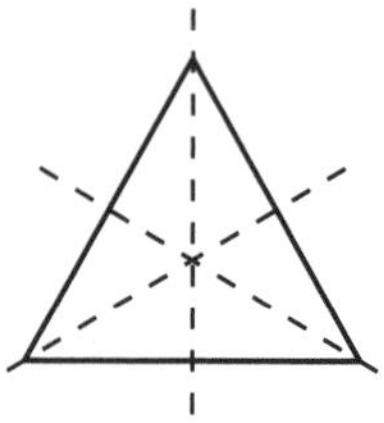

Shape P:

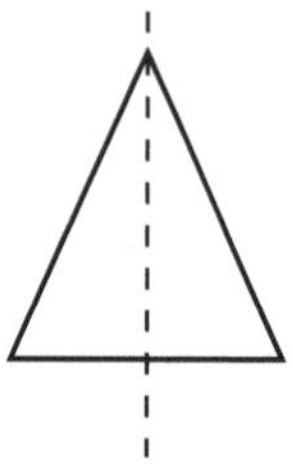

2. Only Shape A has rotation symmetry. Shape A can be turned 120°, 240°, and 360°. (Angle measures will come up later).

3. Shapes I and T have no reflection or rotation symmetry.

B. 1. Shapes B, G, H, J, K, R, and V have reflection symmetry. (Figure 1)

2. All of the parallelograms have rotation symmetry (180° and 360°).

3. The quadrilaterals O, Q, S, and U have no reflection symmetry or rotation symmetry.

C. Shapes C–F have rotation symmetry and reflection symmetry. Shapes C–F are also polygons with equal side lengths and equal angle measures.

D. There are many possible answers: for example, the chalkboard has reflection symmetry and rotation symmetry (180° and 360°). See Shapes G, H, and J for examples. The end of some unsharpened pencils have rotation symmetry and reflection symmetry. See Shape D for an example.

Figure 1

Shape B:

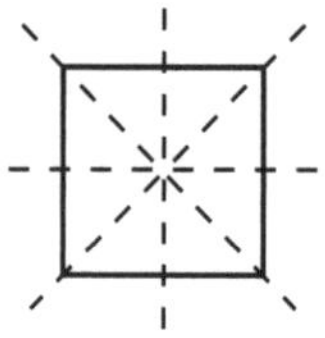

Shape G:

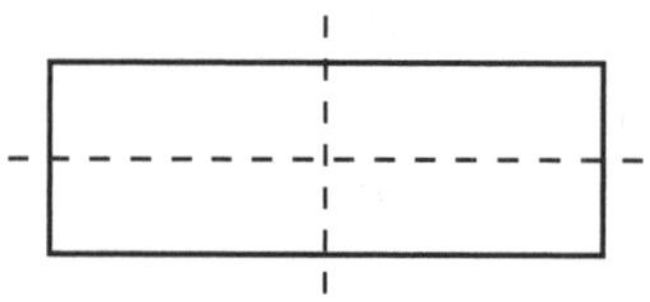

Shape H:

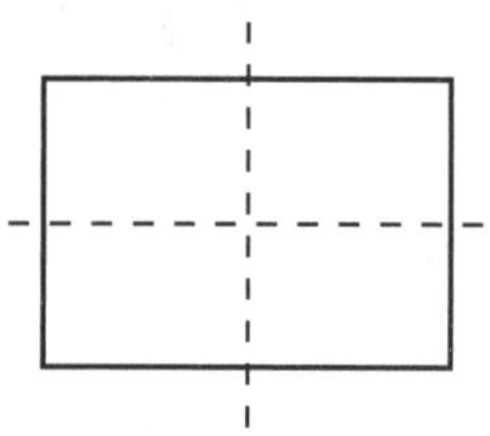

Shape J:

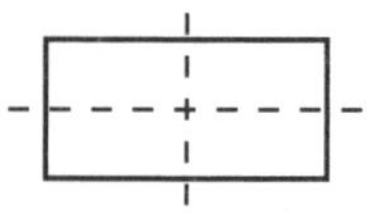

Shape K:

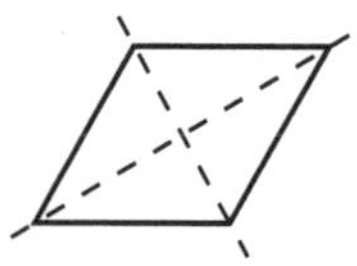

Shape R:

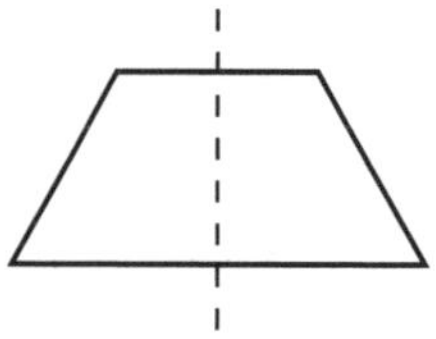

Shape V:

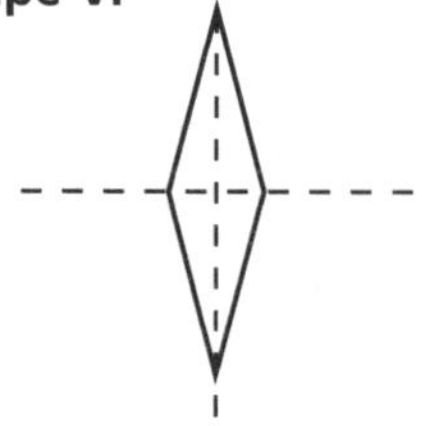

1.3 Tiling a Beehive

Goal

- Decide which shapes will tile a surface and what common properties these shapes may have

Launch 1.3

Show students Transparency 1.1B of the honeycomb with regular hexagons. Ask the class what they notice (i.e., they fit exactly around a point, sides match, angles appear to have the same size).

Define regular polygons. Some students may have sorted by shapes that have equal side lengths in Problem 1.1. If so, refer back to this set. Ask the class if there are any other regular polygons that bees could use. First they may focus on just one regular polygon and then combinations of regular polygons.

Students can work in groups of 2–4, but each student should have a record of the results.

Explore 1.3

Look for strategies that students are using to determine a tiling.

Going Further

If some groups get done early, challenge them to explore whether non-regular triangles or quadrilaterals tile.

Summarize 1.3

When all groups have found shapes and combinations of shapes that work and don't work, have groups share their results. Here are some students' findings from previous classes:

squares

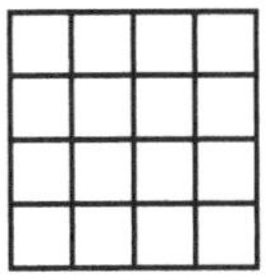

triangles

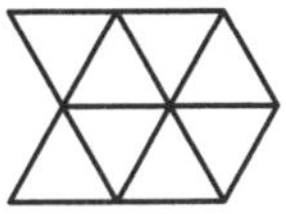

squares and triangles

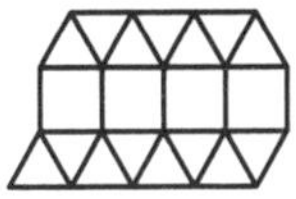

Some teachers use this opportunity to explain to students a short hand notation for describing the shapes and combinations of shapes used to tessellate. For example, to describe the tiling of squares a student would write 4, 4, 4, 4 and for the triangles 3, 3, 3, 3, 3, 3. To describe the combination of shapes presented, you could write 4, 3, 3, 3, 4. The notation identifies the shape by its number of sides. It also tells the number of shapes, and the order in which the shapes surround a point. You could suggest that the class look for interesting tiling patterns in their homes or in school. Have them make a sketch of any designs they find.

1.3 Tiling a Beehive

At a Glance

PACING 1 day

Mathematical Goal

- Decide which shapes will tile a surface and what common properties these shapes may have

Launch

Show students Transparency 1.1B of the honeycomb with regular hexagons.

- *What do you notice about the honeycomb and the shapes that are formed?*

Define regular polygons. Some students may have sorted by shapes that have equal side lengths in Problem 1.1. If so, refer back to this set.

- *Are there any other regular polygons that the bee could have used?*

First they may focus on just one regular polygon and then combinations of regular polygons. If not, ask:

- *Are there any combinations of regular polygons that bees could use?*

Students can work in groups of 2–4, but each student should have a record of the results.

Materials

- Transparency 1.1B
- Overhead Shapes Set (Transparency 1.1E)

Vocabulary

- regular polygon
- tiling

Explore

If some groups get done early, challenge them to explore whether non-regular triangles or quadrilaterals tile.

Materials

- Shapes Set (1 per group)

Summarize

Have groups share their results.

Some teachers use this opportunity to explain to students a shorthand notation for describing the shapes and combinations of shapes used to tessellate.

For example, to describe the tiling of squares one would write 4, 4, 4, 4 and for the triangles 3, 3, 3, 3, 3, 3. The notation identifies the shape by its number of sides. It also tells the number of shapes, and the order in which the shapes surround a point.

You could suggest that the class look for interesting tiling patterns in their homes or in school. Have them make a sketch of any designs they find.

Materials

- Student notebooks

ACE Assignment Guide for Problem 1.3

Core 13–16

Other *Applications* 12, *Connections* 28, *Extensions* 34–36; unassigned choices from previous problems

Adapted For suggestions about adapting ACE exercises, see the CMP *Special Needs Handbook.*

Answers to Problem 1.3

A. 1. Examples of tilings:

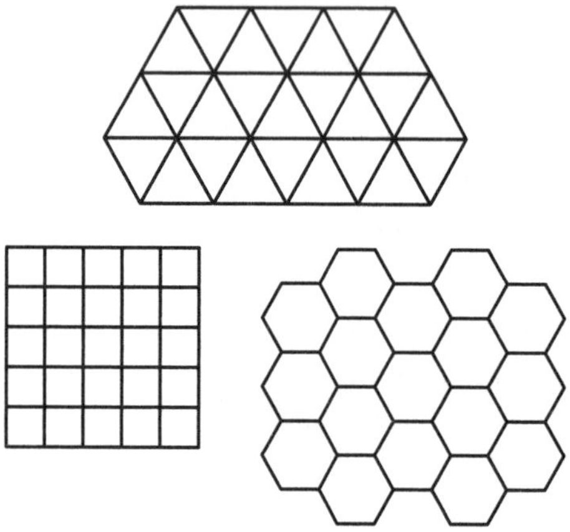

2. Equilateral triangles, squares, and regular hexagons are the only regular polygons that tile a plane by themselves. In a triangle tiling, there are six triangles around each vertex. A square tiling has four around each vertex. Each vertex in hexagon tiling has three hexagons. The pentagon, heptagon, and octagon will not tile because multiple copies of their angles do not sum to 360°.

B. Squares and equilateral triangles, regular octagons and squares, and regular hexagons and equilateral triangles work nicely together. Examples:

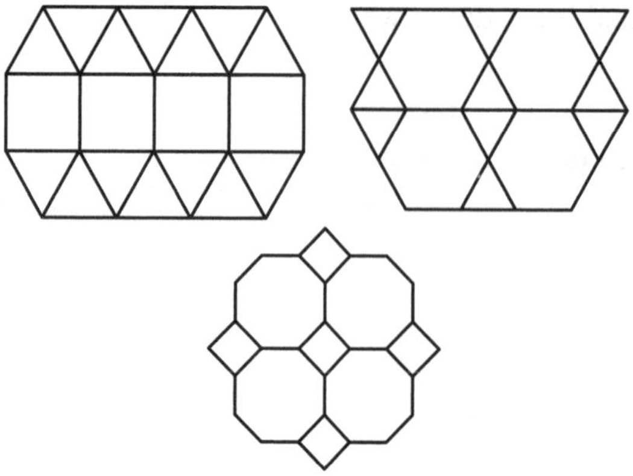

In addition to the three examples shown here, there are 5 more examples which include the following groups of regular polygons around a point: (1) square, triangle, triangle, square, triangle, (2) square, hexagon, square, triangle, (3) dodecagon, hexagon, square, (4) dodecagon, dodecagon, triangle, and (5) 4 triangles and a hexagon.

C. 1. Students will select a point on each tiling.

2. Squares and equilateral triangles tiled together must have two square tiles and three triangles (they can be in different orders) at each vertex. In the octagon and square example, each vertex has two octagons and a square around it. For a hexagon and triangle tiling, one example would be one hexagon and four triangles at a vertex and another would be two hexagons and two triangles at each vertex.

3. No. For example, the two hexagons and two triangles tiling, note that the order around a point may be different. The order at one point may be hexagon, hexagon, triangle, and triangle, whereas the order at another point may be hexagon, triangle, hexagon, and triangle. See the diagrams below.

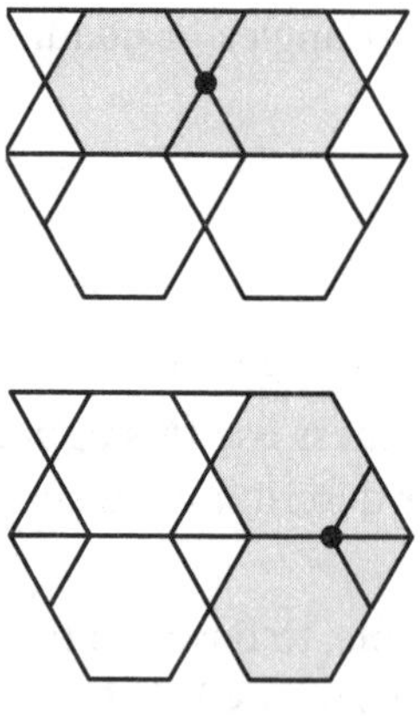

Investigation 1

Bees and Polygons

Honeybees build nests in the wild called *hives.* About 60,000 bees live in a hive. Bees are fairly small insects, but packing a hive with 60,000 bees and their honey is tricky.

Bees store their honey in a honeycomb, which is filled with tubes. An interesting pattern appears on the face of a honeycomb. It is covered with a design of identical six-sided shapes that fit together like tiles on a floor.

You can also find many different shapes in art, architecture, and nature.

What shapes can you identify in Auguste Herbin's painting below?

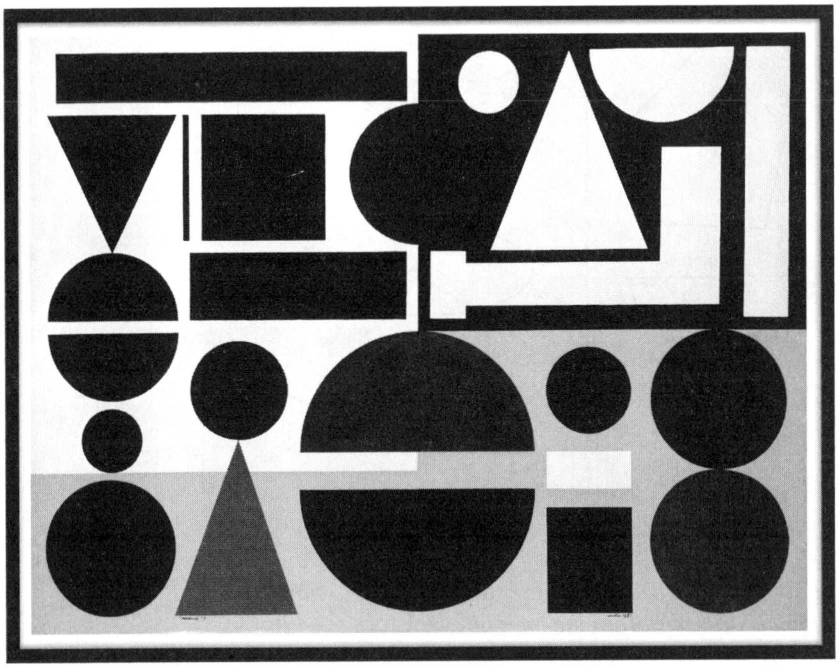

STUDENT PAGE

Notes

In this unit, you will investigate properties that make two-dimensional shapes useful. The unit will focus on *polygons.* First, let's review some basic concepts. A line is a familiar object. In mathematics, *line* means a straight line that has no end in either direction. You can use arrows to show that a line has no ends. A **line segment,** or *segment,* consists of two points of a line and all the points between these two points.

Getting Ready for Problem 1.1

A *polygon* is a group of line segments put together in a special way. For example, some of the shapes below are polygons and some are not.

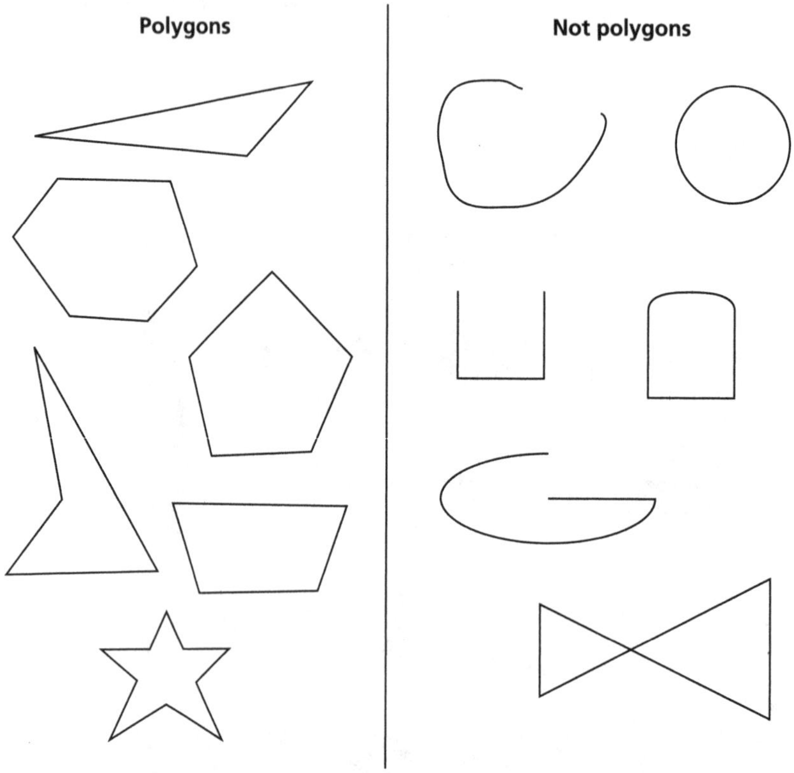

In order to be a polygon, what properties does a shape need to have?
Draw a polygon that is different from the ones above.
Then draw a shape that is not a polygon.

Notes

The line segments in polygons are called **sides.** The points where two sides of a polygon meet are called **vertices.** Polygons have special names based on the number of sides and angles they have. For example, a polygon with six sides and six angles is called a *hexagon*. The table below shows the names of some common polygons.

Common Polygons

Number of Sides and Angles	Polygon Name
3	triangle
4	quadrilateral
5	pentagon
6	hexagon
7	heptagon
8	octagon
9	nonagon
10	decagon
12	dodecagon

You can label a polygon by using a single letter or numeral for the entire shape or by marking each corner, or vertex, with a different letter. To refer to a polygon with lettered vertices, start with any letter and list the letters in order as you move around the polygon in one direction. For the rectangle below, you could say rectangle *CDAB* or rectangle *DCBA* (but not rectangle *ACDB*).

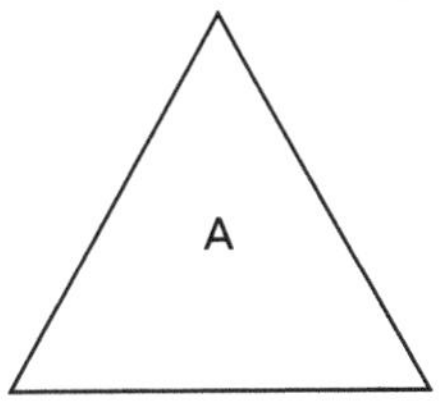

Triangle A

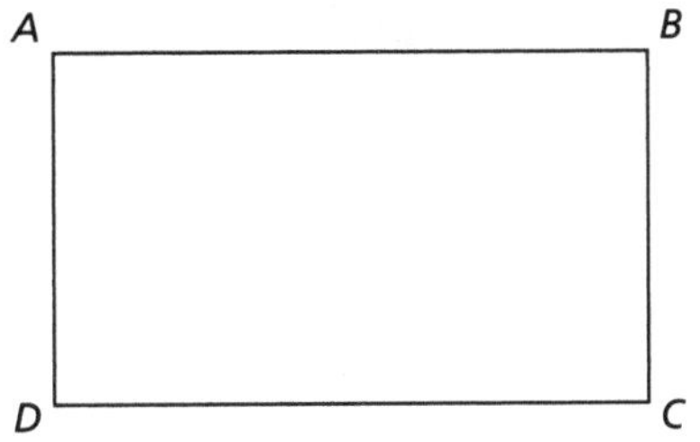

Rectangle *ABCD*

STUDENT PAGE

Notes

1.1 Sorting Shapes

Below are a variety of polygons. Many of these polygons have common properties.

Shapes Set

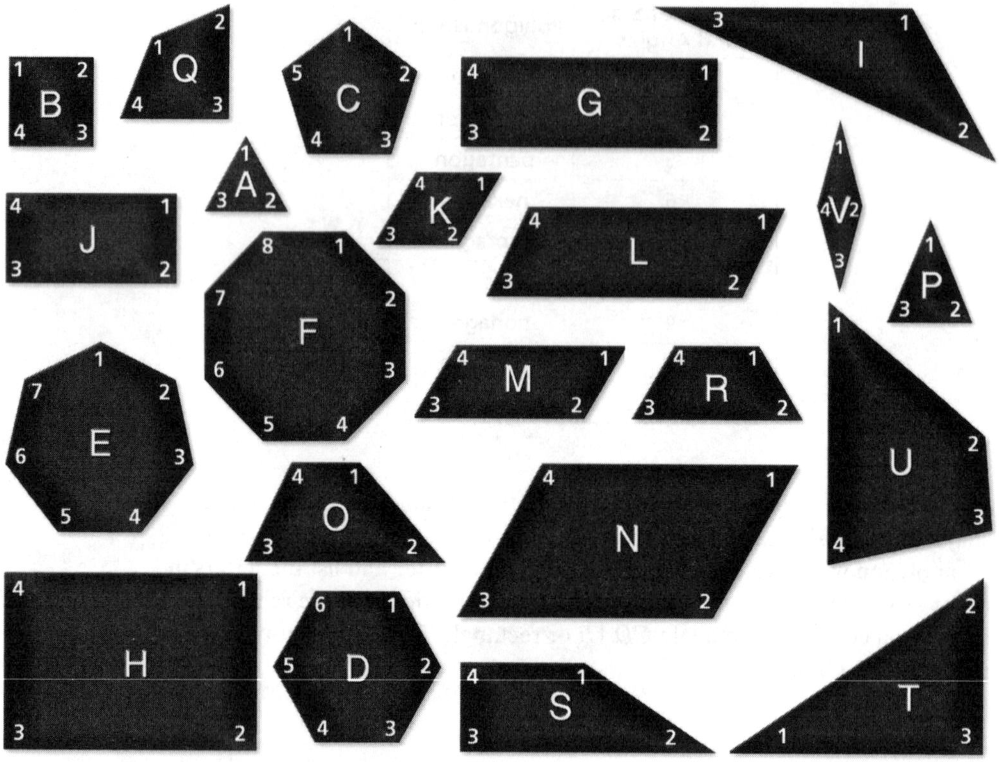

Problem 1.1 Sorting Shapes

A. Sort the polygons in the Shapes Set into groups so that the polygons in each group have one or more properties in common. Describe the properties the polygons have in common and give the letters of the polygons in each group.

B. Take all the triangles and sort them into two or more groups. Describe the properties you used to form the groups and give the letters of the triangles in each group.

Notes

C. Take all the quadrilaterals and sort them into two or more groups. Describe the properties you used to form the groups and give the letters of the quadrilaterals in each group.

D. Rose put Shapes R, O, and S into the same group. What properties do these polygons have in common? Would Shape U belong to this group? Explain.

ACE **Homework starts on page 17.**

In Problem 1.1, you may have sorted the triangles according to the number of equal-length sides they have. An **equilateral triangle** has three sides the same length. An **isosceles triangle** has two sides the same length. A **scalene triangle** has no sides the same length. (The small marks on the sides of each triangle indicate sides that are the same length.)

Equilateral Triangle

Isosceles Triangle

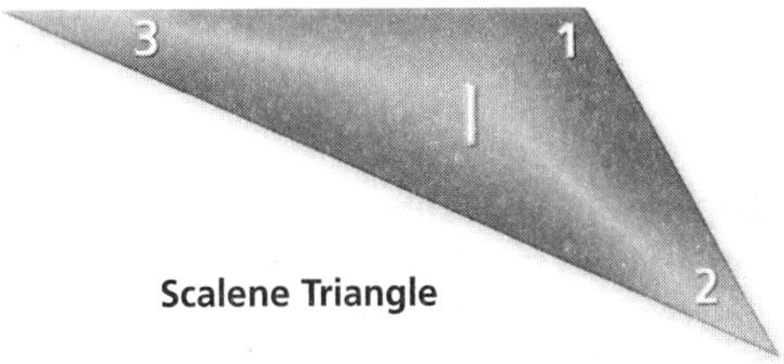

Scalene Triangle

You may have sorted the quadrilaterals according to the number of sides with the same length or the number of angles of the same measure. A **square** is a quadrilateral with four sides the same length and four angles of the same measure. A **rectangle** is a quadrilateral with opposite sides the same length and four angles of the same measure. A **parallelogram** is a quadrilateral with opposite sides the same length and opposite angles of the same measure. (Note: angles 1 and 3 and angles 2 and 4 are opposite angles in the quadrilaterals below.) You will be seeing these shapes throughout this unit.

Square

Rectangle

Parallelogram

Notes

1.2 Symmetries of Shapes

As you study the polygons in this unit, look for ways that different combinations of side lengths and angle sizes give different shapes. In particular, look for shapes that have attractive *symmetries*.

Reflection Symmetry

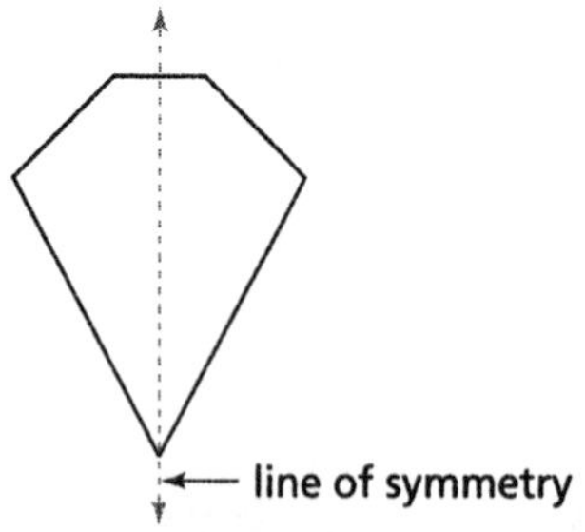

A shape with **reflection symmetry** has two halves that are mirror images of each other. If the shape is folded over its **line of symmetry,** the two halves of the shape match exactly.

Rotation Symmetry

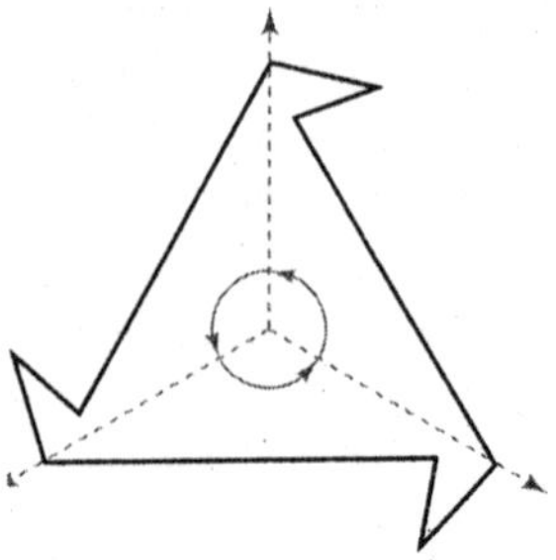

If you rotate any shape a full turn, it will look like it did before you rotated it. When you rotate a shape *less* than a full turn about its center point and it looks exactly as it did before it was rotated, it has **rotation symmetry.**

In the polygon shown above, there are three places in the rotation where the polygon will look exactly the same as when you started.

Reflection symmetry is sometimes called *line* or *mirror symmetry.* (Can you see why?) Rotation symmetry is sometimes called *turn symmetry.*

Notes ______

Getting Ready for Problem 1.2

- Which of the following shapes have reflection symmetry?
- Which of the following shapes have rotation symmetry?

Problem 1.2 Symmetry

Use the Shapes Set from Problem 1.1.

A. Look at the triangles.

1. Which triangles have reflection symmetry? Trace these triangles and draw all the lines of symmetry.

2. Which triangles have rotation symmetry?

3. Which triangles have no symmetries?

B. Look at the quadrilaterals.

1. Which quadrilaterals have reflection symmetry? Trace these quadrilaterals and draw all the lines of symmetry.

2. Which quadrilaterals have rotation symmetry?

3. Which quadrilaterals have no symmetries?

C. Look at the remaining polygons (the polygons that are not triangles or quadrilaterals). What is special about these shapes?

D. Find shapes with symmetry in your classroom. Sketch each shape and describe its symmetries.

ACE **Homework starts on page 17.**

Notes

1.3 Tiling a Beehive

A **regular polygon** is a polygon in which all the sides are the same length and all the angles have the same measure. In an **irregular polygon,** all sides are *not* the same length or all the angles are *not* the same measure. The shapes below are regular polygons.

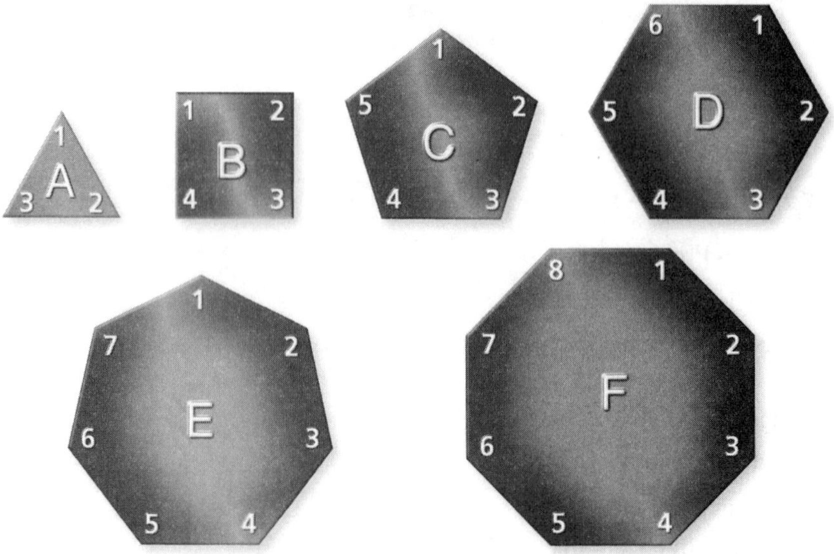

You can find an interesting pattern of regular hexagons on the face of a honeycomb. The hexagons fit together like tiles on a floor.

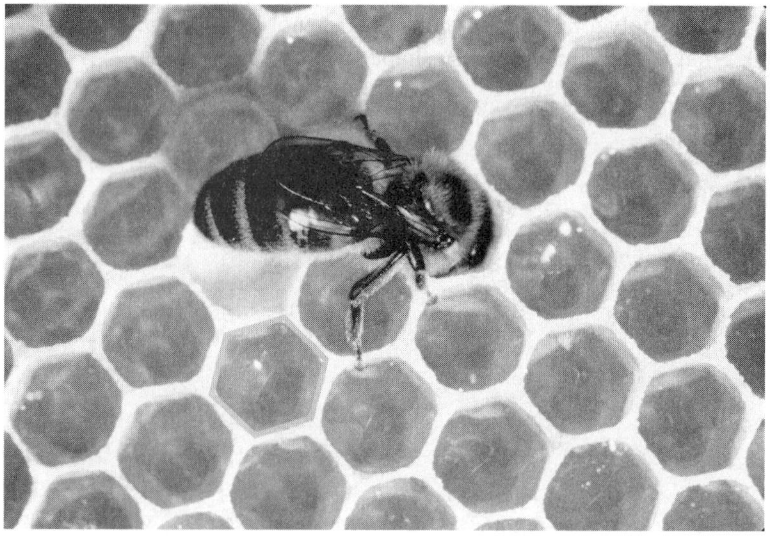

STUDENT PAGE

STUDENT PAGE

Notes

Tiling means covering a flat surface with shapes that fit together without any gaps or overlaps.

Which regular polygons can be used to tile a surface?

Problem 1.3 Tiling With Regular Polygons

Use Shapes A–F from your Shapes Set or cutouts of those shapes. As you work, try to figure out why some shapes cover a flat surface, while others do not.

A. **1.** First, form tile patterns with several copies of the *same* polygon. Try each of the regular polygons. Sketch your tilings.

2. Which regular polygons fit together, without gaps or overlaps, to cover a flat surface?

B. Next, form tile patterns using combinations of two or more different shapes. Sketch your tilings.

C. The following tiling may be one that you found. Look at a point where the vertices of the polygons meet.

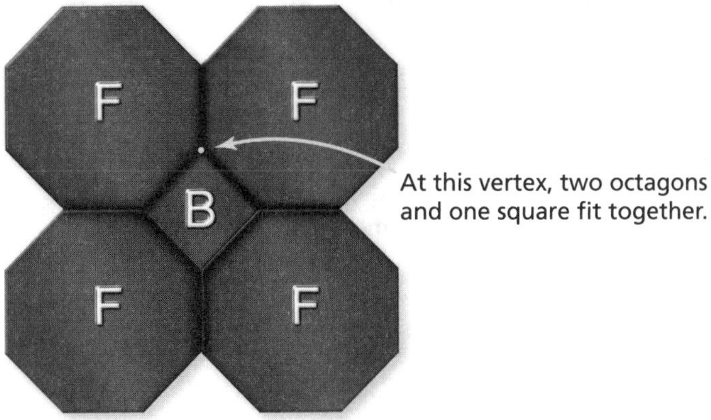
F
F
B
F
F
At this vertex, two octagons and one square fit together.

1. Look back at each tiling you made. Find a point on the tiling where the vertices of the polygons meet.

2. Describe exactly which polygons fit around this point and the pattern of how they fit together.

3. Is this pattern the same for all other points where the vertices of the polygons meet in this tiling?

ACE Homework starts on page 17.

STUDENT PAGE

STUDENT PAGE

Notes

Did You Know?

Tilings are also called *tessellations*. Artists, designers, and mathematicians have been interested in tessellations for centuries. The Greek mathematician and inventor Archimedes (c. 287–212 B.C.) studied the properties of regular polygons that tiled the plane. Beginning in the middle of the eighth century, Moorish artists used tessellating patterns extensively in their work.

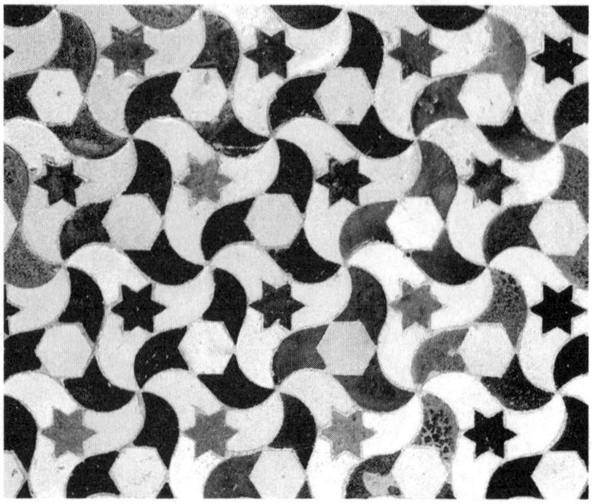

The Dutch artist M.C. Escher (1898–1972), inspired by Moorish designs, spent his life creating tessellations. He altered geometric tessellating shapes to make birds, reptiles, fish, and people.

Go Online
PHSchool.com
For: Information about tessellations
Web Code: ame-9031

STUDENT PAGE

STUDENT PAGE

Notes

Applications Connections Extensions ACE

Applications

1. Tell whether each shape is a polygon. If it is, tell how many sides it has.

a.

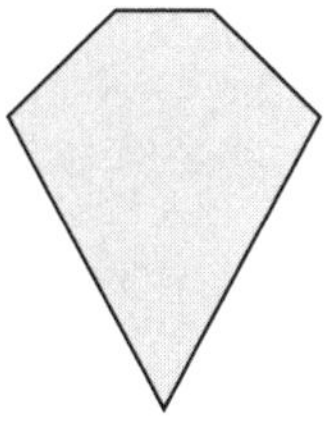

b.

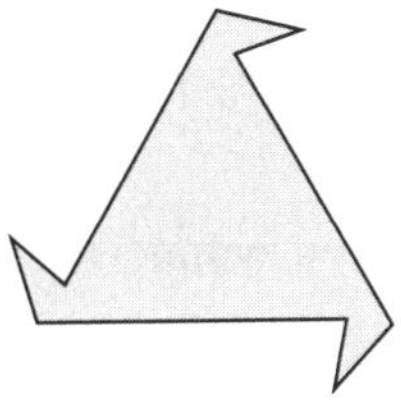

2. Tell whether each figure is a polygon. Explain how you know.

a.

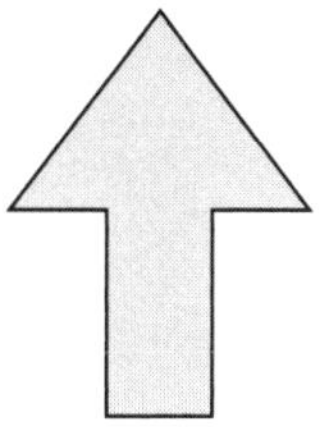

b.

c.

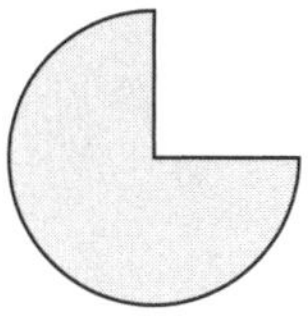

d.

3. Examine Shapes L, R, and N from the Shapes Set (or look at the drawings from Problem 1.1). How are these polygons alike? How are they different?

4. Examine Shapes A, I, P, and T from the Shapes Set (or look at the drawings from Problem 1.1). How are these polygons alike? How are they different?

5. Tell whether each statement is *true* or *false.* Justify your answers.

a. All squares are rectangles.

b. All rectangles are parallelograms.

c. All rectangles are squares.

d. All parallelograms are rectangles.

Notes

6. a. Copy the shapes below. Draw all the lines of symmetry.

Homework Help Online
PHSchool.com
For: Help with Exercise 6
Web Code: ame-3106

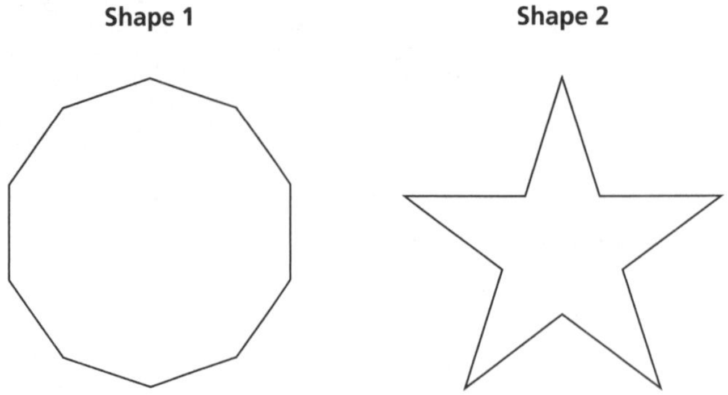

b. Do these shapes have rotation symmetry? Explain.

7. Half of the figure below is hidden. The vertical line is a line of symmetry for the complete figure. Copy the part of the figure shown. Then draw the missing half.

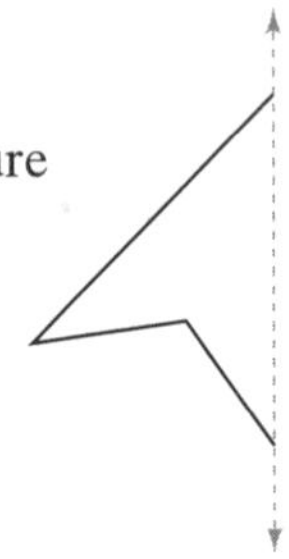

8. Below is a rug design from the Southwest United States.

a. Name some of the polygons in the rug.

b. Describe the symmetries of the design.

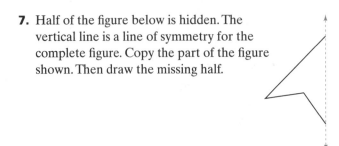

STUDENT PAGE

Notes

9. Here are three state flags.

Arizona

Ohio

New Mexico

a. Describe the lines of symmetry in each whole flag.

b. Do any of the shapes or designs within the flags have rotation symmetry? If so, which ones?

c. Design your own flag. Your flag should have at least one line of symmetry. Your flag should also include three shapes that have rotation symmetry. List the shapes in your flag that have rotation symmetry.

For Exercises 10 and 11, use these quilt patterns.

Pattern A

Pattern B

10. Name some of the polygons in each quilt pattern.

11. Describe the symmetries of each quilt pattern.

12. a. Does a circle have any symmetries? If so, explain and show some examples.

b. Can you make a tiling pattern with circles? If so, explain and show some examples.

13. Choose a rectangle from your Shapes Set, or draw your own. Find two ways that copies of your rectangle can be used to tile a surface. Sketch your tilings.

Notes

14. Choose a parallelogram from your Shapes Set, or draw your own. Find two ways that copies of your parallelogram can be used to tile a surface. Sketch your tilings.

15. Choose a scalene triangle from your Shapes Set, or draw your own. Find two ways that copies of your triangle can be used to tile a surface. Sketch your tilings.

16. Find three examples of tilings in your school, home, or community. Describe the patterns and make a sketch of each.

Connections

For each fraction, find two equivalent fractions. One fraction should have a denominator less than the one given. The other fraction should have a denominator greater than the one given.

17. $\frac{4}{12}$ 18. $\frac{9}{15}$ 19. $\frac{15}{35}$ 20. $\frac{20}{12}$

Copy the fractions and insert <, >, or = to make a true statement.

21. $\frac{5}{12}$ ■ $\frac{9}{12}$ 22. $\frac{15}{35}$ ■ $\frac{12}{20}$ 23. $\frac{7}{13}$ ■ $\frac{20}{41}$ 24. $\frac{45}{36}$ ■ $\frac{35}{28}$

Go Online
PHSchool.com
For: Multiple-Choice Skills Practice
Web Code: ama-3154

25. **Multiple Choice** Choose the correct statement.

A. $\frac{5}{6} = \frac{11}{360}$ **B.** $\frac{3}{4} = \frac{300}{360}$ **C.** $\frac{1}{4} = \frac{90}{360}$ **D.** $\frac{3}{36} = \frac{33}{360}$

Alberto's little sister Marissa decides to take a ride on a merry-go-round. It is shaped like the one shown. Marissa's starting point is also shown.

26. **Multiple Choice** Choose the point where Marissa will be after the ride completes $\frac{4}{8}$ of a full turn.

F. point C **G.** point D

H. point E **J.** point G

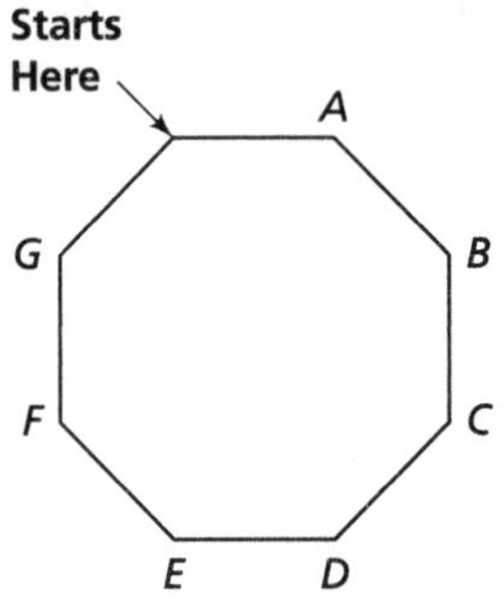

27. **Multiple Choice** Where will Marissa be after the ride completes $\frac{1}{2}$ of a full turn?

A. point B **B.** point C

C. point D **D.** point F

Notes

28. Find all the possible rectangles with whole number side lengths that can be made with the given number of identical square tiles. Give the dimensions of each rectangle.

a. 30 square tiles

b. 24 square tiles

c. 36 square tiles

d. 17 square tiles

e. How are the dimensions of the rectangles for a given number of square tiles related to factor pairs of the number?

f. Which of the rectangles you made were squares? Give the dimensions of the squares you made.

Extensions

For Exercises 29–33, one diagonal of each quadrilateral has been drawn. Complete parts (a) and (b) for each quadrilateral.

a. Is the given diagonal a line of symmetry? Why or why not?

b. Does the figure have any other lines of symmetry? If so, copy the figure and sketch the symmetry lines.

29.

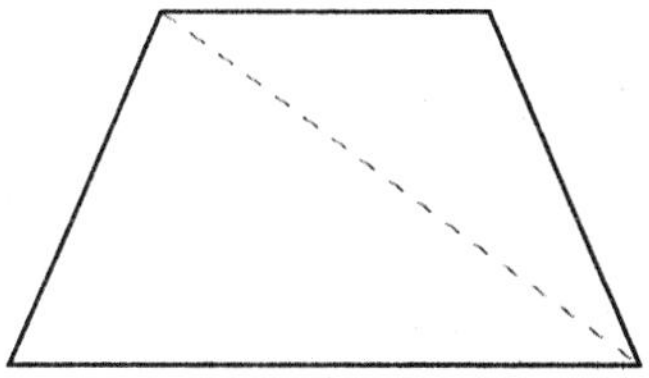

30.

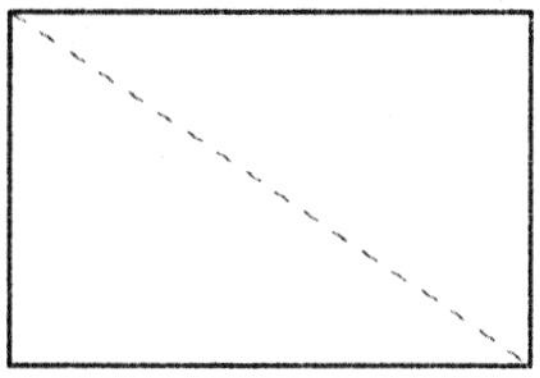

31.

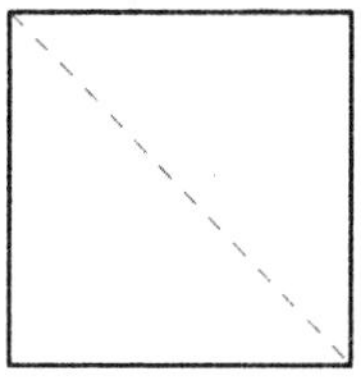

32.

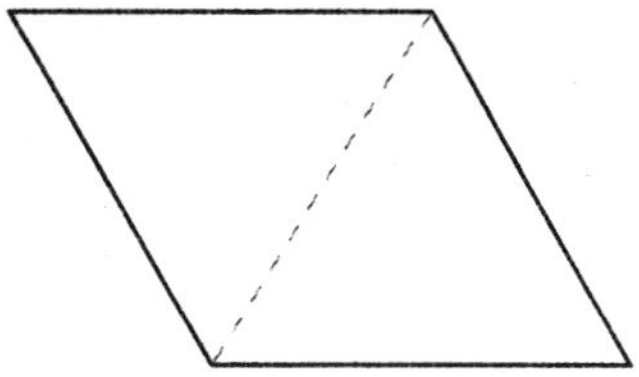

33.

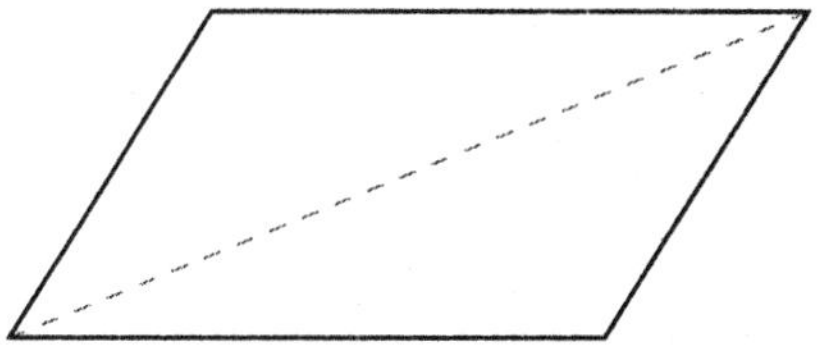

Notes

For Exercises 34 and 35, use the two given shapes to form a tiling pattern. Trace and cut out the shapes, or use shapes from your Shapes Set. Sketch your tilings.

34.

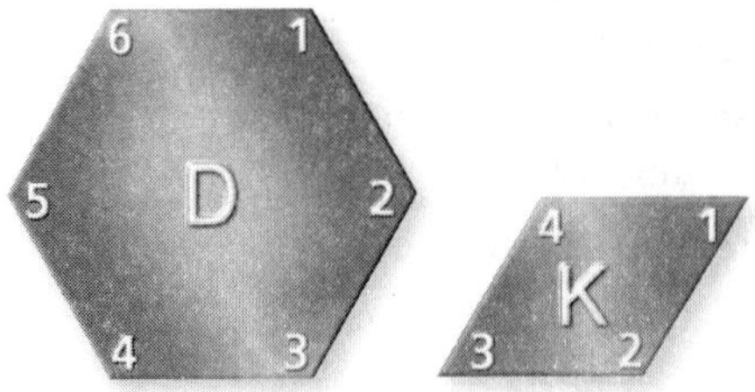

35.

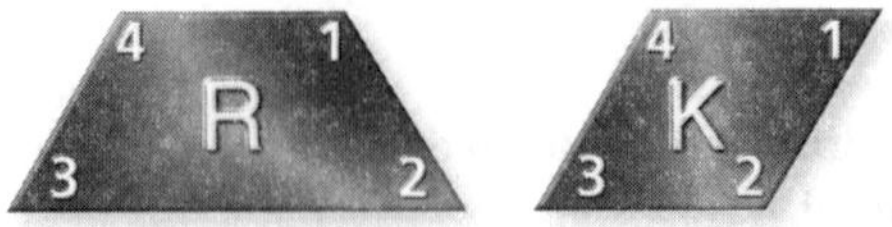

36. Choose an irregular quadrilateral from your Shapes Set, such as Q or U, or draw your own. Cut out several copies of your quadrilateral. See whether you can use the copies to tile a surface. Sketch your findings. Test other irregular quadrilaterals to see if they can be used to tile a surface. Summarize what you find about using irregular quadrilaterals to tile a surface.

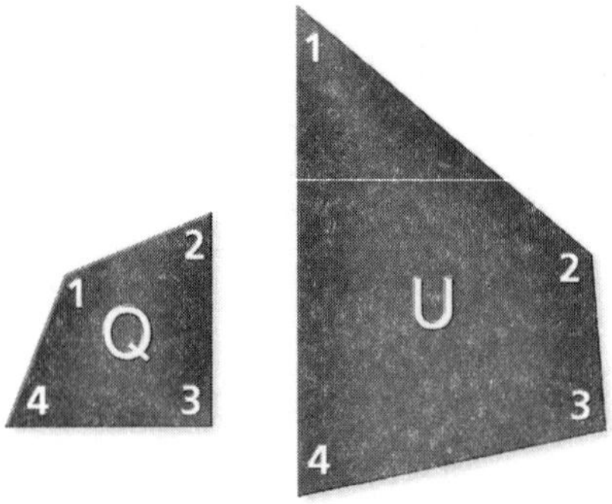

Notes

Mathematical Reflections 1

In this investigation, you explored some properties of polygons. You saw that some polygons have reflection or rotation symmetry, while others have no symmetries. You also discovered that some polygons fit together like tiles to cover a flat surface, while others do not. These questions will help you summarize what you have learned.

Think about your answers to these questions. Discuss your ideas with other students and your teacher. Then write a summary of your findings in your notebook.

1. a. What does it mean for a figure to have reflection symmetry? Give an example.

b. What does it mean for a figure to have rotation symmetry? Give an example.

2. a. Using one shape at a time, which regular polygons will fit together to tile a surface? Which regular polygons cannot tile a surface?

b. Why do you think that some shapes make tilings and some do not?

Unit Project What's Next?

What information about shapes can you add to your *Shapes and Designs* project?

STUDENT PAGE

STUDENT PAGE

Notes

Investigation 1

ACE Assignment Choices

Differentiated Instruction
Solutions for All Learners

Problem 1.1

Core 1–5
Other *Connections* 17–25

Problem 1.2

Core 6–9
Other *Applications* 10, 11; *Connections* 26–27; *Extensions* 29–33; unassigned choices from previous problems

Problem 1.3

Core 13–16
Other *Applications* 12, *Connections* 28, *Extensions* 34–36; unassigned choices from previous problems

Adapted For suggestions about adapting Exercise 6 and other ACE exercises, see the CMP *Special Needs Handbook*.
Connecting to Prior Units 17–27: *Bits and Pieces I*

Applications

1. a. The shape is a polygon with five sides.
   b. The shape is a polygon with nine sides.
2. a. Yes. This figure is a polygon because it is a closed figure with straight sides.
   b. No. This figure is not a polygon because it is not closed.
   c. No. This figure is not a polygon because some of its sides are curved.
   d. No. A circle is not a polygon because it has curved lines.
3. They are alike in that they have four sides and at least one pair of parallel (students may not know this term yet and can explain it in other ways) sides. Shapes L and N are different than Shape R since they have two pairs of parallel sides whereas R only has one pair.
4. They are all triangles. Shape A has all sides of the same length (equilateral); Shape P has two sides of the same length (isosceles); Shapes I and T have no sides of the same length (scalene).
5. a. True. Squares have all of the properties of rectangles: two pairs of opposite sides with the same length and four right angles.
   b. True. All rectangles are quadrilaterals with opposite sides of the same length and parallel.
   c. False. In a rectangle all sides do not have to be equal; for example see Shape J.
   d. True. All rectangles are parallelograms. See part (b). [Note: Logically, this statement is the negation of the statement in part (b).]
6. a. Shape 1 (a decagon) has ten lines of symmetry. Shape 2 (also known as a pentagram) has five lines of symmetry.
   b. Both shapes have rotation symmetry. Shape 1 can be repeatedly rotated $\frac{1}{10}$ of a turn and Shape 2 can be repeatedly rotated $\frac{1}{5}$ of a turn.
7. 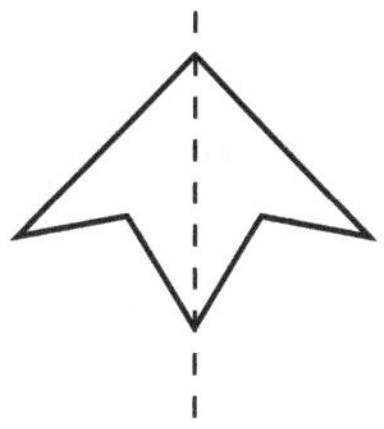
8. a. Triangles, parallelograms, dodecagons, 36-gons
   b. The rug has 180° and 360° rotation symmetries. The 36-gons inside the rug also have 180° and 360° rotation symmetries.

9. **a.** Arizona's flag and New Mexico's flag have vertical lines of symmetry through the middle. Ohio's flag does not have a horizontal line of symmetry because the stars don't all match up. New Mexico's flag has a horizontal line of symmetry.

   b. The circle in the Ohio flag, the stars in the Ohio and Arizona flags and the design in the New Mexico flag all have rotation symmetry through the middle.

   c. Answers will vary.

10. Possible Answers: Pattern A: squares, rectangles, triangles, and octagons
Possible Answers: Pattern B: triangles, squares, rectangles, and octagons

11. Pattern A: The quilt has reflection symmetry around a vertical line in the center, a horizontal line in the middle, and two diagonal lines. (Note: Some students may disagree since the colors may not match up, but if they focus on the shapes there is both reflection and rotation symmetry.) Also the quilt has 90°, 180°, 270°, and 360° rotation symmetry.
Pattern B: Again, disregarding color, the quilt is in the shape of a square and has a vertical line of symmetry, a horizontal line of symmetry and two diagonal lines of symmetry. It also has 90°, 180°, 270°, and 360° rotation symmetry.

12. **a.** The circle is full of reflection (or line) symmetries as well as rotation symmetries. Any line through the center of the circle (a diameter) is a line of symmetry. Any amount of turn around the center of the figure will make the figure fit into exactly the same position.

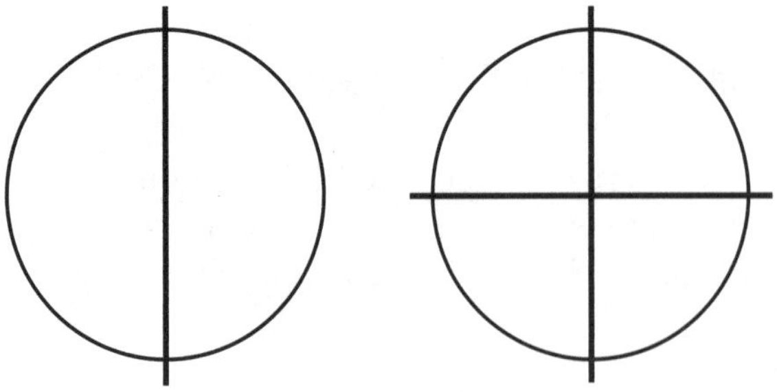

   b. No, it is not possible to tile with circles only. There would always be some overlap or gap.

13. Answers will vary. Possibilities include:

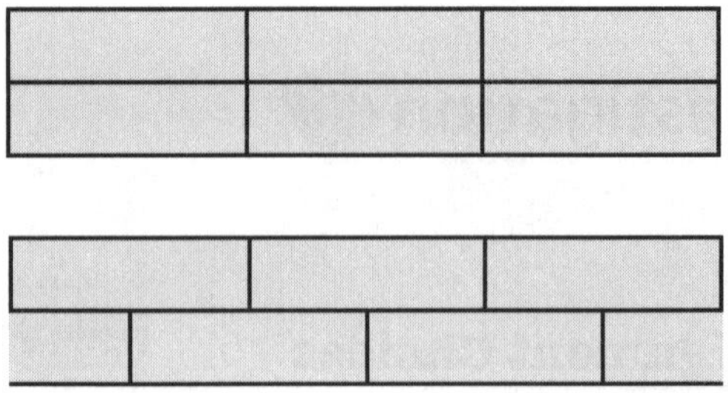

14. Answers will vary. Possible answers include:

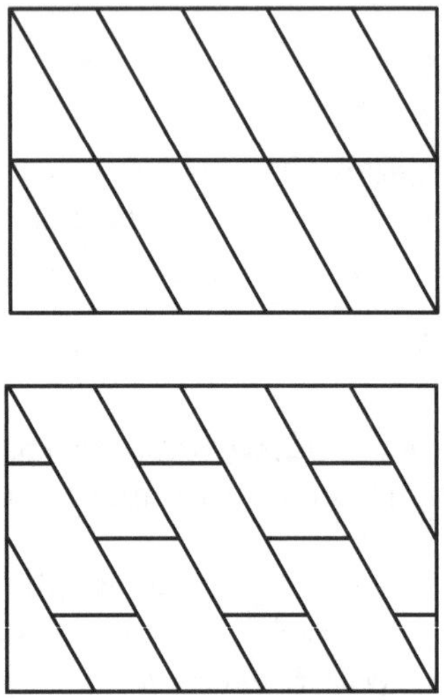

15. Answers will vary. One possible answer:

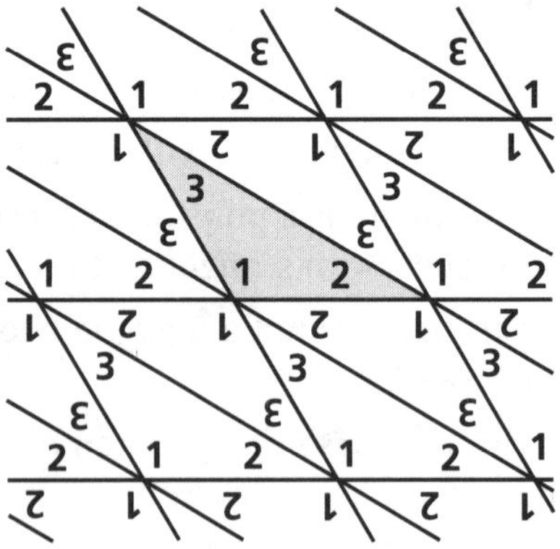

Note: If the triangle is scalene, each vertex of the tiling must have two occurrences of each angle.

16. Answers will vary. Possible answers:

a. Our hardwood floor is made of long rectangles tiled together.

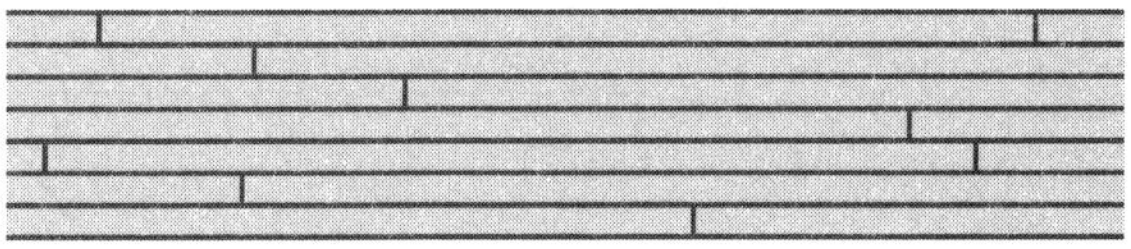

b. The dropped ceiling in my classroom is a tile of squares and long rectangles.

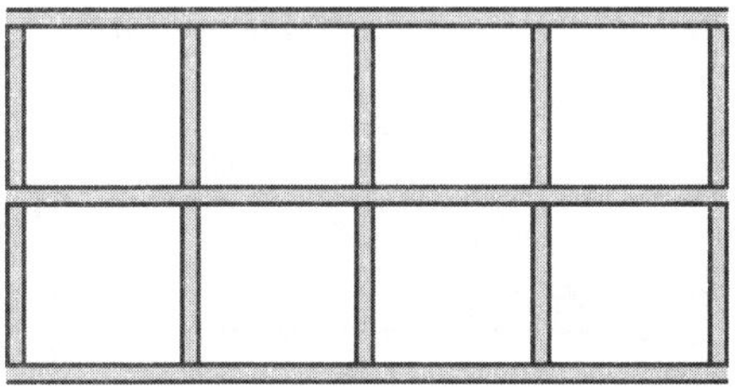

c. The Log Cabin quilt on my bed is made of different-size rectangles. Here's a small portion of it.

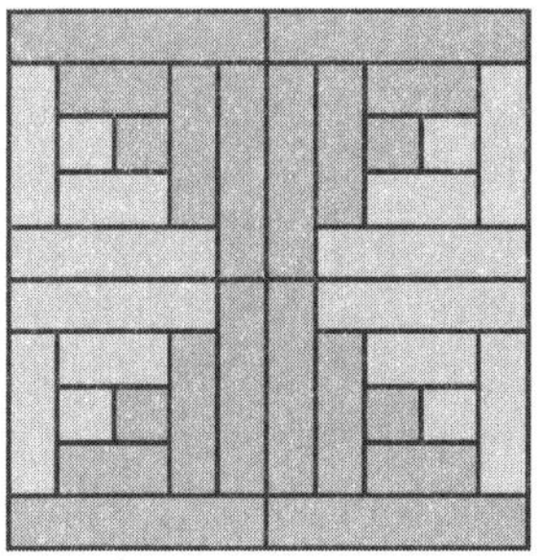

Connections

Possible answers:

17. $\frac{8}{24}, \frac{2}{6}$ **18.** $\frac{18}{30}, \frac{3}{5}$ **19.** $\frac{30}{70}, \frac{3}{7}$ **20.** $\frac{40}{24}, \frac{10}{6}$

21. $<$ **22.** $<$ **23.** $>$ **24.** $=$

25. C **26.** G **27.** C

28. For the answers a to d, some students may or may not list both, for example, 1×30 and 30×1. For the purposes of this exercise, it is not necessary to list both.

a. $1 \times 30, 2 \times 15, 3 \times 10, 5 \times 6, 10 \times 3, 15 \times 2, 30 \times 1$

b. $1 \times 24, 2 \times 12, 3 \times 8, 4 \times 6, 6 \times 4, 8 \times 3, 12 \times 2, 24 \times 1$

c. $1 \times 36, 2 \times 18, 3 \times 12, 4 \times 9, 6 \times 6, 9 \times 4, 12 \times 3, 18 \times 2, 36 \times 1$

d. $1 \times 17, 17 \times 1$

e. The dimensions are the same as the factor pairs because they are the numbers you multiply to get their products, which are also the number of square tiles.

f. 36 square tiles form a square whose dimensions are 6 tiles by 6 tiles.

Extensions

29. a. No. This is not a line of symmetry, because the part of the figure on the one side of it does not look like it is being reflected in a mirror to form the part on the other side of the line.

b. Vertical line through the middle of top and bottom sides.

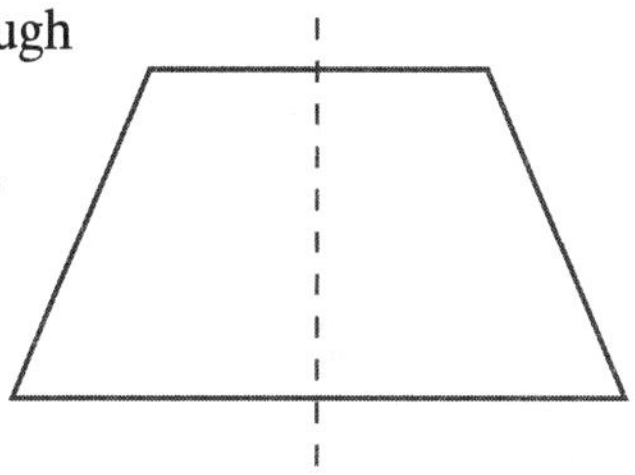

30. a. No. This is not a line of symmetry because the part of the figure on the one side of it does not look like it is being reflected in a mirror to form the part on the other side of the line.

b. Horizontal and vertical lines through the middle.

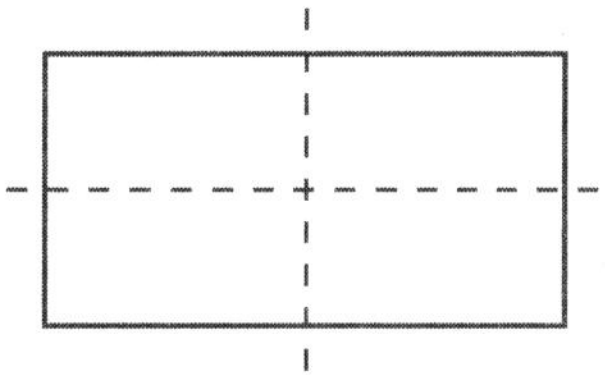

31. a. Yes. This is a line of symmetry because the part of the figure on the one side of it does look like it is being reflected in a mirror to form the part on the other side of the line.

b. Horizontal, vertical, and a diagonal line from right to left, all going through the center.

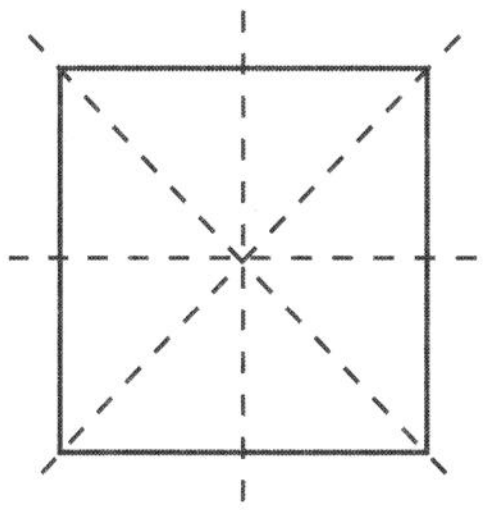

32. **a.** Yes. This is a line of symmetry because the part of the figure on the one side of it does look like it is being reflected in a mirror to form the part on the other side of the line.

b. The rhombus has the other diagonal as a line of symmetry.

33. **a.** No. This is not a line of symmetry because the part of the figure on the one side of it does not look like it is being reflected in a mirror to form the part on the other side of the line.

b. The parallelogram has no lines of symmetry.

34. Two examples:

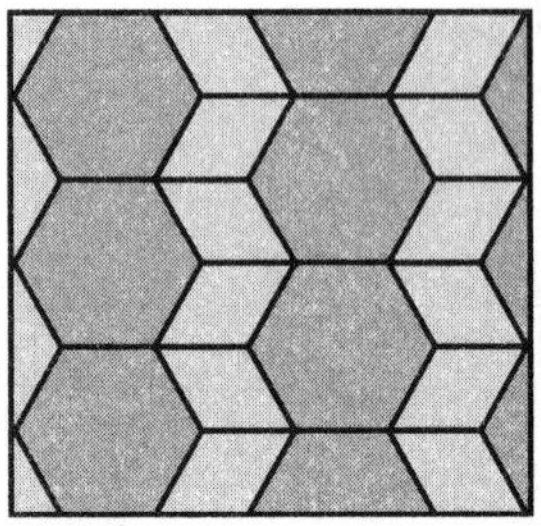

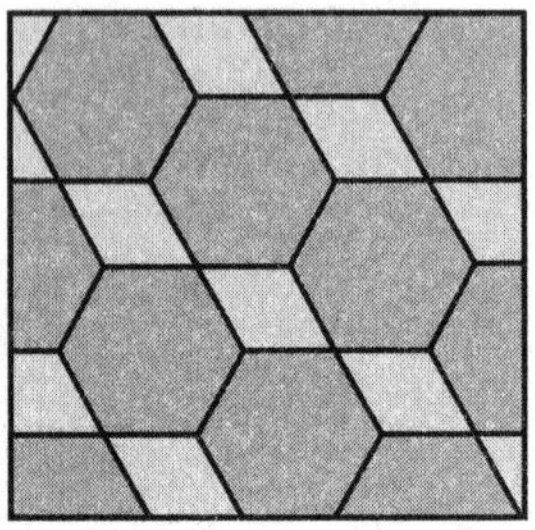

35. Two examples:

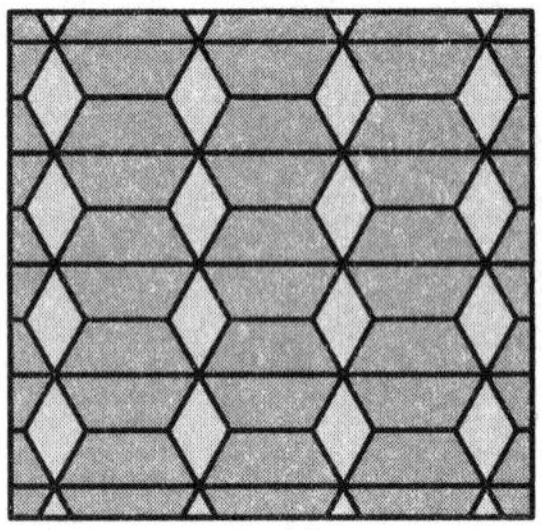

36. The irregular quadrilateral will tile a floor. Because there are 360° in the angles of a quadrilateral, you need to be sure that you have each angle around each vertex point. As with the scalene triangle, you need to put together edges that are the same length. To help students see the pattern and to see that the pattern works for any quadrilateral, label the sides and the vertices. This shows that there are copies of each of the angles of the quadrilateral around each vertex. It also shows that the sides are always placed so that the lengths match and the labels are reversed.

It will not be easy for students to see how to use the irregular quadrilateral. If no one discovers how to do a tiling with that shape (or even one of the others), we recommend that you leave it as an open question for students to work on rather than showing students yourself.

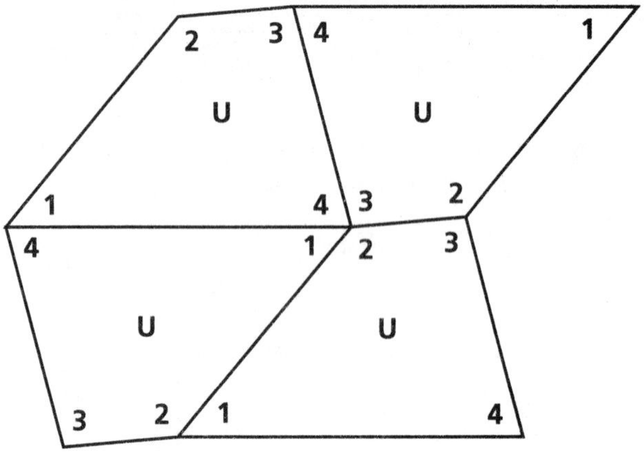

Possible Answers to Mathematical Reflections

1. **a.** A polygon with reflection symmetry has two halves that are mirror images of each other. If the polygon is folded over the line of symmetry, the two halves of the shape match exactly. There are many possible examples since all regular polygons have reflection symmetries. Other examples may include: isosceles triangles, rectangles, parallelograms with all sides of equal length, and trapezoids with non-parallel sides of equal length.

b. A polygon with rotation symmetry can be turned around its center point less than 360° and still look exactly the same for certain angles of rotation. All regular polygons and all parallelograms have rotation symmetries.

2. **a.** Equilateral triangles, squares, and regular hexagons can tile a surface. Other regular polygons cannot, such as regular octagons and pentagons.

b. Shapes that tile have angles that completely surround the vertex with no gaps or overlaps. Their angle measures are factors of 360, like 60, 90, or 120 (angles and their measures will be discussed further in Investigation 2).

Investigation 2 Polygons and Angles

Mathematical and Problem-Solving Goals

- Use and develop benchmarks to estimate the size of angles
- Increase the ability to reason with shapes
- Practice measuring angles and realize when precision in measurement is important.
- Realize that as the sides of an angle are extended, the angle size or the amount of the turn does not change, but the distance between the two sides does change
- Explore the patterns among angles created when two or more parallel lines are cut by another line
- Develop a better understanding of parallel lines and parallelograms

Summary of Problems

Problem 2.1 Understanding Angles

Students estimate angles by comparing them to 90° or a right angle turn.

Problem 2.2 Developing Angle Benchmarks

Students play a game on circular grids. This helps them to develop angle sense using rotations of 30° and 45° and their multiples.

Problem 2.3 Using an Angle Ruler

Students practice using an angle ruler (a movable protractor) to measure angles of some of the shapes in the Shapes Set.

Problem 2.4 Analyzing Measurement Errors

Students analyze the effects of measurement error in computing the angle Amelia Earhart needed to fly to reach her next destination.

Problem 2.5 Angles and Parallel Lines

Students explore some interesting patterns among the angles created when two or more parallel lines are cut by a line.

	Suggested Pacing	Materials for Students	Materials for Teachers	ACE Assignments
All	$7\frac{1}{2}$ days	Calculators, student notebooks	Blank transparencies, angle ruler	
2.1	1 day		Transparency 2.1	1–3, 27–29
2.2	1 day	Labsheet 2.2 (1 per group)	Transparencies 2.2A and 2.2B	4–9, 30–36, 41
2.3	2 days	Shapes Sets (1 per group), angle rulers (1 per student)	Transparency 2.3, overhead Shapes Set (Transparency 1.1E)	10–17, 37
2.4	1 day	Angle rulers (1 per student), rulers, Labsheet 2.4	Transparency 2.4	18–20, 38–40
2.5	2 days	Shapes Sets (1 per group), angle rulers (1 per student), Labsheet 2.5	Transparencies 2.5A and 2.5B	21–26, 42–44
MR	$\frac{1}{2}$ day			

2.1 Understanding Angles

Goal

- Use a right angle as a benchmark to estimate the size of angles

Students are shown what a one-degree angle looks like and are introduced to the measurement of angles. A complete turn is broken into 360 small turns, each of which is called 1° of turn or an angle measuring 1°. This means that a right angle, which is one-fourth of a turn, would be $\frac{1}{4}$ of 360° or 90° in measure. This is the first time students are being asked to deal with numbers of degrees as a way to identify angles. They will now equate right angles with 90° and use estimation skills to help sketch angles of other degrees.

Launch 2.1

Talk about the Getting Ready for Problem 2.1 that introduces angles as turns, wedges, or two sides with a common vertex with students.

You can have them examine the room to find examples of each kind of angle. Here are possible examples that students may find:

- *The corner of the door between the top edge and one of the vertical edges might be called a wedge (actually makes a 90° wedge). The angle of turn might be the swinging or opening of the door. When Josh holds the door open to talk with his friend before class begins, the door and the wall with the hinge could be the sides of an angle with a common vertex.*

What you want to do is to get the students thinking about angles as turns, wedges, and two sides with a common vertex and get them looking for examples. Students should be encouraged to continue to look for interesting angles in the world while they study the rest of the unit. You may want to display students' examples of the angles they find in the classroom.

Suggested Questions In order to introduce students to right angles and the meaning of one degree, you could ask the following:

- *We all know what a square corner is. We also know that another name for a square corner is a right angle. Who can find a right angle in this room?*
- *Who can find an angle less than a right angle in this room?*
- *Who can find an angle greater than a right angle in this room?*
- *How can we tell when an angle is less than a right angle?*
- *Draw an example and explain how you know it is less than a right angle.*

Here you are focusing the students on right angles and ways of making comparisons. The students may say that you can just fold a square corner and compare it to the angle. Tell the students that the standard system of measuring angles breaks the full turn into 360 small turns, each of which is 1° of a turn. This means that a right angle, which is one-fourth of a turn, would be $\frac{1}{4}$ of 360° or 90° in measure.

Suggested Questions Draw an angle on the overhead and ask:

- *Is the angle larger than a right angle, equal to a right angle, or smaller than a right angle?*
- *Estimate about how many degrees you think are in the measure of the angle.*

Extend the sides of the angle and ask:

- *Does the measure of the angle change?* (When a reasonable answer has been found, let the class work on Problem 2.1.)

Have students work on this problem individually.

Explore 2.1

Students can share strategies and answers with their classmates. If students finish early, have them draw angles and estimate their size.

Summarize 2.1

There are many ways to check students' sketches. One possibility is to display a transparency containing the correct angles so that students can compare them to their sketches. You may want to pass the transparency around so that students can check their work by placing the transparency over their angles. Make sure students understand that their sketches do not have to be a perfect match.

You might want to have a class discussion about why 90° was chosen as the measure of a right angle. Use the Did You Know? as part of the discussion.

Emphasize to students that when we measure an angle, we are measuring the opening or turn between the sides of the angle. The lengths of the two sides (rays) that form the angle do not affect the measure of the angle. For example, these are all 30° angles:

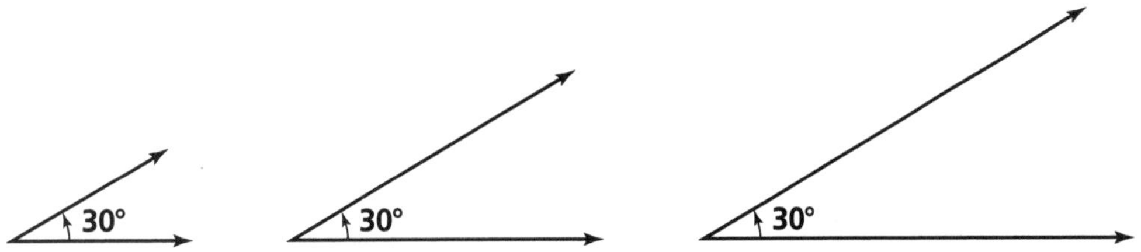

INVESTIGATION 2

2.1 Understanding Angles

At a Glance

PACING 1 day

Mathematical Goal

- Use a right angle as a benchmark to estimate the size of angles

Launch

Talk about the Getting Ready. Have students find examples of each kind of angle. Introduce students to right angles and the meaning of one degree:

- *We all know what a square corner is. Another name for a square corner is a right angle. Who can find a right angle in this room?*
- *Who can find an angle less than a right angle in this room?*
- *Who can find an angle greater than a right angle?*
- *How can we tell when an angle is less than a right angle? Draw an example and explain how you know it is less than a right angle.*

Focus the students on right angles and on making comparisons.

- *The standard system of measuring angles breaks the full turn into 360 small turns, each of which is 1° of a turn. This means that a right angle, which is one-fourth of a turn, would be $\frac{1}{4}$ of 360° or 90° in measure.*

Draw an angle on the overhead and ask:

- *Is this angle larger than a right angle, equal to a right angle, or smaller than a right angle?*
- *Estimate about how many degrees you think are in the measure of the angle.*

Have students work on this problem individually.

Materials

- Blank transparencies
- Transparency 2.1

Vocabulary

- ray
- vertex
- degrees
- right angle

Explore

As you move around the room, look for more clues about students' prior knowledge of shapes. Students can put their results on poster paper.

Summarize

To check students' sketches, display a transparency containing the correct angles so that students can compare them to their sketches. Pass the transparency around so that students can check their work by placing the transparency over their angles. Sketches do not have to be a perfect match.

- *Why do you think 90° was chosen as the measure of a right angle?*
- *Why do you think a full turn is 360°?*
- *When we measure an angle, we are measuring the opening or turn between the sides of an angle. If we extend the sides of an angle, does the angle measure change?*

Draw three examples of 30° angles with different length rays on the overhead and explain why they all measure 30°.

Materials

- Student notebooks

ACE Assignment Guide for Problem 2.1

Differentiated Instruction
Solutions for All Learners

Core 1, 2, 29
Other *Applications* 3, *Connections* 27, 28

Adapted For suggestions about adapting ACE exercises, see the CMP *Special Needs Handbook.*
Connecting to Prior Units 28: *Prime Time*; 29: *Bits and Pieces I*

Answers to Problem 2.1

A. 1. 30°

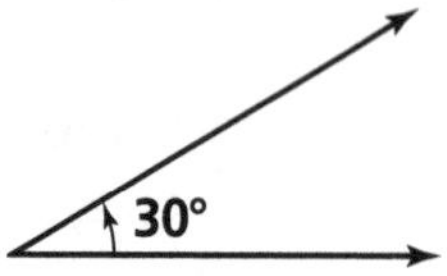

2. 60°

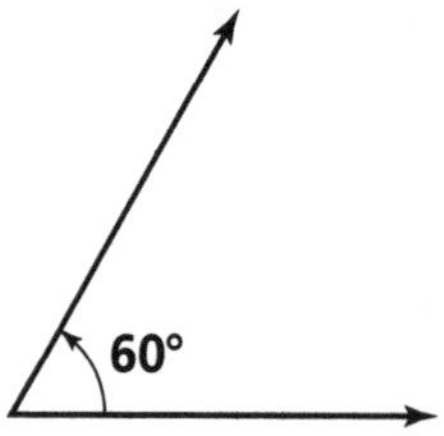

3. 22.5°

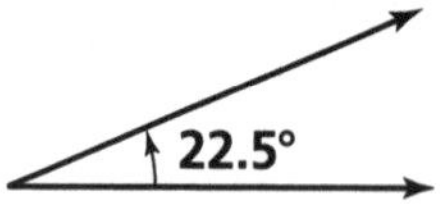

4. 135°

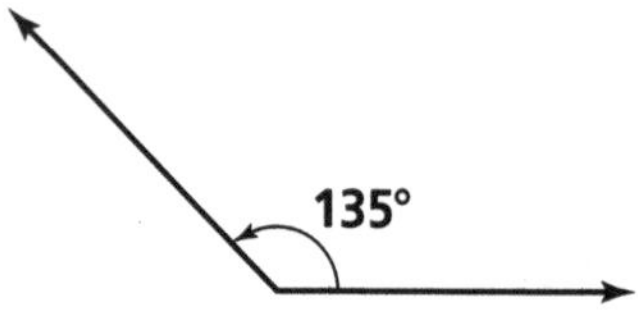

5. 180°

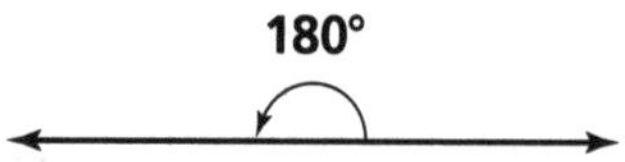

6. 270°

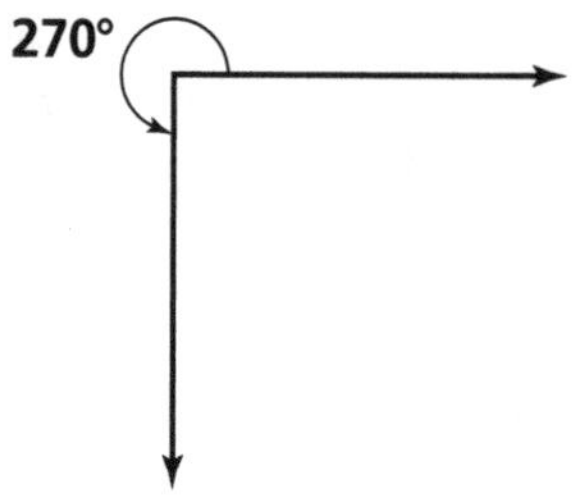

B. 1.

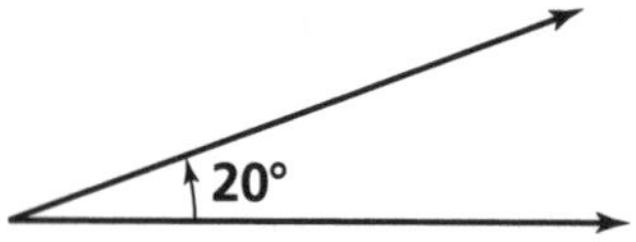

2.

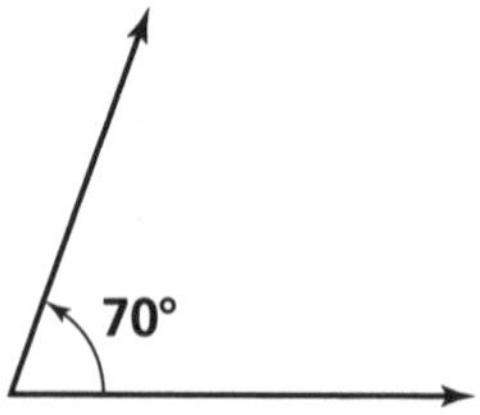

3.

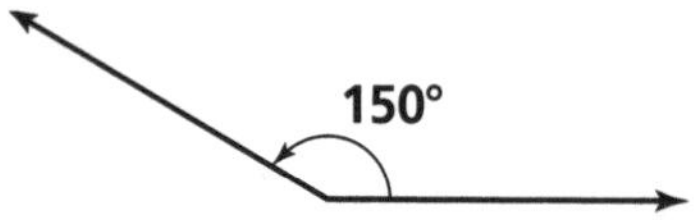

4.

5.

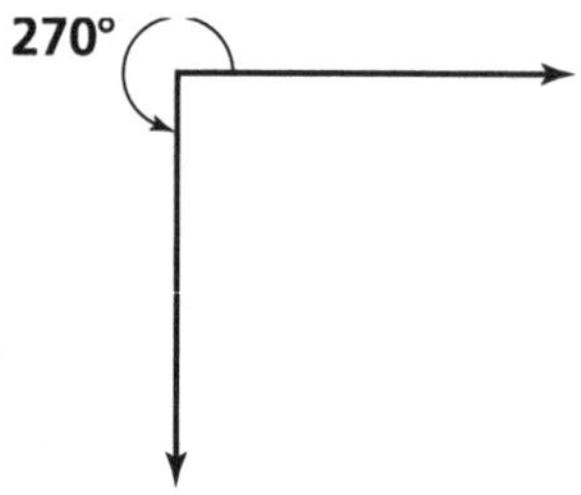

6.

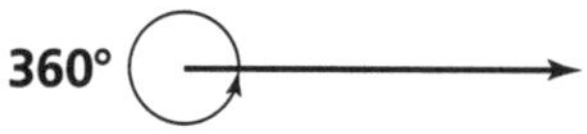

C. 1. 35°

2. 150°

3. about 235°

2.2 Developing Angle Benchmarks

Goal

- Develop angle benchmarks

We will look at two grids on which the polar coordinate system can be used to locate points. We still use two numbers. However, the first number tells how far to move in the x direction (horizontal direction) to locate a circle around the center of the plane, and the second number tells how many degrees to turn to locate the point on the circle that represents the location of the point. This system of locating points is called the polar coordinate system.

Launch 2.2

Briefly review rectangular coordinates and ordered pairs with your students. Refer them to the rectangular coordinate grid in the student edition. There is an alternative launch to this problem, given below, which uses rectangular coordinates.

- *In this problem, we are going to explore a different way of locating points.*

Suggested Questions Refer students to the two grids on Transparency 2.2A. Point out that these grids have circles and lines that form angles. Have students look closely at the grid on the left.

- *What are the measures of some of the angles in this grid? Look especially at angles with a vertex at the center of the grid.* (Point out the 45°, 90°, 135° angles and so on.)

Help students to see that the angles are all multiples of 45°.

Use two polystrips to form an angle. Start with an angle of zero degrees and then gradually open it up. Continue to rotate one of the polystrips, creating larger and larger angles. Stop after a 45°, 90°, 135°, and 180° angle and ask about the measure of the angles.

Suggested Questions Now have students look at the grid on the right and ask:

- *What are the measures of some of the angles in this grid?*

Point out the 30°, 60°, 90°, 120° angles and so on. Help students to see that the angles are all multiples of 30°.

- *Using these grids, describe a point by giving two numbers. The first number tells how far to move from the center of the grid. The second number tells the amount of turn measured in degrees. How would I find the point (3, 90°)?*

Using either grid, help students to see that to locate this point, you move out 3 units along the 0° line (x-axis) in the positive direction and then moving counterclockwise through a turn of 90° along that circle.

Playing the game as a class helps students learn how to locate other points on both grids and understand how the grids work. You can use one of the grids on Transparency 2.2A.

We are going to play a game of tic-tac-toe on this new grid. To win, you will need four marks in a row, although four in a row may mean around a circle or on a line. We will play the left half of the room against the right half. The left half of the room will be X's, and the right half will be O's. Can someone on the left side of the room give me the coordinates of a point on this grid?

When a student gives you a point, count out from the center for the first number, then measure the turn on the circle for the second number. Mark this with an X.

- *Now I need someone on the right side of the room to give me the coordinates of a point.*

Again, count out to the right from the center, then measure around the circle. Mark the intersection with an O. Continue until one team gets four in a row.

Have the students play the game in pairs or two against two.

Alternative Launch

You could launch this problem by playing a version of four-in-a-row with rectangular coordinates. This would be a way to review or introduce students to rectangular coordinates. Start by drawing four vertical lines and four horizontal lines that intersect the vertical lines. The left vertical line is the y-axis and the lower horizontal line is the x-axis. But do not label the lines nor label any points on the lines.

Divide the class into two teams. Ask one team for a pair of numbers. Start counting at the lower left corner and try to locate the point. If the coordinates are not on the grid, start counting at the origin and pretend to fall off the grid. For example, if the first group gives the pair of numbers, (5, 1), start counting at the origin and go along the x-axis until you reach 4 and then oops—fall off the line. Students quickly understand that they need to give a pair of numbers that include 0, 1, 2, 3, or 4. Alternate taking a pair of numbers from each team and mark O or X. The first team to get four in a row wins.

Have the students play the game in pairs or two against two.

Explore 2.2

Hand out Labsheet 2.2. As you work with the groups, be sure they are using the grid appropriately. The game should increase students' estimation and reasoning skills with angles. Have them note any winning strategies they discover. If students finished early, you can hand out sheets with grids using 15° intervals from Transparency 2.2B or wait until the summary.

Summarize 2.2

Students can report on winning strategies they found or moves they hoped others would make to put them at an advantage. They should be able to discuss whether going first gives a noticeable advantage. Ask questions to focus the discussion on what they have learned about angles. Choose different points on the grid and ask students how to locate these points. You may want to use another grid in the summary such as one with rays at 15° intervals (Transparency 2.2B).

Have students tell you how to find your way to points on this grid.

2.2 Developing Angle Benchmarks

At a Glance

PACING 1 day

Mathematical Goal

- Develop angle benchmarks

Launch

Materials
- Transparency 2.2A

Briefly review rectangular coordinates and ordered pairs with your students. A rectangular coordinate grid is in the student edition.

- *In this problem, we are going to explore a different way of locating points.*

Refer students to the two grids on Transparency 2.2A. Point out that these grids have lines and circles that form angles. Have students look closely at the grid on the left.

- *What are the measures of some of the angles in this grid? Look especially at angles with a vertex at the center of the grid.*

Now have students look at the grid on the right and ask:

- *What are the measures of some of the angles in this grid?*

Point out the 30°, 60°, 90°, 120° angles and so on. Help students to see that the angles are all multiples of 30°.

- *Using these grids, you describe a point by giving two numbers. The first number tells how far to move from the center of the grid. The second number tells the amount of turn measured in degrees. How would I find the point (3, 90°)?*

Using either grid, help students to see how to locate this point.

- *We are going to play a game of tic-tac-toe on this new grid.*
- *To win, you will need four marks in a row—although four in a row may mean around a circle or on a line.*
- *We will play the left half of the room against the right half. The left half of the room will be X's and the right half will be O's.*

When a student on the left half of the room gives you a point, count out from the center for the first number, then measure the turn on the circle for the second number. Mark this with an X. Ask a student on the right side of the room for a point. Continue until one team gets four in a row. Have the students play the game in pairs or two against two.

Alternative Launch:

You could launch this problem by playing a version of four-in-a-row with rectangular coordinates.

Explore

Materials
- Labsheet 2.2 (1 per group)

Hand out Labsheet 2.2. As you work with the groups, be sure they are using the grid appropriately. Have them note winning strategies.

Summarize

Students can report on winning strategies they found or moves they hoped others would make to put them at an advantage. They should be able to discuss whether going first gives a noticeable advantage. Choose different points on the grid and ask students how to locate these points. On Transparency 2.2B is another grid with rays at 15° intervals that can also be used.

Materials
- Student notebooks
- Transparency 2.2B

ACE Assignment Guide for Problem 2.2

Differentiated Instruction
Solutions for All Learners

Core 4, 5, 36
Other *Applications* 6–9, *Connections* 30–35, *Extensions* 41; unassigned choices from previous problems

Adapted For suggestions about adapting Exercises 6–9 and other ACE exercises, see the CMP *Special Needs Handbook*.
Connecting to Prior Units 30–35: *Bits and Pieces I*

Answers to Problem 2.2

A. One possible strategy: (0, 0°) is useful because it has to be a part of any win on the straight lines.

B. Some examples: *A* (3, 150°), *B* (1, 0°), *C* (2, 30°)

2.3 Using an Angle Ruler

Goals

- More practice with estimation
- Increase the ability to reason with shapes
- Practice measuring angles with an angle ruler

This section gives students practice with using angles they are familiar with (such as the right angle) to estimate the measures of other angles and gives students experience measuring angles. This problem also introduces a measuring tool for angles that has a long history, especially in medicine, but little prior use in mathematics education. The angle ruler's formal name is goniometer, which means "angle measurer."

Mathematics Background

For background on how to use a goniometer, see pages 6 and 7.

Launch 2.3

More Estimation with Regular Polygons

In this problem, students use Shapes A, B, D, K, R, and V (from the Shape Set), and combinations of these shapes, to estimate and to find the measure of every angle in each shape.

Suggested Questions First have students look at the indicated shapes as you ask questions:

- *Which of these shapes has the angle with the smallest measure?* (Shape V)
- *Which shape has the angle with the largest measure?* (Shape V)
- *Can you find a 90° angle in one of these shapes? How do you know it is 90°?* (Shape B. It appears to have a square corner.)
- *How do the angles of Shape D compare to a right angle? Are their measures greater or less?* (greater)
- *What would be a reasonable estimate of the measure of the greatest angle of Shape D? How do you know this is reasonable?* (any angle between 100° and 135°)

Introducing the Angle Ruler

When you are satisfied that students have some strategies to begin reasoning about the angles of the shapes, pick one shape, and have students estimate its angle measures. Then demonstrate how to use the angle ruler. Instructions for using the angle ruler can be found in the student edition. Demonstrate how to measure one of the angles as students follow along at their desks. Have them measure two or three separate angles on a polygon with you and record the angle measures they read. Students will get slightly different measures, and this will allow you to talk about the fact that all measures are approximations. There is always some error in the measurements we make, no matter how precise the tool we are using.

To avoid a common error in using the angle ruler, make sure students understand that the top arm of the angle ruler needs to be rotated counterclockwise from the ruler arm to get an accurate measurement.

When you feel that students understand how to use the angle ruler by placing the vertex of the angle at the rivet, have them measure an angle they have already measured by aligning the angle's sides with the insides of the angle ruler's arms. Students should see that this method gives the same results except for errors of measurement. See pages 6 and 7 for more details.

Tell students that in Problem 2.3 they will first estimate the size of an angle of a shape and then check the estimate with the angle ruler. Students should note how they estimated the angle size.

Students can work in pairs for Questions A and B.

Explore 2.3

Each student should have a record of how they estimated the size of the angles in the shapes. Remind them to sketch each shape and to label its angle measures on the shape. As you work with the groups, look for interesting ways of reasoning that you want to be sure are shared in the summary. Students should measure their own angles for Question C and draw their own angles for Question D.

Summarize 2.3

Question A

Have students report their findings in a class discussion. Take time to explore all the strategies they used to arrive at their answers.

Here is one way a student worked with the square and the rhombus (Shape V):

- *Roberto knew that the four angles of the square are each 90°. Using that benchmark, he placed the rhombus (Shape V) on the square, aligning a vertex and side of one of the smaller rhombus angles with a vertex and side of the square. The angles did not match, but Roberto found that, by using two more rhombus shapes, three of the small angles together matched one angle of the square. He concluded that since three of the rhombus angles were equal to 90°, a single angle measured 30°. He could now use the 30° angle to help him find the measures of the angles in the other shapes.*

You may want to display these benchmark strategies for students to refer to as they proceed through the unit.

Question B

Have students record their measurements for some of the angles. Look for large discrepancies. If they occur, have the group measure again. You might want to ask students for suggestions for using the angle ruler to get a more accurate measurement. Save the angle measures for the regular polygons for Problem 3.1.

Question C

Up until now, students have used the angle ruler to measure angles that aligned with the ruler's 5° interval marks. In Question C, they need to measure between the 5° intervals. Ask students for answers and discuss what might account for any differences they may have found in the measurements. Students do not need to agree on the degree measurements, but their measurements should be close. Through their discussion, students will begin to understand the issues involved in making precise measurements. Use Transparency 2.3 to display the angles and their measures from Question C.

Suggested Questions You may want to ask the following:

- *How do you decide the number of degrees for angles between the 5° intervals on the ruler?*
- *What things do you check to make sure you are making accurate measurements?*

Be sure students notice the extra scale on the measuring circle of the angle ruler, which helps the user to measure with greater accuracy.

At a Glance

2.3 Using an Angle Ruler

PACING 2 days

Mathematical Goals

- More practice with estimation
- Increase the ability to reason with shapes
- Practice measuring angles with an angle ruler

Launch

Have students look at Shapes A, B, D, K, R, and V (from the Shapes Set) as you ask questions:

- *Which of these shapes has the angle with the smallest measure?*
- *Which shape has the angle with the largest measure?*
- *Can you find a 90° angle in one of these shapes?*
- *How do you know it is 90°?*
- *How do the angles of Shape D compare to a right angle? Are their measures greater or less?*
- *What is a reasonable estimate of the measure of the greatest angle of Shape D? How do you know this is reasonable?*

Pick one shape and have students estimate its angle measures. Demonstrate how to use the angle ruler. Instructions are in the student edition. Have them measure and record the measures for two or three separate angles on a polygon with you. If they want, they could trace around the polygon and measure on their sketch.

After you feel students understand how to use the angle ruler by placing the vertex of the angle at the rivet, have them measure an angle of a polygon they have already measured by aligning the angle's sides with the insides of the angle ruler's arms. Students should see that this method gives the same results except for errors of measurement.

Students can work in pairs for Questions A and B and individually for Questions C and D.

Materials

- Overhead Shapes Set (Transparency 1.1E)
- Shapes Set (1 per group)
- Angle rulers (1 per student)

Explore

Make sure each student records how they estimated the angle sizes. Remind them to sketch each shape and to label its angle measures on the sketch.

Have students measure and draw their own angles for Questions C and D.

Summarize

During a class discussion, look for large discrepancies in angle measurements. If they occur, have the group measure again.

- *How do you get a more accurate measure with the angle ruler?*

Materials

- Student notebooks
- Transparency 2.3

continued on next page

Summarize

continued

Save the angle measures for the regular polygons for Problem 3.1. In Question C, they need to measure between the 5° intervals. Use Transparency 2.3 to display the angle measures from Question C.

- *How do you decide the number of degrees for angles between the 5° intervals on the ruler?*
- *What things do you check to make sure you are making accurate measurements?*

Be sure students notice the extra scale on the measuring circle of the angle ruler, which helps the user to measure with greater accuracy.

ACE Assignment Guide for Problem 2.3

Differentiated Instruction
Solutions for All Learners

Core 15–17 (students will need angle rulers for these exercises)
Other *Applications* 10–14; *Connections* 37 (students will need angle rulers); unassigned choices from previous problems

Adapted For suggestions about adapting ACE exercises, see the CMP *Special Needs Handbook*.
Connecting to Prior Units 37: linear measurement in elementary school

Answers to Problem 2.3

A. Estimates should be within 5° of the actual angle measures listed below.

B. **1.** Shape A has three 60° angles.
Shape B has four 90° angles.
Shape D has six 120° angles.

Shape K

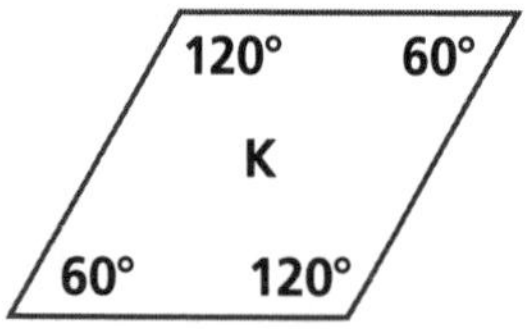

Shape R

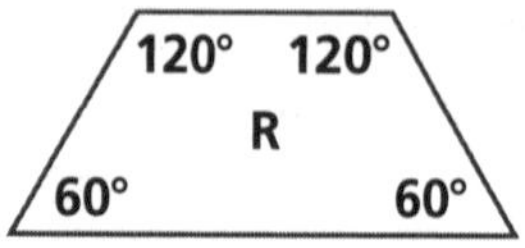

Shape V

C. **1.** 52–53°

2. 95–97°

3. 128–130°

4. 70°

D. **1.** A possible answer includes angles that measure between 0° and 52°, or an angle whose measure is less than the one found in part (1) of Question C.

2. A possible answer includes angles whose measure is greater than the answer in part (3) of Question C (128–130°).

2.4 Analyzing Measurement Errors

Goals

- Realize when precision in measurement is important
- Realize that as the sides of an angle are extended, the angle size or the amount of the turn does not change, but the distance between the two sides does change

The issue of the measure of an angle not being dependent on the lengths of the sides of the rays is a very important one. Students tend to have a hard time holding on to what is being measured when we measure an angle. You will see in the upcoming problems that we are confronting this problem in a number of ways. In Analyzing Measurement Errors, students will see that as you move further out on the edge of a ray, the distance to a corresponding point on the other ray does indeed get bigger. This is a chance to sort out what is being measured: the angle does not change, but the distance between points that are the same distance from the vertex on each of the rays will get much farther apart.

Launch 2.4

Draw an angle on the overhead and have students estimate its size. Extend the rays of the angle. Ask students if the angle measure changed when the sides were extended. Tell the story of the Amelia Earhart crash. Focus students on the issues raised in the problem. Ask students to guess how far off course they think that Amelia Earhart was.

Students can work in pairs, but each student needs to make their own measurements.

Explore 2.4

Suggest to students that they check their measurements. Remind them how to use the angle ruler and the extra circle on the ruler for greater precision.

Going Further

- *How close could Howland Island be for Amelia to land on it given that the measurement error had occurred?*

Summarize 2.4

Have group representatives report on the findings of their group (if you have chosen to use transparencies or large sheets of paper, let them present their work).

On Labsheet 2.4, the crash site is about 9° from Howland Island. The angle measure that reaches from one side of Howland to the other is about 2°. So if Amelia Earhart were aiming for the center of the island, she could be off 1° in either direction.

Students could also discuss whether Amelia Earhart could have spotted the island if she were 2° or 3° off in either direction.

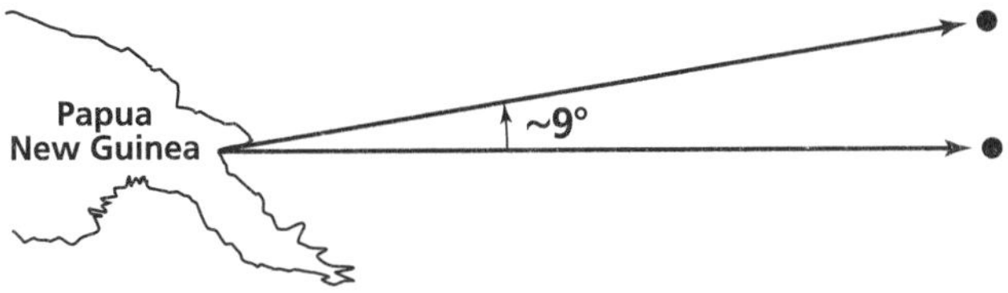

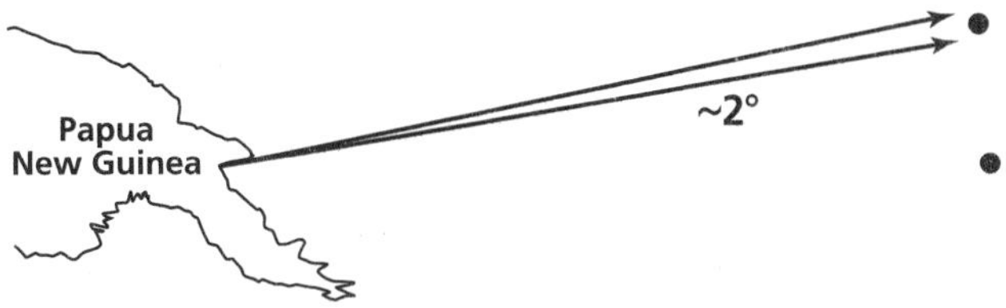

INVESTIGATION 2

Question B provides the opportunity to discuss a troubling aspect of angles that students come across. That is, as the sides of an angle are extended, the angle size or the amount of the turn does not change, but the distance between the two sides does change. This is one of the goals of the problem. (Figure 1)

Encourage students to get as close an estimate as they can on part C. The angles that they are dealing with are very small.

Figure 1

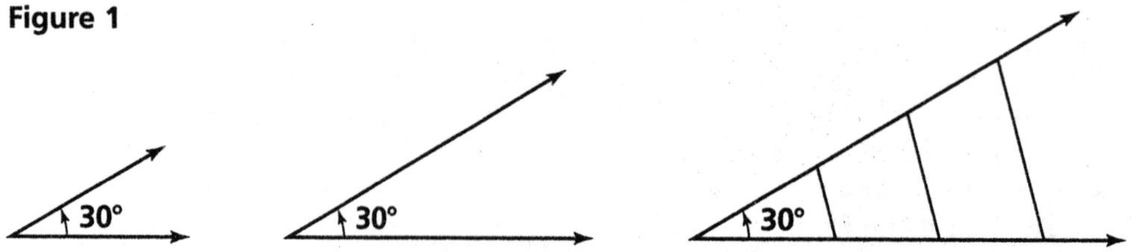

2.4 Analyzing Measurement Errors

At a Glance

PACING 1 day

Mathematical Goals

- Realize when precision in measurement is important
- Realize that as the sides of an angle are extended, the angle size or the amount of the turn does not change, but the distance between the two sides does change

Launch

Draw an angle on the overhead and have students estimate its size. Extend the rays of the angle. Ask students:

- *Did the angle measure change when the sides were extended?*

Tell the story of the Amelia Earhart crash. Focus students on the issues raised in the problem. Ask students:

- *How far off course do you think that Amelia Earhart was?*

Students can work in pairs, but each student needs to make their own measurements.

Material
- Transparency 2.4

Explore

Suggest to students that they check their measurements. Remind them how to use the angle ruler and the extra circle on the ruler for greater precision.

Going Further

- *How close could Howland Island be for Amelia to land on it given that the measurement error had occurred?*

Materials
- Labsheet 2.4
- Angle rulers (1 per student)
- Rulers

Summarize

Have group representatives report on the findings of the group (if you have chosen to use transparencies or large sheets of paper, let them present their work).

On Labsheet 2.4, the crash site is about 9° from Howland Island. The angle measure that reaches from one side of Howland to the other is about 2°. So, if Amelia Earhart was aiming for the center of the island, she could be off 1° in either direction.

Students could also discuss whether Amelia Earhart could have spotted the island if she was 2° or 3° off in either direction.

Question B provides the opportunity to discuss a troubling aspect of angles that students come across.

- *As the sides of an angle are extended, the angle size or the amount of the turn does not change. But what happens to the distance between the two sides?*
- *What does that mean for someone trying to navigate a plane?*

Encourage students to get as close an estimate as they can on Question C since the angles that they are dealing with are very small.

Materials
- Student notebooks
- Blank transparencies or large sheets of paper (optional)

ACE Assignment Guide for Problem 2.4

Differentiated Instruction
Solutions for All Learners

Core 18–20 (students will need angle rulers for some of these exercises)
Other *Connections* 38–40; unassigned choices from previous problems

Adapted For suggestions about adapting ACE exercises, see the CMP *Special Needs Handbook.*

Answers to Problem 2.4

A. about 9°

B. They are about 100 mi apart at points *A* and *D*, approximately 175 mi apart at points *B* and *E*; about 260 mi apart at points *C* and *F*. (There could be measurement error.) The important idea that students should notice is that the distance is increasing as they move further out on the ray.

C. She would fly over the Soloman Islands and probably land somewhere north of the Samoa islands.

2.5 Angles and Parallel Lines

Goals

- Explore the patterns among angles created when two or more parallel lines are cut by another line
- Develop a better understanding of parallel lines and parallelograms

Mathematics Background

For background on parallel lines and angles formed by transversal lines, see page 7.

Launch 2.5

Draw two intersecting lines. Label the angles *a, b, c, d.*

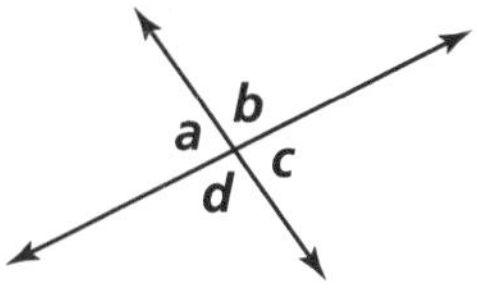

Suggested Questions

- *What can you say about the sum of the measures of angles a and b? (The sum is 180° because the two angles form a straight line.)*
- *What else can you say about these four angles?*

Use Transparency 2.5B to introduce students to parallel and non-parallel lines. One pair is parallel, one pair is intersecting, and the other pair is not parallel, but not quite intersecting yet.

- *What are parallel lines?* (Parallel lines are lines that no matter how far they are extended in the plane, they never intersect.)

A plane is a term that students might have heard before, but do not need to know the formal definition for. The term, however, is important to ensure that the definition of parallel lines is mathematically correct.

For the pair of parallel lines, label them L_1 and L_2. Draw a transversal and label the eight pairs of angles that are formed—*a, b, c, d, e, f, g,* and *h*. Tell the class that they are to measure these angles and look for patterns.

Have students work in pairs. Give each student a copy of Labsheet 2.5.

Explore 2.5

Each student needs a record of the patterns and angle measures they find. Look for some interesting strategies to discuss in the summary.

For Question E, if students are having difficulty seeing the connection between the parallel lines cut by a transversal and parallelograms, have them extend the sides of the parallelograms.

Ask students what patterns do they notice about vertical angles like angles *a* and *c* or *b* and *d* and for supplementary angles like angles *a* and *b* or *c* and *d*.

Summarize 2.5

Collect answers and then make a list of the conjectures that the students have found. They will find many pairs of equal angles, such as those discussed in the Mathematics Background on page 7. They will also find pairs of angles whose sum is 180°. These angles are called supplementary angles. They do not need the names for these angles (unless your district or state requires the name). They should have their angles marked in some way so they can communicate their findings. The angles to concentrate on are the alternate interior angles, vertical angles, corresponding angles, and supplementary angles.

Have students check their conjectures with another pair of parallel lines cut by a transversal.

Discuss parallel lines and parallelograms. Ask the class to examine some of the shapes in the Shapes Set. Help them see the connection between parallel lines and parallelograms. Previously parallelograms have been defined as quadrilaterals with opposite sides the same length and opposite angles the same measure. Another definition for a parallelogram is a quadrilateral with opposite sides parallel. A parallelogram can be formed by drawing two parallel lines that are cut by two parallel transversals. So opposite interior angles are equal and adjacent angles are supplementary (their sum is 180°). In the Mathematics Background on page 7: angles *a* and *b* are adjacent since they share a common ray between them.

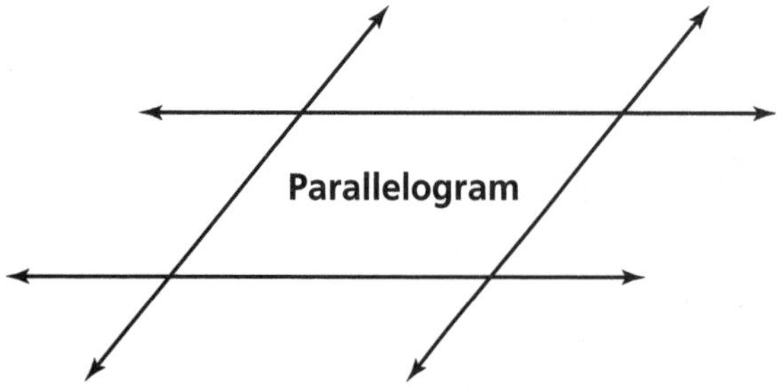

Suggested Questions Look for some rectangles in the set. Ask:

- *Are rectangles parallelograms? Why?* (Rectangles are parallelograms because opposite sides are equal in length and opposite angles are the same measure, or rectangles are parallelograms because opposite sides are parallel)
- *How can you sketch a parallelogram?* (Drawing two parallel lines that are cut by two parallel transversals can make a parallelogram)

Check for Understanding

- *Draw two parallel lines and a transversal. Label one of the angle measures 50°. What are the measures of the other angles? Explain your reasoning.* (Students should be able to use their knowledge of straight angles, vertical angles, and alternate interior angles to find the measures of the other seven angles, which measure either 50° or 130°.)

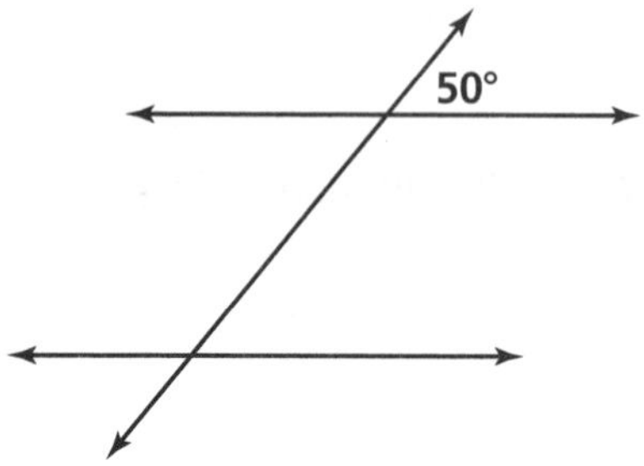

Answer:

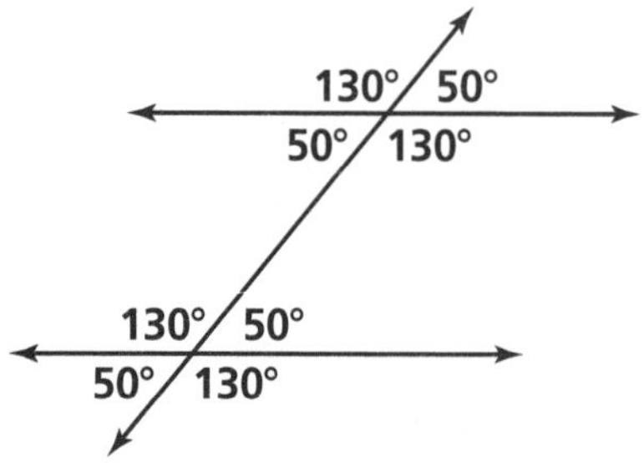

2.5 Angles and Parallel Lines

At a Glance

PACING 2 days

Mathematical Goals

- Explore the patterns among angles created when two or more parallel lines are cut by another line
- Develop a better understanding of parallel lines and parallelograms

Launch

Use Transparency 2.5B to introduce students to parallel and non-parallel lines.

Parallel lines are lines that never intersect, no matter how far they are extended in the plane. For the pair of parallel lines, label them L_1 and L_2. Draw a transversal and label the eight pairs of angles that are formed—*a*, *b*, *c*, *d*, *e*, *f*, *g*, and *h*.

- *You are going to measure these angles and look for patterns.*

Have students work in pairs.

Materials

- Transparencies 2.5A and 2.5B

Vocabulary

- parallel lines
- transversal

Explore

Each student needs a record of the patterns and angle measures they find. For Question E, if students are having difficulty seeing the connection, have them extend the sides of the parallelograms. What patterns do you notice about vertical angles like angles *a* and *c* or *b* and *d* and for supplementary angles like angles *a* and *b* or *c* and *d*?

Materials

- Shapes Set (1 per group)
- Angle rulers (1 per group)
- Labsheet 2.5

Summarize

Make a list of the students' conjectures. They will find many pairs of equal angles. They will also find pairs of angles that sum to 180° (*supplementary angles*).

Have students check their conjectures with another pair of parallel lines cut by a transversal. Discuss parallel lines and parallelograms. Ask the class to examine some of these shapes in the Shapes Set. Previously parallelograms have been defined as quadrilaterals with opposites sides the same length and opposite angles the same measure. Another definition for parallelogram is a quadrilateral with opposite sides parallel. A parallelogram can be formed by drawing two parallel lines that are cut by two parallel transversals. So opposite interior angles are equal and adjacent angles are supplementary (See the Mathematics Background on page 7.) Look for some rectangles in the set. Ask:

- *Are rectangles parallelograms? Why? How can you sketch a parallelogram?*

Check for Understanding

- *Draw two parallel lines and a transversal. Label one of the angle measures 50°. What are the measures of the other angles? Explain your reasoning.*

Materials

- Student notebooks

ACE Assignment Guide for Problem 2.5

Differentiated Instruction
Solutions for All Learners

Core 21, 22, 24, 25, 26

Other *Applications* 23 (students will need an angle ruler), *Extensions* 42–44; unassigned choices from previous problems

Adapted For suggestions about adapting ACE exercises, see the CMP *Special Needs Handbook*.

Answers to Problem 2.5

Figure 1

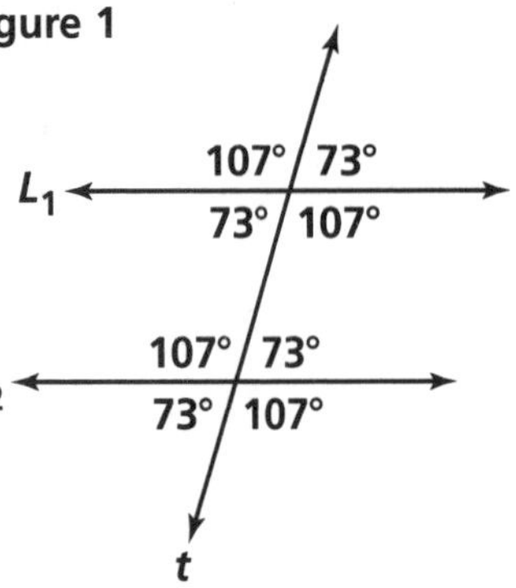

Figure 3

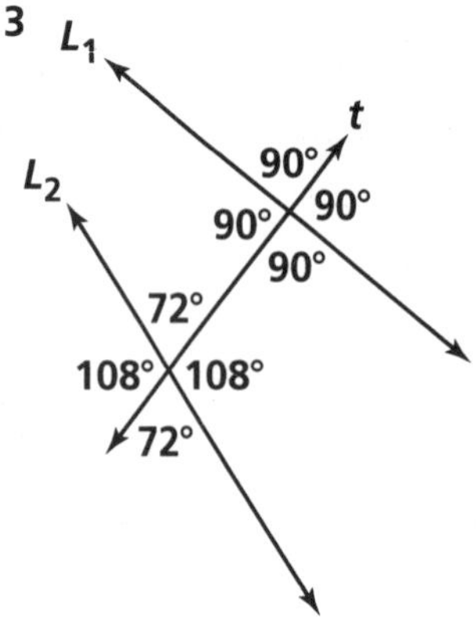

A. Some possible patterns that were observed (Note: students are not expected to use language like alternate interior, corresponding, adjacent, or supplementary):

The measures of the angles inside the parallel lines (interior) that are on opposite sides of the transversal are equal. (These are called alternate interior angles.)

When four angles are made by two intersecting lines, the angles across from each other, that do not share a side, have the same measure. (These are called vertical angles.)

When two parallel lines are intersected by a transversal, the four angles created by the top parallel line and the transversal have measures that are equal to the four corresponding angles created by the intersection of the bottom parallel line and the transversal. (These are called corresponding angles.)

The sum of two angles that share a side and whose two other sides form a straight line is 180°. These angles form a straight line. (They are both adjacent and supplementary angles.)

B. Angle measures will vary according to the different transversals that are drawn. However, the patterns are the same as in Question A.

C. Except for the above-noted patterns in Question A, ii, and Question A, iv, the patterns for Figure 3 are not the same as the patterns for Figures 1 and 2.

D. One possible answer: two angles that are on the inside or interior part of the parallel lines, and are on the same side of the transversal, have measures that add up to 180°. (They are supplementary.)

E. **1.** They are parallelograms because they have opposite sides that are parallel.

2. Using the example of Shape M, the top and bottom are parallel and the sides are transversals of these two parallel lines, or vice versa, the top and bottom are transversals to the parallel sides.

3. Possible answers: Opposite angles have the same measures. The sum of the angles on the same side of the parallelogram is 180°. (They are supplementary.)

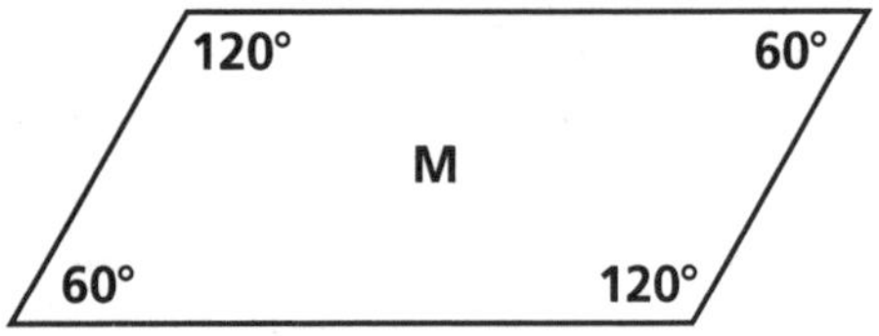

The student edition pages for this investigation begin on the next page.

STUDENT PAGE

Notes

Investigation 2

Polygons and Angles

Both the regular decagon and the five-point star below have ten sides of equal length.

What makes these two polygons different?

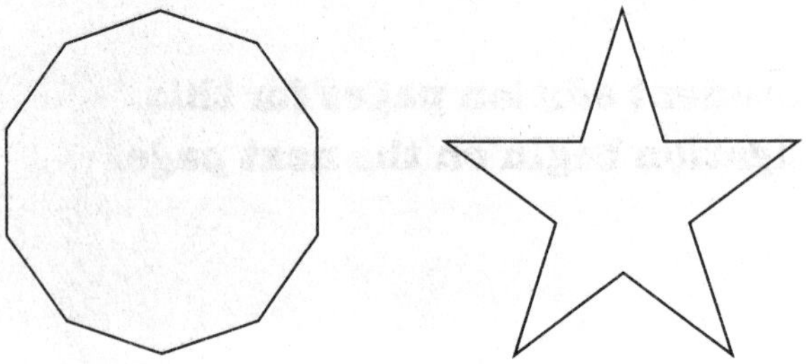

2.1 Understanding Angles

The workers in a honeybee hive fly great distances to find flowers with nectar. They use nectar to make honey. When a bee finds a good patch of flowers, it returns to the hive and communicates the location of the flowers to the other bees.

Did You Know?

Honeybees live in colonies. Each honeybee colony has a single queen and thousands of worker bees. The worker bees find flowers to get nectar. The nectar is used to make honey. Worker bees build the honeycomb and keep the beehive clean. They feed and groom the queen bee and take care of the baby bees. They also guard the hive against intruders.

Scientific observation has shown that honeybees have an amazing method for giving directions to flowers: they perform a lively dance!

Go Online
PHSchool.com
For: Information about honeybees
Web Code: ame-9031

Notes

During the direction dance, a honeybee moves in a combination of squiggly paths and half circles. The squiggly paths in the dance indicate the direction of the flowers. If the flowers are in the direction of the sun, the middle path of the bee's dance is straight up and down.

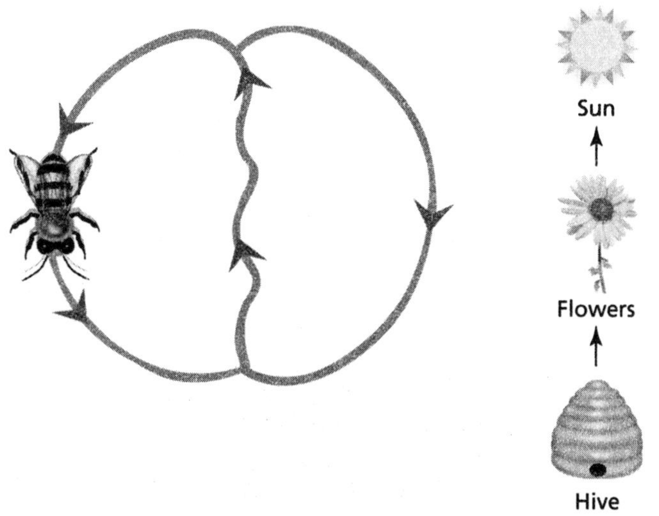

If the flowers are not in the direction of the sun, the direction of the honeybee's dance is tilted. The angle of the tilt is the same as the angle formed by the sun, the hive, and the flowers.

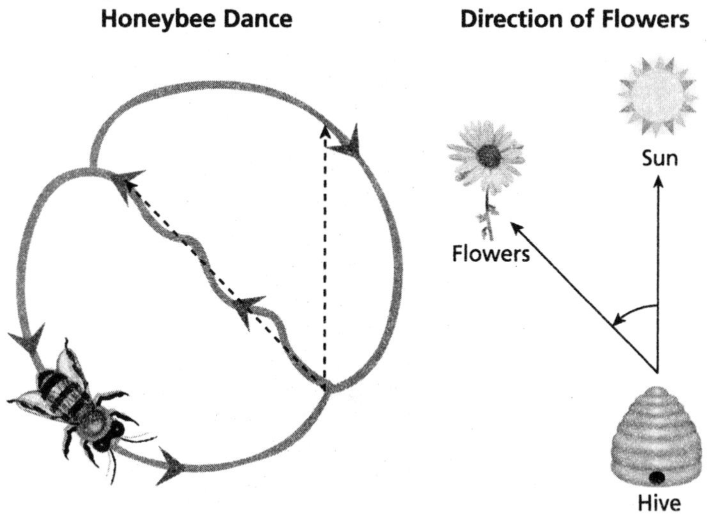

STUDENT PAGE

STUDENT PAGE

Notes

The bee dance illustrates one way to think about an angle—as a *turn*. When the honeybee dances in a tilted direction, she is telling the other bees how far to *turn* from the sun to find the flowers.

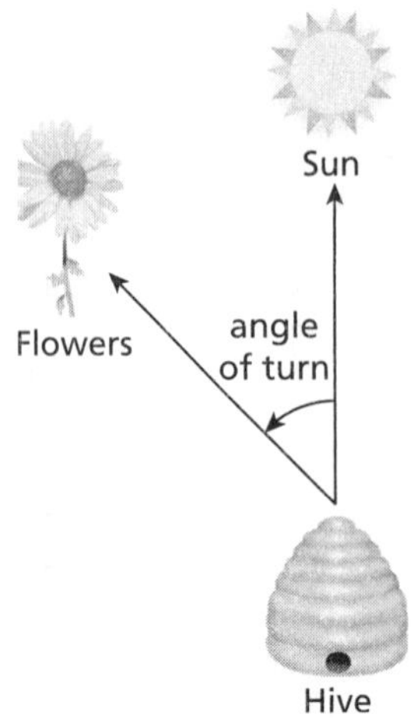

You can also think of an angle as the sides of a *wedge*, like the cut sides of a slice of pizza. Or, you can think of an angle as a point with two sides extending from the point, like branches on a tree.

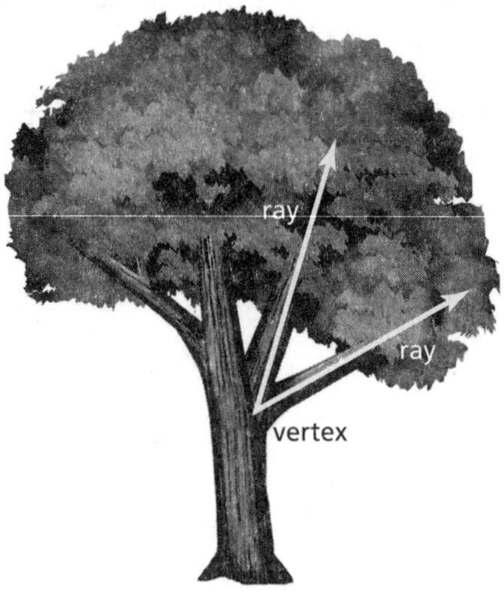

In all of these examples, since each side extends from a point in only one direction, the sides are called **half lines** or **rays.** The point is called the **vertex** of the angle.

Notes

In many figures, like in the triangle below, you will see angles without the arrows to indicate the rays.

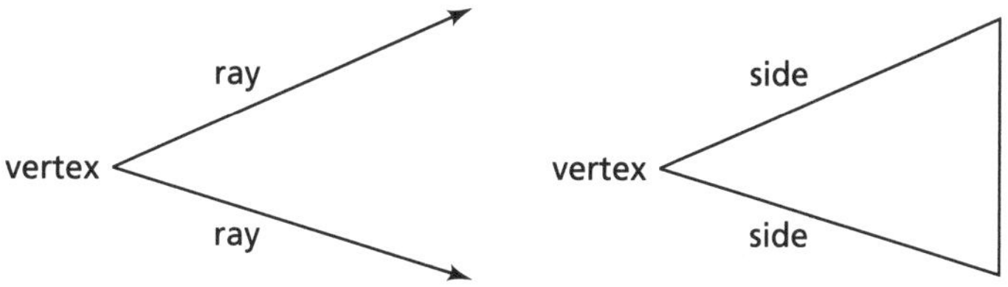

Getting Ready for Problem 2.1

Think of some examples of angles that can be found in your school, your home, in other buildings, or outside. Give at least one example of each type of angle described.

- An angle that occurs as the result of a *turning motion,* such as the opening of a door
- An angle that occurs as a *wedge,* such as a slice of pizza
- An angle that occurs as *two rays with a common vertex,* such as the branches on a tree

How could you compare the size of these angles?

There are several ways to describe the size of an angle. The most common way uses units called **degrees.** An angle with measure 1 degree (also written 1°) is a very small turn, or a very narrow wedge.

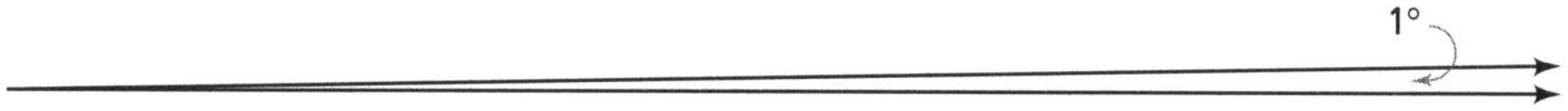

Did You Know?

The ancient Babylonians measured angles in degrees. They set the measure of an angle that goes all the way around a point to 360°. They may have chosen 360° because their number system was based on the number 60. They may have also considered the fact that 360 has many factors.

Go Online
PHSchool.com
For: Information about Babylonians
Web Code: ame-9031

Notes

An angle with a measure of 170° results from a very large turn. You can fit 170 wedges that measure 1° in this angle!

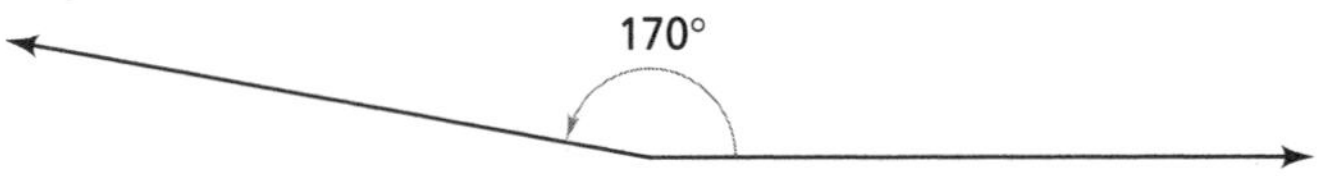

The angles below have sides that meet to form a square corner. Such angles are called right angles. A **right angle** has a measure of 90°. A right angle is sometimes marked with a small square as shown on the angle at the right. When you see an angle marked this way, you can assume it has a measure of 90°.

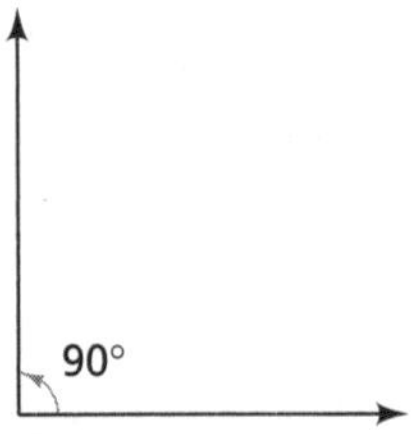

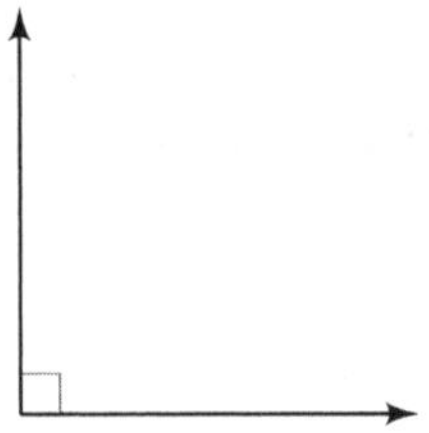

The angle below is one-half the size of a right angle. So, its measure is 45°.

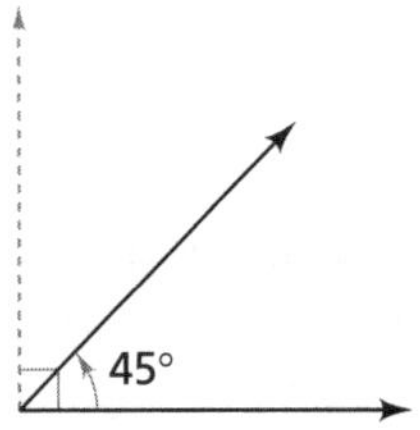

Problem 2.1 Understanding Angles

A. Sketch the angles made by these turns. For each sketch, include a curved arrow indicating the turn and label the angle with its degree measure.

1. One third of a right-angle turn
2. Two thirds of a right-angle turn
3. One quarter of a right-angle turn
4. One and a half right-angle turns
5. Two right-angle turns
6. Three right-angle turns

Notes

B. In parts (1)–(6), sketch an angle with *approximately* the given measure. For each sketch, include a curved arrow indicating the turn.

1. 20°

2. 70°

3. 150°

4. 180°

5. 270°

6. 360°

C. Estimate the measure of each angle.

1.

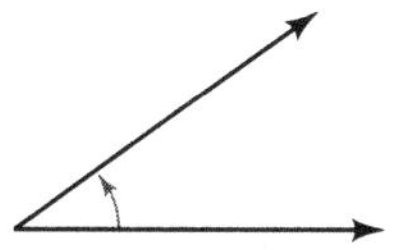

2.

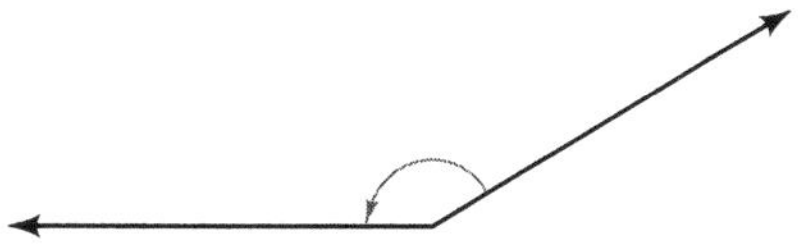

3.

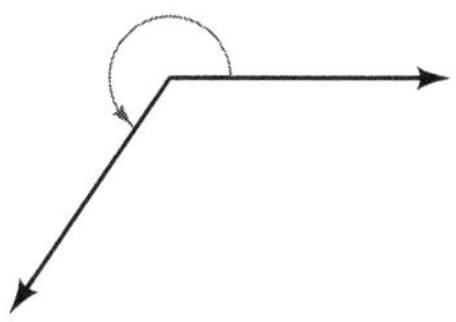

ACE Homework starts on page 40.

2.2 Developing Angle Benchmarks

You may know how to locate points on a grid by using ordered pairs of coordinates. Given the ordered pair (1, 4), you first start at (0, 0) and move to the right the number of units given by the first coordinate, 1. From this point, you move up the number of units given by the second coordinate, 4.

On the grid at right, point *A* has coordinates (1, 4). Point *B* has coordinates (3, 2). Point *C* has coordinates (5, 6).

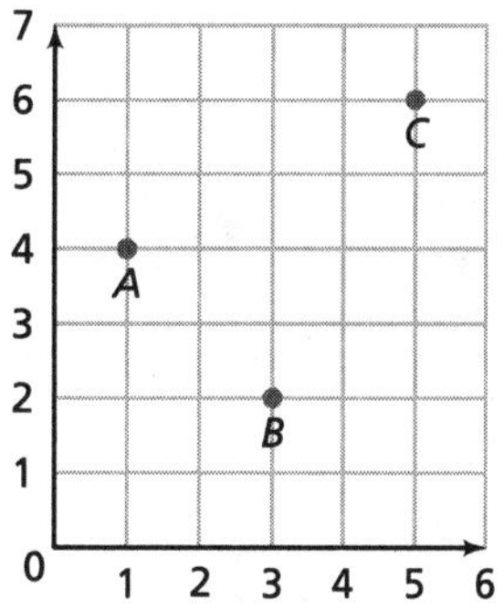

Notes

Mathematicians and scientists find it useful to locate points using different kinds of coordinate grids. One way to locate points is to use a circular grid. On this kind of grid, angle measures help describe the location of points.

Two examples of circular grids are shown below. The grid on the left has lines at 45° intervals. The grid on the right has lines at 30° intervals. The circles are numbered, moving out from the center at 0.

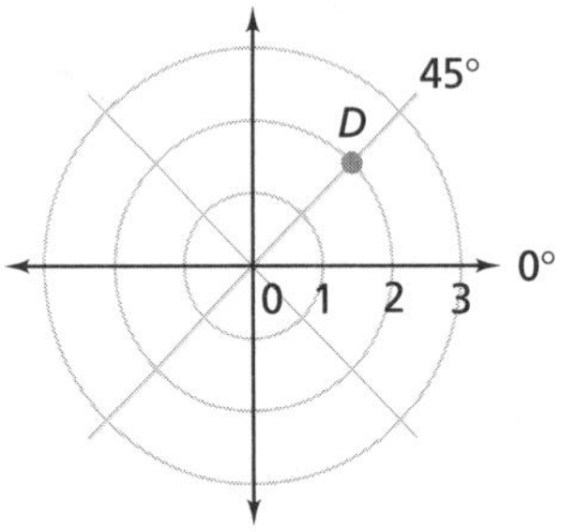

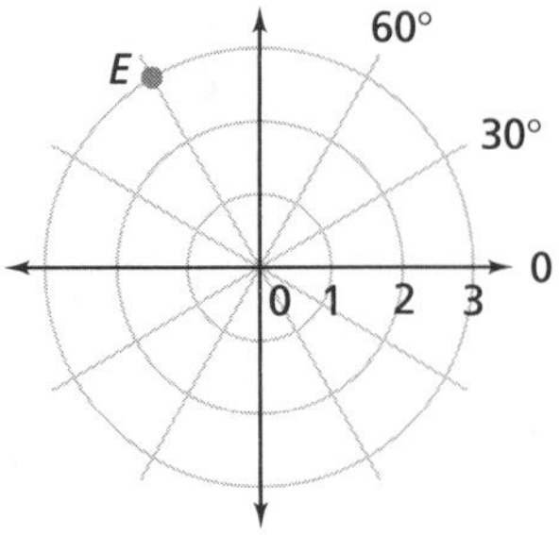

Points on a circular grid are described by giving a distance and an angle. For example, point *D* has coordinates (2, 45°). To locate a point, start at the center of the grid and move to the right the number of units indicated by the first coordinate. Then, move counterclockwise along that circle the number of degrees given by the second coordinate. To locate (2, 45°), move to the right 2 units on the 0° line and then move up (around the circle) to the 45° line.

Can you find the coordinates of point E above?

You can use circular grids to play a game called Four in a Row. Two players or two teams can play the game.

STUDENT PAGE

STUDENT PAGE

Notes

Four in a Row Rules

Choose one of the circular grids, either with 30° intervals or 45° intervals.

- Player A chooses a point where a circle and a grid line meet and says the coordinates of the point aloud.
- Player B checks that the coordinates Player A gave are correct. If they are, Player A marks the point with an X. If they are not, Player A does not get to mark a point.
- Player B chooses a point and says its coordinates. If the coordinates are correct, Player B marks the point with an O.
- Players continue to take turns, saying the coordinates of a point and then marking the point. The first player to get four marks in a row, either along a grid line or around a circle, wins the game.

Problem 2.2 Developing Angle Benchmarks

A. Play Four in a Row several times. Play games with the 30° grid and the 45° grid. Write down any winning strategies you discover.

B. On one of the circular grids, label points *A*, *B*, and *C* that fit the following descriptions:

- The angle measure for point *A* is greater than 120°.
- The angle measure for point *B* is equal to 0°.
- The angle measure for point *C* is less than 90°.

ACE **Homework starts on page 40.**

STUDENT PAGE

Notes

Did You Know?

Circular grids are examples of *polar coordinate grids*. Sir Isaac Newton introduced polar coordinates. In some real-life settings, such as sea and air navigation, a rectangular coordinate system is not always useful. In these settings, a system similar to a polar coordinate system works better.

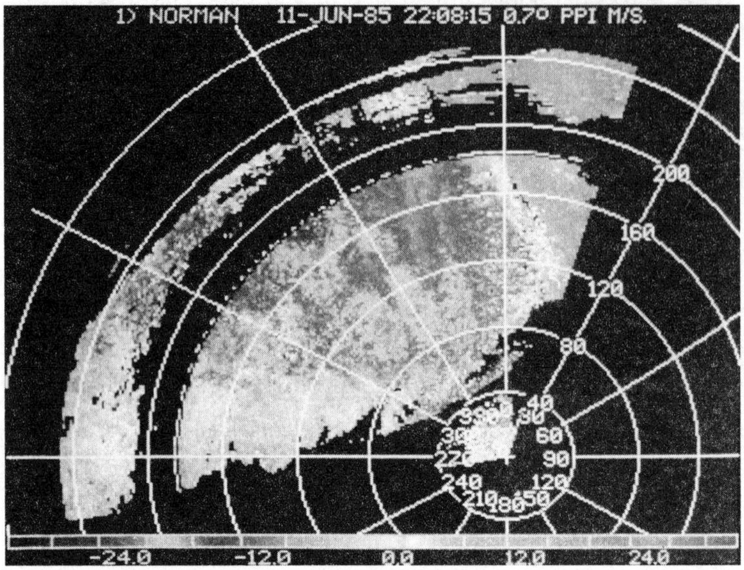

You may have seen grids similar to these polar coordinate grids shown as radar grids in movies or on television. This is because certain types of radar use polar coordinates in order to locate objects. This type of radar is used to find weather patterns, airplanes, and ships at sea.

Go Online
PHSchool.com
For: Information about radar
Web Code: ame-9031

An object appearing on radar will have an angle measure. It will be based on the direction of the object from the radar site. You measure the angle of the direction by turning clockwise from North.

2.3 Using an Angle Ruler

In many situations in which distance and angles are measured, estimates are good enough. But sometimes it is important to measure precisely. If you were navigating an ocean liner, an airplane, or a rocket, you would want precise measurements of the angles needed to plot your course.

STUDENT PAGE

STUDENT PAGE

Notes

There are several tools for measuring angles. One of the easiest to use is the *angle ruler*. An angle ruler has two arms, like the sides of an angle. A rivet joins the arms. This allows them to swing apart to form angles of various sizes. One arm is marked with a circular ruler showing degree measures from 0° to 360°.

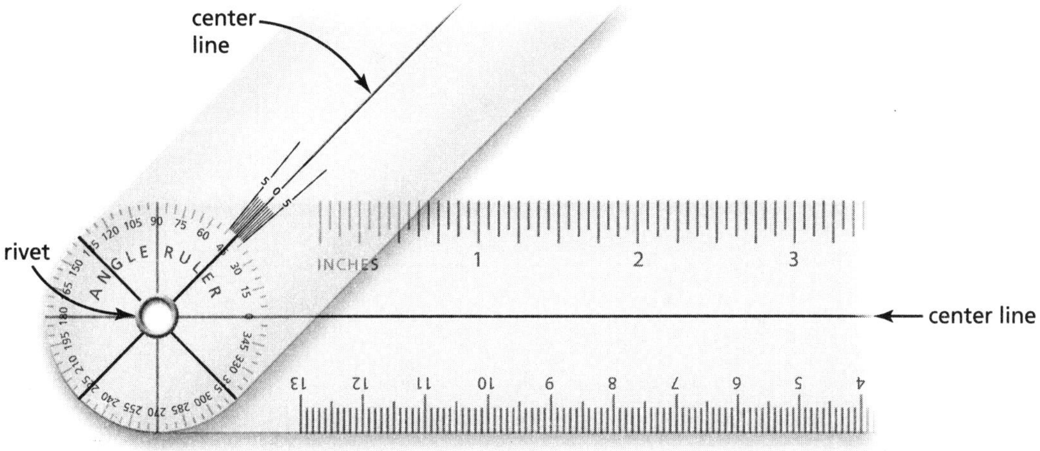

To measure an angle with an angle ruler, first place the rivet over the vertex of the angle. Then set the *center line* of the arm with the ruler markings on one side of the angle. Swing the other arm around counterclockwise until its center line lies on the second side of the angle. The center line on the second arm will pass over a mark on the circular ruler. This tells you the degree measure of the angle.

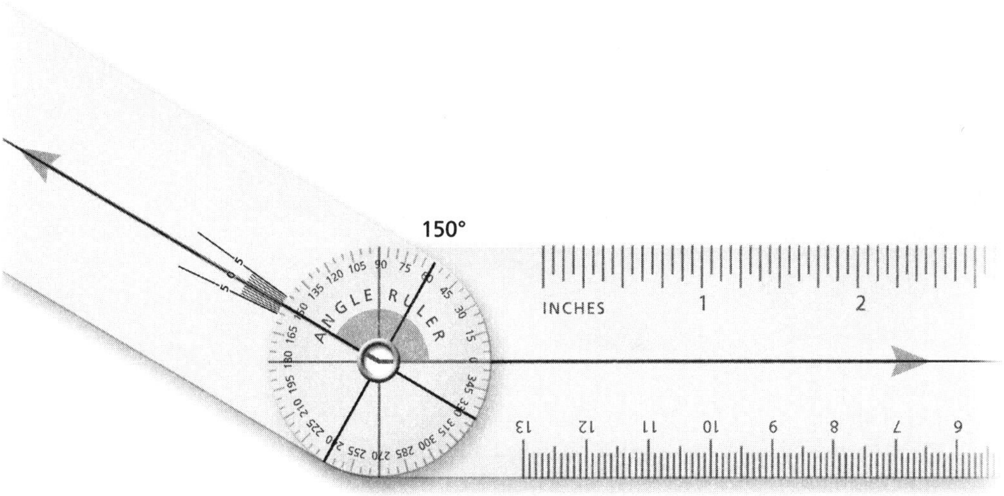

Notes

When you are measuring an angle on an actual object, you can place the object between the two arms of the angle ruler as shown here. Then read off the size of the angle. Angle 1 in shape R measures 120°.

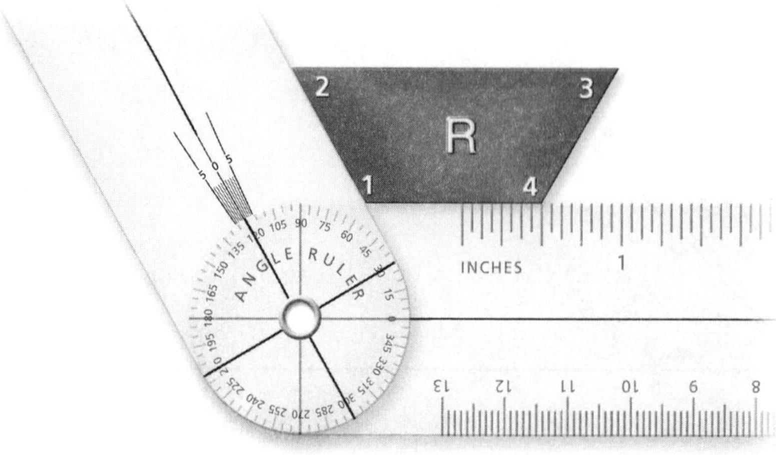

In Problems 2.1 and 2.2, you used 90°, 45°, and 30° angles as benchmarks, or references, to sketch angles and estimate angle measures. In Problem 2.3, you will use these benchmark angles to estimate the angle measures for some of the shapes in the Shapes Set. You can then use an angle ruler to measure the angles.

Problem 2.3 Measuring Angles

For this problem set you will need Shapes A, B, D, K, R, and V from the Shapes Set.

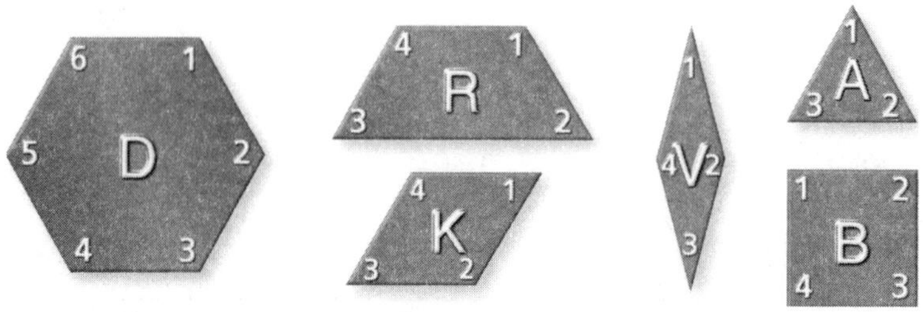

A. Copy Shapes A, B, D, K, R, and V onto a sheet of paper. *Estimate* the measure of each angle in the shapes. Label each angle with your estimate.

STUDENT PAGE

Notes

B. **1.** Use an angle ruler to *measure* each angle of the six shapes. On your drawing of the shapes, label each angle with its measure. Use a different color than you used on Question A.

2. How do your measurements compare with your estimates?

C. Use an angle ruler to find the measure of each angle.

1.

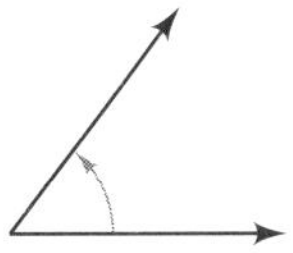

2.

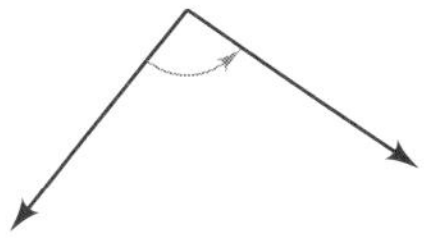

3.

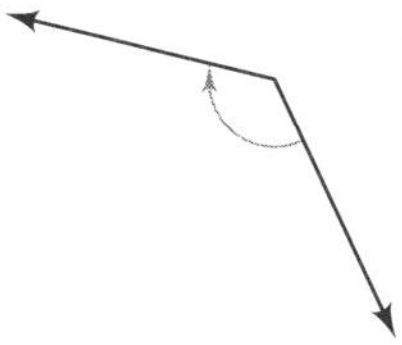

4.

D. **1.** Draw an angle whose measure is less than the measure of any of the angles in Question C.

2. Draw an angle whose measure is greater than the measure of any of the angles in Question C.

ACE **Homework starts on page 40.**

Did You Know?

The angle ruler's formal name is *goniometer* (goh nee AHM uh tur), which means "angle measurer." Goniometers are used by doctors and physical therapists to measure flexibility (range of motion) in joints such as knees, elbows, and fingers.

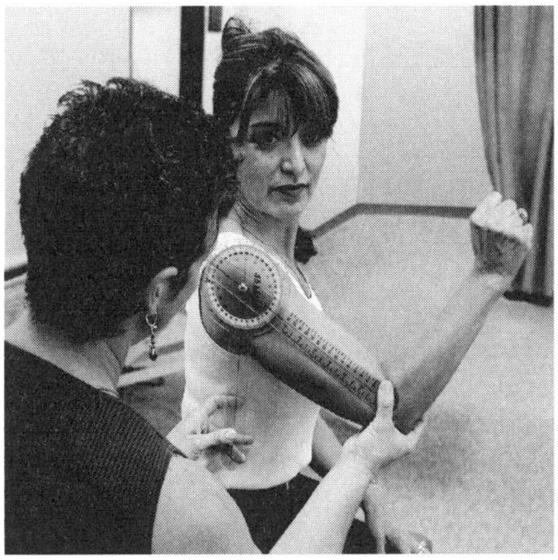

A *protractor* is another device used for measuring angles (see Exercise 21 in Investigation 4). Protractors are an alternative to angle rulers.

Go Online
PHSchool.com
For: Information about physical therapists
Web Code: ame-9031

Notes

2.4 Analyzing Measurement Errors

In Problem 2.3, you and your classmates may have found slightly different measures for some of the angles. Because no instrument gives absolutely precise measurements, there is some error every time you use a measurement tool. However, in some situations, it is important to make measurements that are as precise as possible. For example, when using angle measures to navigate an airplane, even small errors can lead a flight far astray.

In 1937, the famous aviator Amelia Earhart tried to become the first woman to fly around the world. She began her journey on June 1 from Miami, Florida. She reached Lae, New Guinea, and then headed east toward Howland Island in the Pacific Ocean. She never arrived at Howland Island.

In 1992, 55 years later, investigators found evidence that Earhart had crashed on the deserted island of Nikumaroro, far off her intended course. It appears that an error may have been made in plotting Earhart's course.

Notes

Problem 2.4 Analyzing Measurement Errors

The map below shows Lae, New Guinea; Howland Island (Earhart's intended destination); and Nikumaroro Island (the crash site).

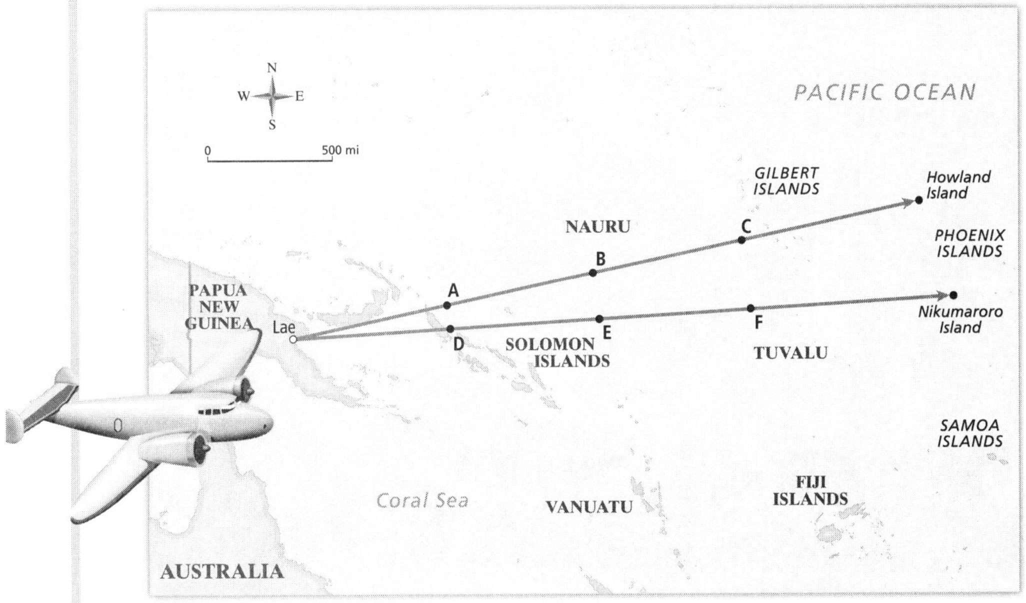

A. How many degrees off course was Earhart's crash site from her intended destination?

B. Suppose two planes fly along the paths formed by the rays of the angle indicated on the map. Both planes leave Lae, New Guinea, at the same time and fly at the same speed. Find the approximate distance in miles between the planes at each pair of points labeled on the map (A and D, B and E, and C and F).

C. Amelia Earhart apparently flew several degrees south of her intended course. Suppose you start at Lae, New Guinea, and are trying to reach Howland, but you fly 20° south. Where might you land?

ACE **Homework starts on page 40.**

STUDENT PAGE

STUDENT PAGE

Notes

2.5 Angles and Parallel Lines

In mathematics, *plane* means a flat surface that extends forever without edges. **Parallel lines** are lines in a plane that never meet. Remember that lines are straight and extend forever in two directions.

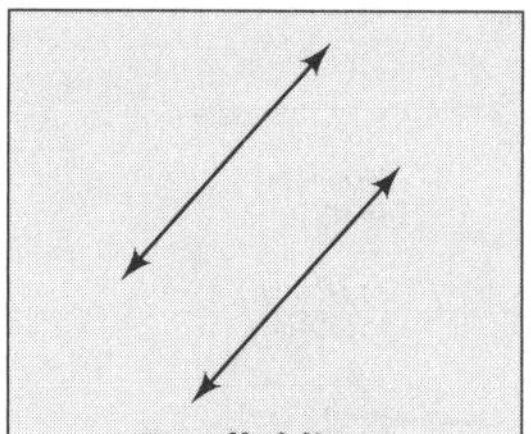
Parallel lines

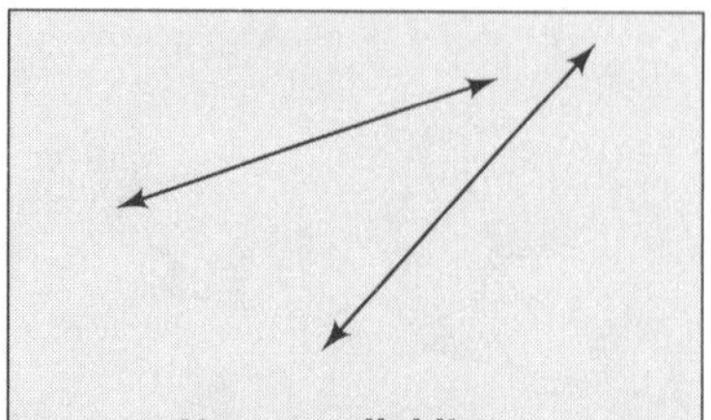
Non-parallel lines

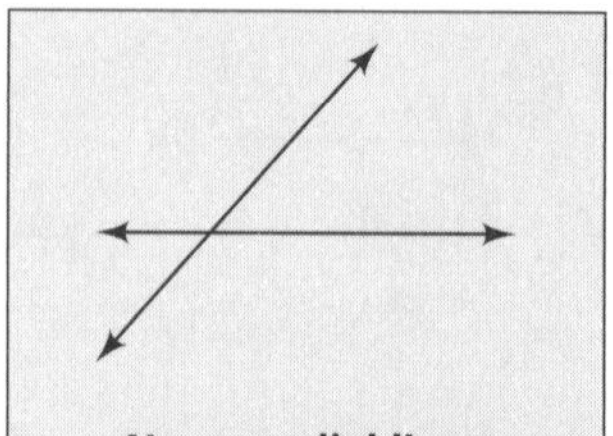
Non-parallel lines

The next problem helps you explore some interesting patterns among angles formed when parallel lines are intersected by a third line. A line that intersects two or more lines is called a **transversal.**

Notes

Problem 2.5 Angles and Parallel Lines

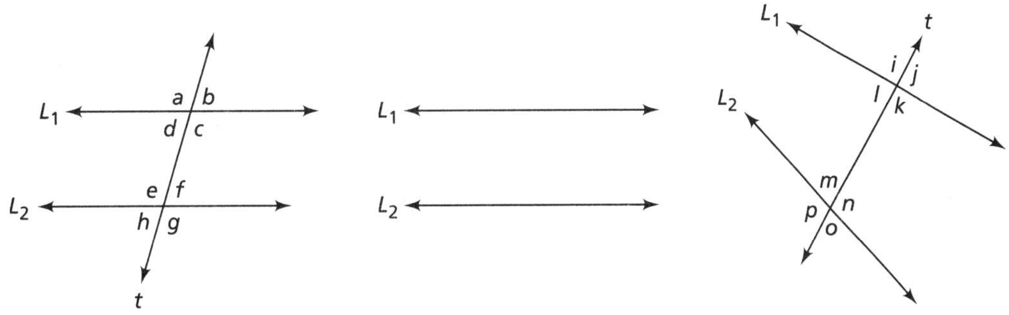

Figure 1 Figure 2 Figure 3

A. In Figure 1, lines L_1 and L_2 are parallel. They are intersected by a transversal t. Measure the angles labeled with small letters. What patterns do you observe among the angle measures?

B. In Figure 2, lines L_1 and L_2 are also parallel.

- Using a copy of Figure 2, draw a transversal t that intersects both lines.
- Measure the angles that are formed.
- What patterns do you observe among the angle measures?

C. In Figure 3, lines L_1 and L_2 are *not* parallel.

- Measure the angles formed by the transversal intersecting lines L_1 and L_2.
- Which patterns you observed in Figures 1 and 2 appear in Figure 3? Explain.

D. Make one or more conjectures about the measures of the angles formed when a transversal intersects two parallel lines.

E. **1.** Explain why Shapes B, G, H, J, K, L, M, N, and V in the Shapes Set are called parallelograms.

2. Trace two of the parallelograms. Are any of the lines in the parallelograms transversals? If so, which lines are transversals?

3. Based on the conjectures that you have made in this problem, what do you think is true about the angle measures of a parallelogram? Check your ideas by choosing a parallelogram from the Shapes Set and measuring its angles.

ACE **Homework starts on page 40.**

STUDENT PAGE

STUDENT PAGE

Notes

Applications

1. Tell whether each diagram shows an angle formed by a wedge, two sides meeting at a common point, or a turn.

a.

b.

c.

2. Give the degree measure of each turn.

a. One right-angle turn

b. Four right-angle turns

c. Five right-angle turns

d. One half of a right-angle turn

e. One ninth of a right-angle turn

f. One fourth of a right-angle turn

Notes ____

3. At the start of each hour, the minute hand of a clock points straight up at the 12. In parts (a)–(f), determine the angle through which the minute hand turns as the given amount of time passes.

Notice that only the minute hand is illustrated on the clock. Make a sketch to illustrate each situation. The curved arrow is pointing clockwise here because that is the direction that the minute hand turns.

a. 15 minutes

b. 30 minutes

c. 20 minutes

d. one hour

e. 5 minutes

f. one and a half hours

4. *Without* using an angle ruler, decide whether the measure of each angle is closest to 30°, 60°, 90°, 120°, 150°, 180°, 270°, or 360°. Be prepared to explain your reasoning.

a.

b.

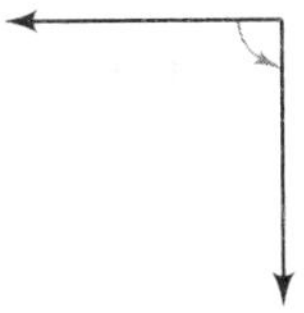

c.

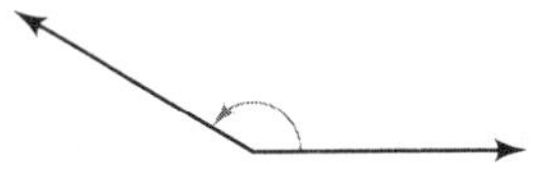

d.

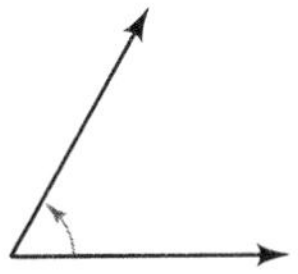

e.

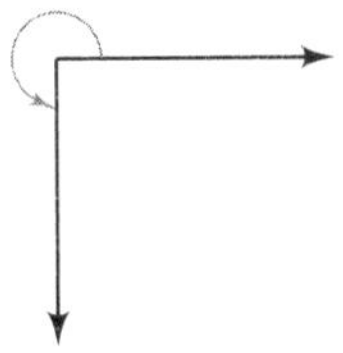

f.

g.

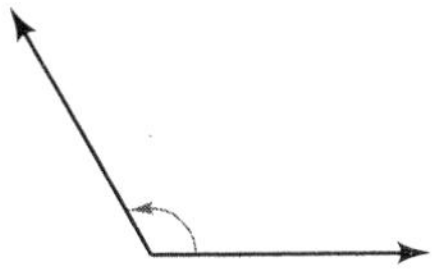

h.

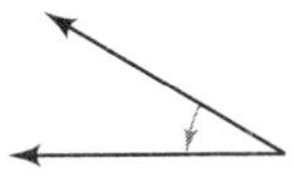

Notes

5. You have learned that a 90° angle is called a *right angle*. An angle with measure less than 90° is an **acute angle.** An angle with measure greater than 90° and less than 180° is an **obtuse angle.** An angle with measure exactly 180° is a **straight angle.** Decide whether each angle in Exercise 4 is right, acute, obtuse, straight, or none of these.

For Exercises 6–9, find the measure of the angle labeled x, *without* measuring.

6.

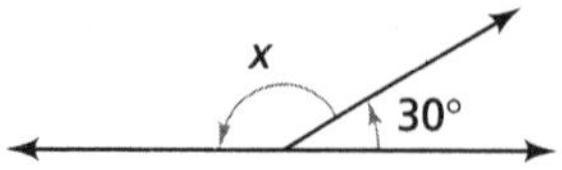

7.

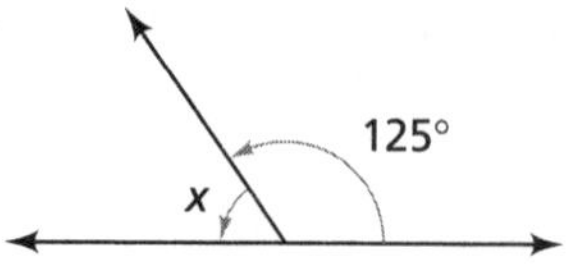

8.

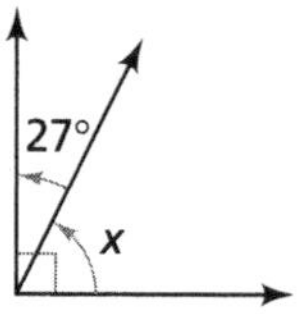

9.

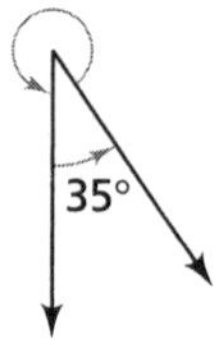

For Exercises 10–13, a worker bee has located flowers with nectar and is preparing to do her dance. The dots represent the hive, the sun, and flowers. Estimate the measure of each angle. Use an angle ruler to check your estimate.

10.

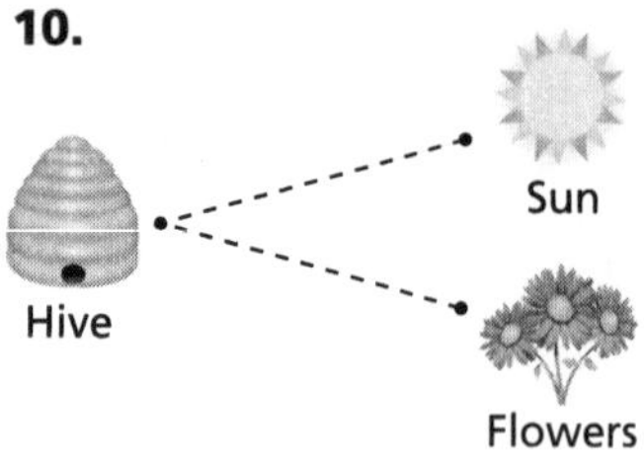

11.

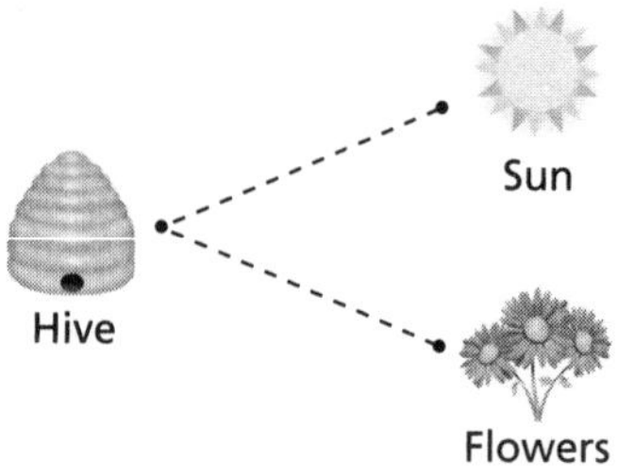

12.

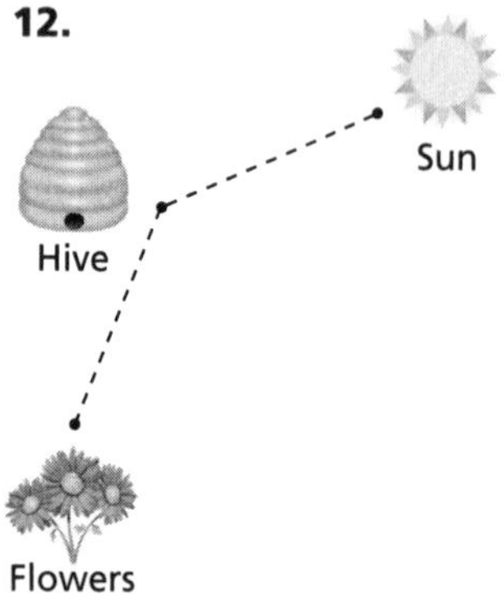

13.

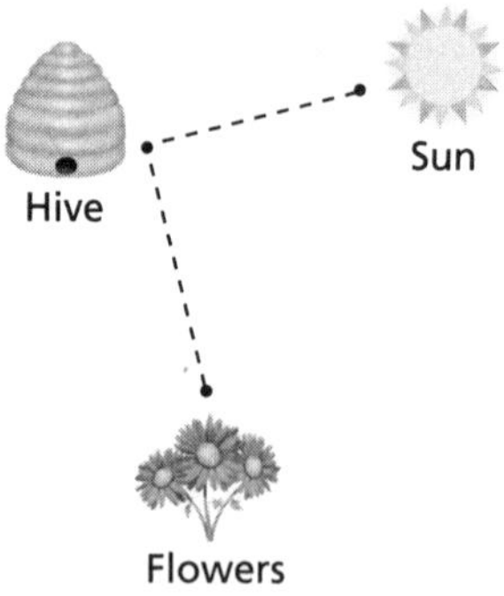

Notes

14. Draw an angle for each measure. Include a curved arrow indicating the turn.

a. 45° **b.** 25° **c.** 180° **d.** 200°

15. *Without* measuring, decide whether the angles in each pair have the same measure. If they do not, tell which angle has the greater measure. Then find the measure of the angles with an angle ruler to check your work.

a.

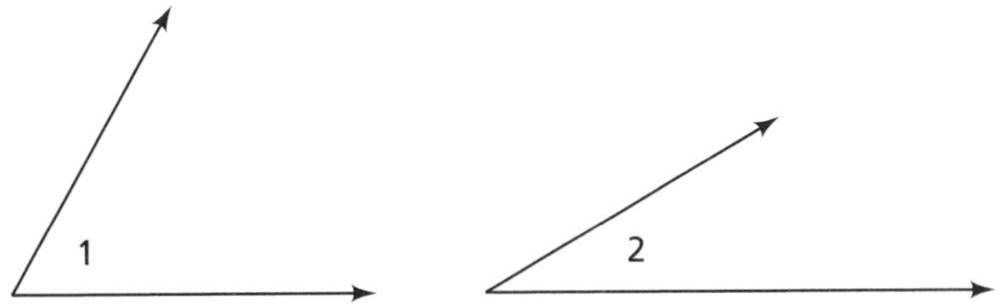

b.

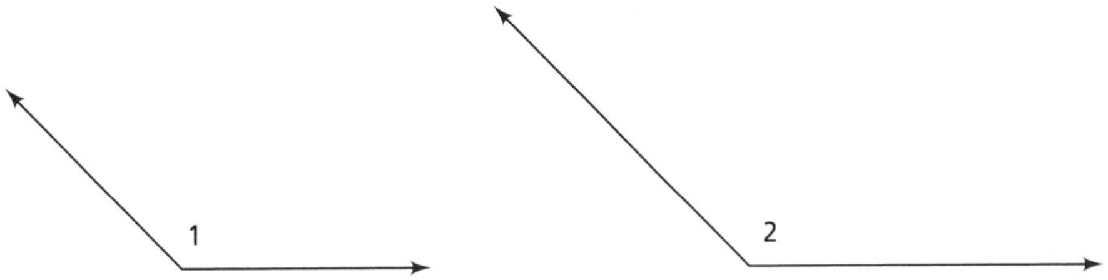

c.

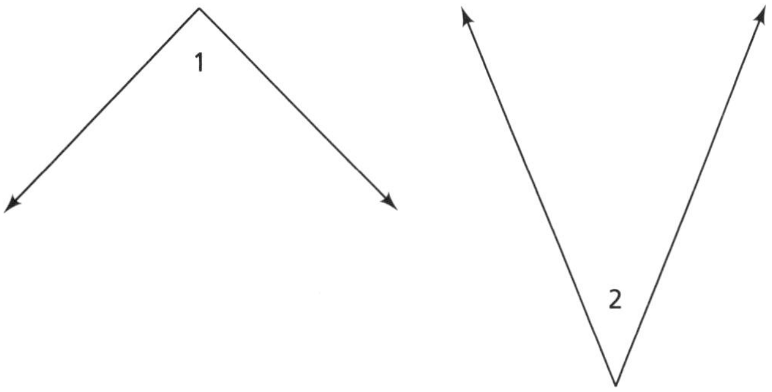

Notes ____________________

16. Estimate the measure of each angle, then check your answers with an angle ruler.

a.

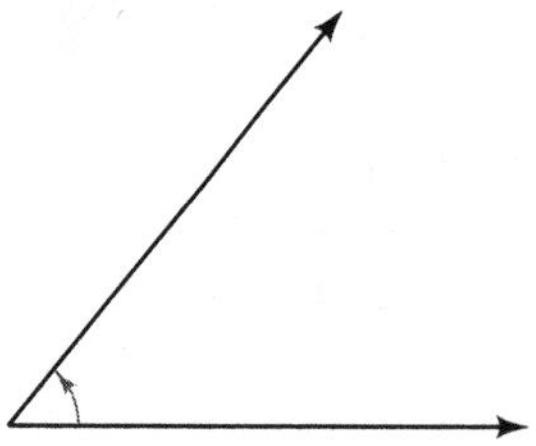

b.

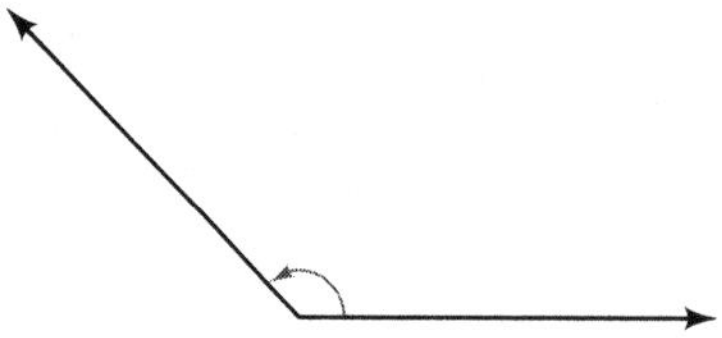

c.

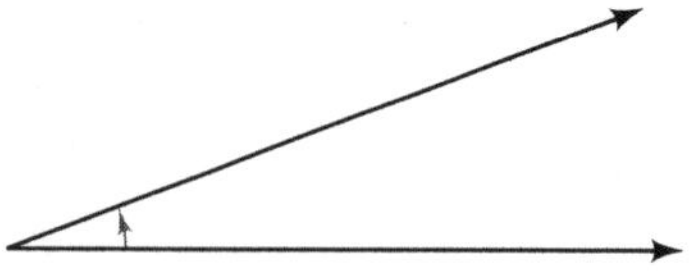

d.

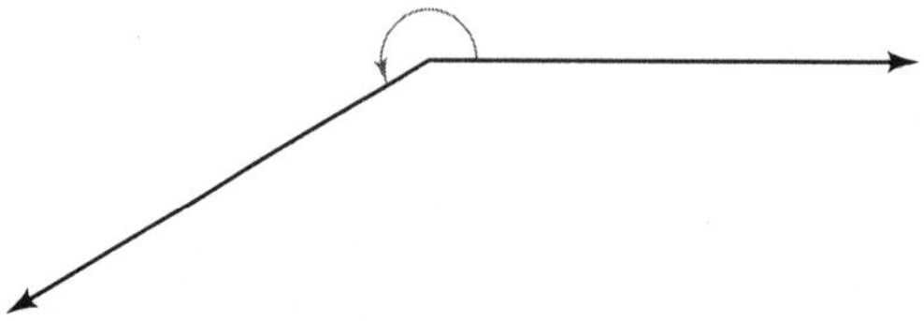

e.

17. For each polygon below, measure the angles with an angle ruler.

a.

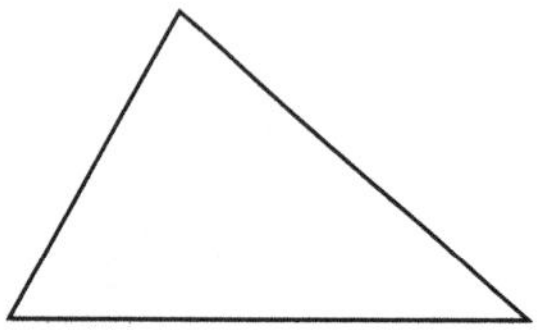

b.

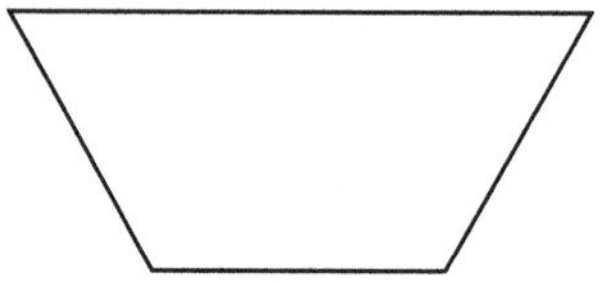

18. You have read about how worker bees communicate the location of flowers. Suppose the angle a worker bee indicates is off by 1°. How will this affect the other bees' ability to locate the flowers? Explain.

STUDENT PAGE

STUDENT PAGE

Notes

19. A bee leaves the hive and wants to fly to a rose but instead ends up at a daisy. How many degrees did the bee travel off course? Estimate your answer. Then check your answer with an angle ruler.

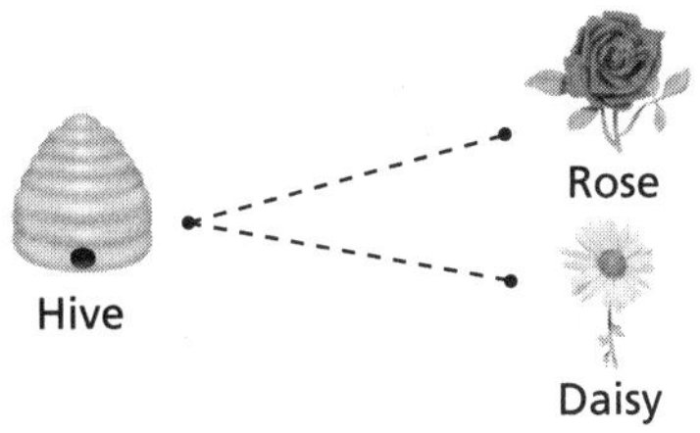

20. Little Bee left point A for a flower patch. Big Bee left point B for the same flower patch. However, both bees were 15° off course. Little Bee landed on the patch and Big Bee did not. Explain why Big Bee did not hit the patch and Little Bee did, if they were both off course by 15°.

Homework Help Online
PHSchool.com
For: Help with Exercise 20
Web Code: ame-3220

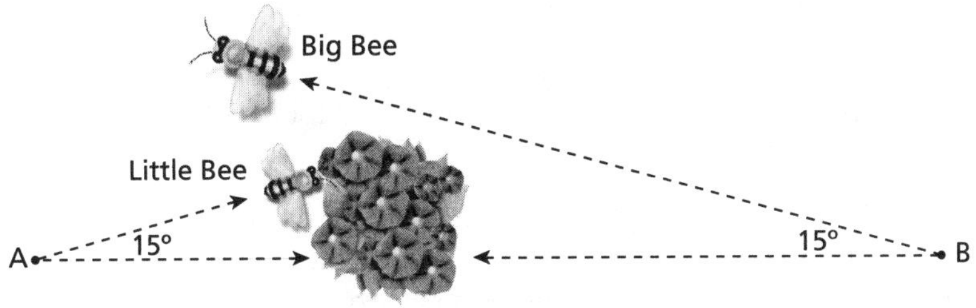

21. Lines L_1 and L_2 are parallel lines cut by a transversal. The measure of one of the angles is given. Based on what you discovered in Problem 2.5, find the measures of the other angles.

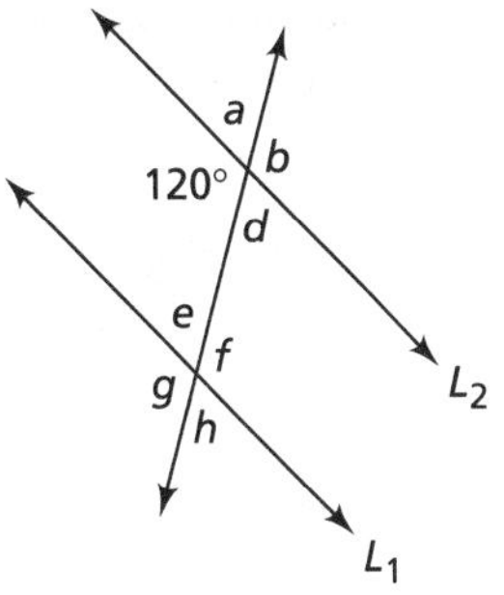

Applications

STUDENT PAGE

STUDENT PAGE

Notes

22. In parts (a)–(c), lines L_1 and L_2 are intersected by a transversal. The measures of some of the angles formed are given. In each part, tell whether you think the lines are parallel. Explain.

a.

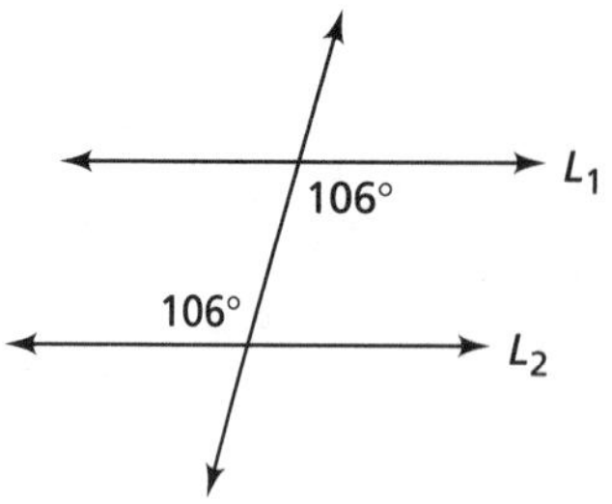

b.

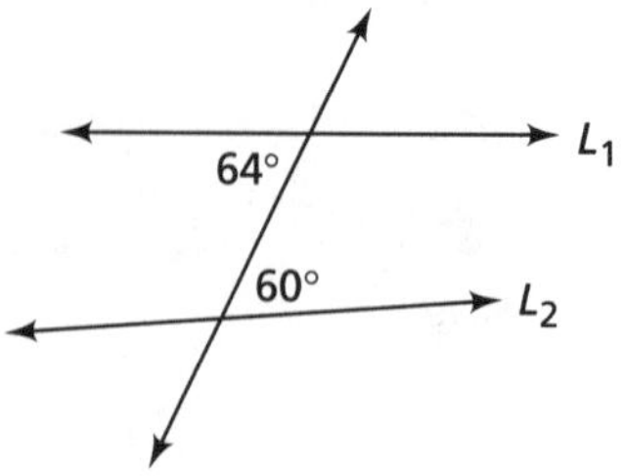

c.

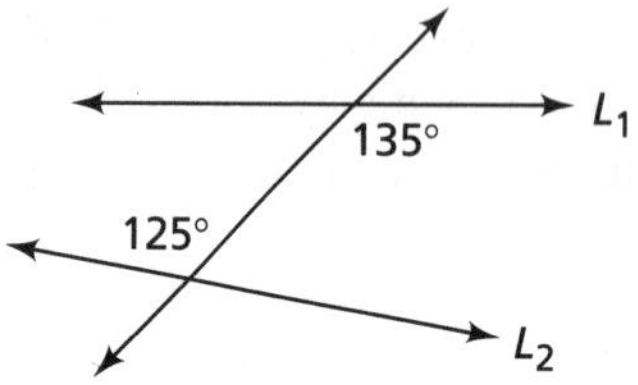

23. **a.** Draw any two intersecting lines, L_1 and L_2. Measure the four angles formed around the point of intersection.
b. What patterns do you observe among the angle measures?
c. Draw two more pairs of intersecting lines and measure the angles formed. Do you observe the same patterns as in part (b)?

24. **Multiple Choice** Use the angle measures to determine which of the following shapes is a parallelogram. The shapes may not be drawn to scale.

A.

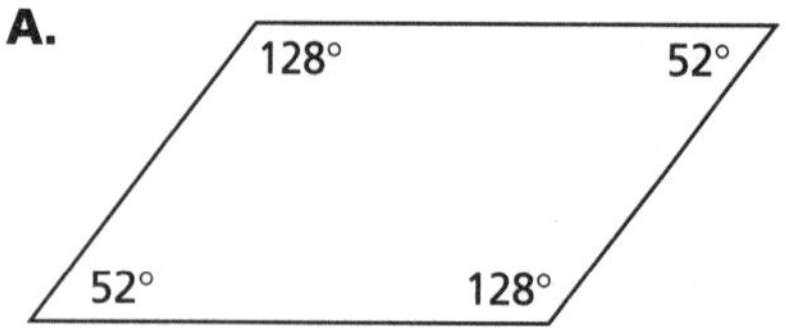

B.

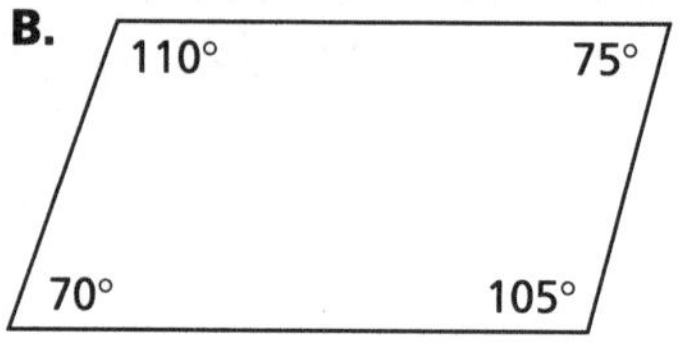

C.

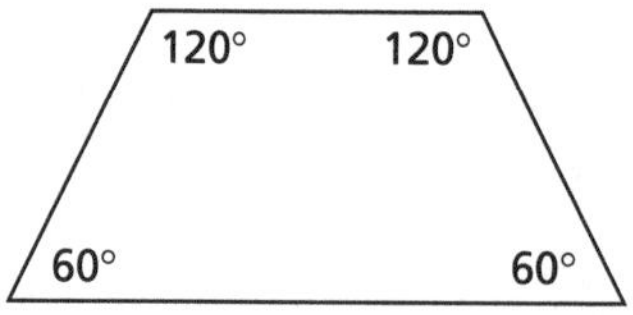

D.

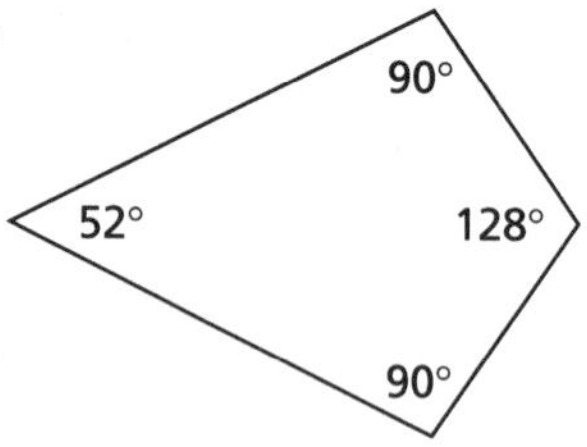

STUDENT PAGE

STUDENT PAGE

Notes

25. How did you know which shape was a parallelogram in Exercise 24?

26. Liang said that an equilateral triangle must have angles totaling 360° because he can cut it into two right triangles, as in the diagram. Is Liang's statement correct? Explain.

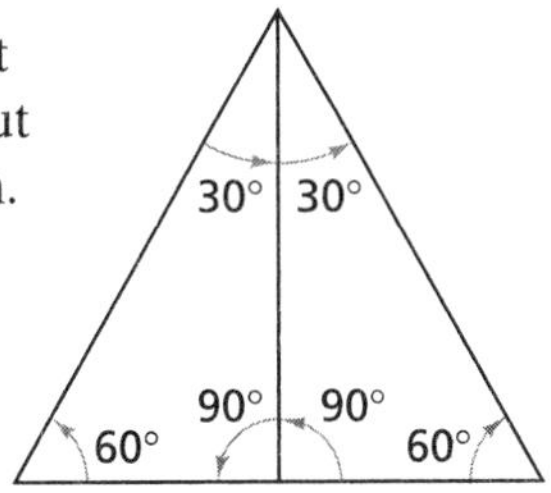

Connections

27. Is the statement below *true* or *false*? Justify your answer.

The region inside a polygon can be tiled by triangles.

28. The number 360 was chosen for the number of degrees in a full turn. The number may have been chosen because it has many factors.

a. List all the factors of 360.

b. What is the prime factorization of 360?

29. A right angle can be thought of as a quarter of a complete rotation.

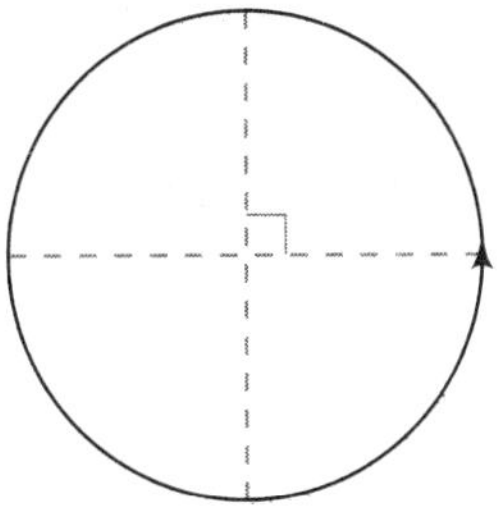

a. How many degrees is $\frac{1}{3}$ of a quarter of a rotation?

b. How many degrees is two times a quarter of a rotation?

c. How many degrees is $2\frac{1}{3}$ times a quarter of a rotation?

Replace the ■ with a number that will make the sentence true.

30. $\frac{1}{2} = \frac{■}{360}$

31. $\frac{1}{10} = \frac{36}{■}$

32. $\frac{1}{■} = \frac{40}{360}$

33. $\frac{■}{3} = \frac{120}{360}$

Go Online
PHSchool.com
For: Multiple-Choice Skills Practice
Web Code: ama-3254

Notes

34. A full turn is 360°. If a bee turns around 180°, like the one at the right, she has made a half turn.

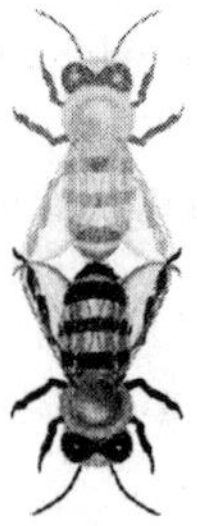

a. What fraction of a turn is 90°?

b. What fraction of a turn is 270°?

c. How many turns is 720°?

d. How many degrees is the fraction $\frac{25}{360}$ of a turn?

35. The minute hand on a watch makes a complete rotation every hour. The hand makes half of a full rotation in 30 minutes.

a. In how many minutes does the hand make $\frac{1}{6}$ of a rotation?

b. In how many minutes does the hand make $\frac{1}{6}$ of half a rotation?

c. What fraction of an hour is $\frac{1}{6}$ of half a rotation?

d. How many degrees has the minute hand moved through in $\frac{1}{6}$ of half a rotation?

36. The circular region is divided into four equal wedges formed by angles with vertices at the center of the circle. Such angles are called **central angles** of the circle. Each central angle shown measures 90°.

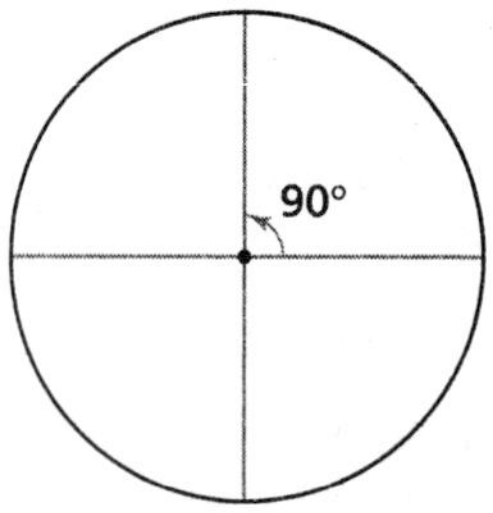

In parts (a)–(c), sketch a circular region divided into the given number of equal wedges. Then find the measure of the central angles.

a. 8 equal edges b. 6 equal wedges c. 3 equal wedges

d. Find another way to divide the circular region into equal wedges so that the central angles have whole number degree measures. Give the number of wedges and the measure of the central angles. What strategy did you use?

STUDENT PAGE

Notes

37. A ruler is used to measure the length of line segments. An angle ruler is used to measure the size of (or turn in) angles.

a. What is the unit of measurement for each kind of ruler?

b. Write a few sentences comparing the method for measuring angles to the method for measuring line segments.

38. Skateboarders use angle measures to describe their turns. Explain what a skateboarder would mean by each statement.

a. I did a 720. **b.** I did a 540. **c.** I did a 180.

39. In the figure below, the blue segments represent half of a polygon. The red vertical line is the line of symmetry for the complete polygon.

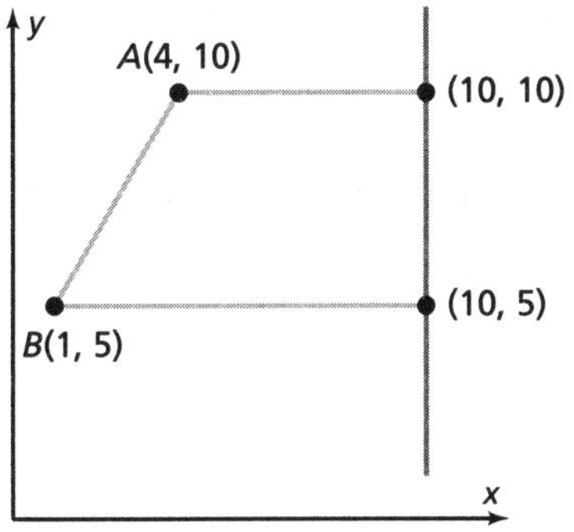

a. Copy the figure onto a sheet of grid paper. Then draw the missing half of the polygon.

b. On the "new" half of the figure, what are the coordinates of the point that corresponds to point A? What are the coordinates of the point that corresponds to point B?

c. Describe some properties of the polygon.

Connections

STUDENT PAGE

Notes

40. Multiple Choice Which choice is a 180° rotation of the figure below?

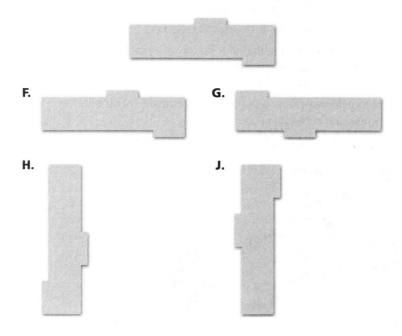

F. 

G. 

H. 

J. 

Extensions

41. Design a new polar coordinate grid for playing Four in a Row. Play your game with a friend or a member of your family. Explain the ideas that led to your new design. Compare playing on your new grid to playing on the grids given in Problem 2.2.

42. The **midpoint** of a line segment is the point that divides it into two segments of equal length. Trace the parallelogram below onto a sheet of paper. Connect the midpoints of two opposite sides. Describe the two quadrilaterals that are formed. Are they parallelograms? Explain.

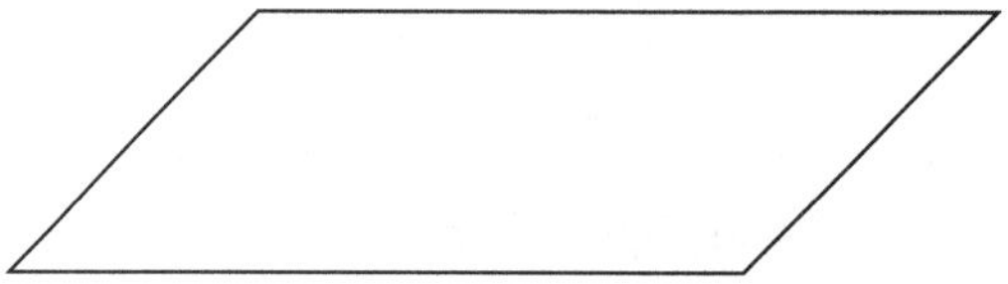

Notes

43. a. In the equilateral triangle below, the midpoints of two of the sides have been marked and then connected by a line segment. How does the length of this segment compare to the length of the third side of the triangle? Does the segment appear to be parallel to the third side of the triangle?

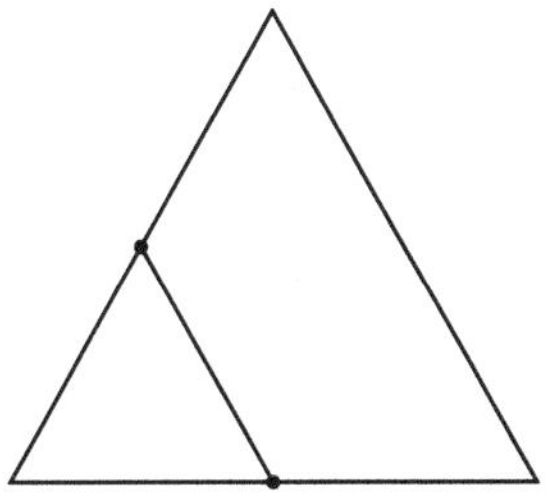

b. Draw an isosceles triangle. Locate the midpoints of two of the sides. Then draw a line segment connecting the midpoints. Compare the segment with the third side of the triangle. Do the observations you made in part (a) also apply in this case? Now connect the midpoints of a different pair of sides. Do the same observations hold?

c. Draw a scalene triangle. Locate the midpoints of two of the sides. Then draw a line segment connecting the midpoints. Compare the segment with the third side of the triangle. Do the observations you made in part (a) also apply in this case? Now connect the midpoints of a different pair of sides. Do the same observations hold?

44. Two lines are **perpendicular** if they intersect to form right angles. Tell whether the statement below is *true* or *false*. Justify your answer.

If a transversal is perpendicular to one line in a pair of parallel lines, then it must also be perpendicular to the other line.

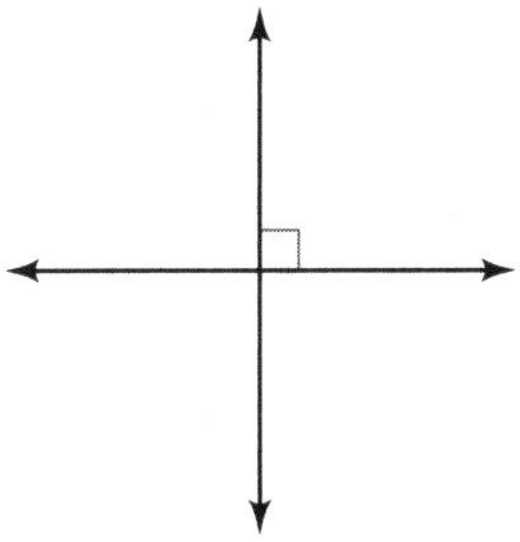

Perpendicular Lines

Connections Extensions

STUDENT PAGE

STUDENT PAGE

Notes

Did You Know?

Astronomers use two types of angles to locate objects in the sky. The *altitudinal* (al tuh too' di nuhl) *angle* is the angle from the horizon to the object. The horizon has an altitudinal angle of 0°. The point directly overhead, called the *zenith*, has an altitudinal angle of 90°.

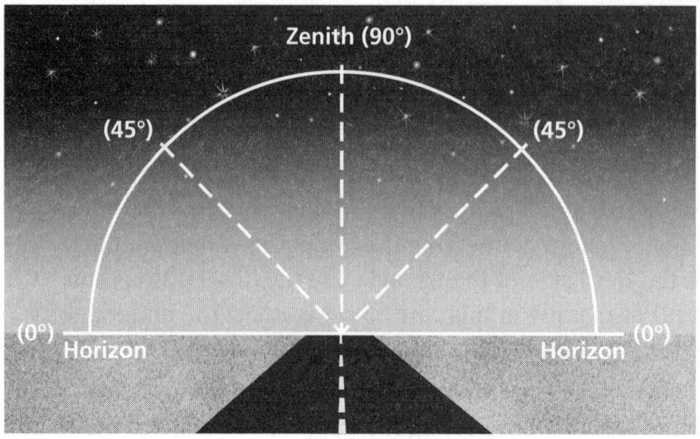

The *azimuthal* (az uh myooth' uhl) *angle* is the angle of rotation from north to the object. To find the azimuthal angle of an object, face north and then rotate clockwise until you are facing the object. The angle through which you turn is the azimuthal angle.

To find the azimuthal angle *between* two objects, face one of the objects and then turn until you are facing the other. The angle through which you turn is the azimuthal angle between the objects.

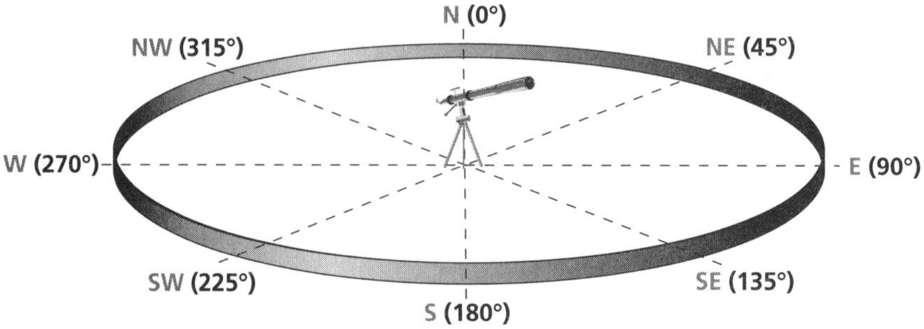

Go Online PHSchool.com **For:** Information about astronomy **Web Code:** ame-9031

STUDENT PAGE

Notes

Mathematical Reflections 2

In this investigation, you thought about angles that involved turns, sides of wedges, and two sides with a common vertex. You learned to estimate angle measures and to use tools to make more precise measurements. These questions will help you summarize what you have learned.

Think about your answers to these questions. Discuss your ideas with other students and your teacher. Then write a summary of your findings in your notebook.

1. **a.** Explain what the measure of an angle is.

   b. Explain how to measure an angle.

2. Describe some ways to estimate the measure of an angle.

3. **a.** What does it mean for two lines to be parallel?

   b. If two parallel lines are intersected by a transversal, what patterns can you expect to find in the measures of the angles formed?

Unit Project What's Next?

What information about shapes can you add to your *Shapes and Designs* project?

Notes

Investigation 2

ACE Assignment Choices

Differentiated Instruction
Solutions for All Learners

Problem 2.1

Core 1–2, 29
Other *Applications* 3, *Connections* 27, 28

Problem 2.2

Core 4, 5, 36
Other *Applications* 6–9, *Connections* 30–35, *Extensions* 41; unassigned choices from previous problems

Problem 2.3

Core 15–17 (students will need angle rulers for these exercises)
Other *Applications* 10–14, *Connections* 37 (students will need angle rulers); and unassigned choices from previous problems

Problem 2.4

Core 18–20
Other *Connections* 38–40; unassigned choices from previous problems

Problem 2.5

Core 21, 22, 24, 25, 26
Other *Applications* 23, *Extensions* 42–44; unassigned choices from previous problems

Adapted For suggestions about adapting Exercises 6–9 and other ACE exercises, see the CMP *Special Needs Handbook.*
Connecting to Prior Units 28: *Prime Time;* 29, 30–35: *Bits and Pieces I;* 37: linear measurement in elementary school

Applications

1. a. wedge
b. two sides meeting at a common point
c. turn

2. a. 90° **b.** 360° **c.** 450°
d. 45° **e.** 10° **f.** 22.5°

3. a. 90°

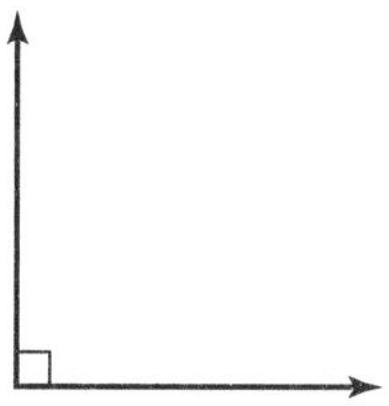

b. 180°

c. 120°

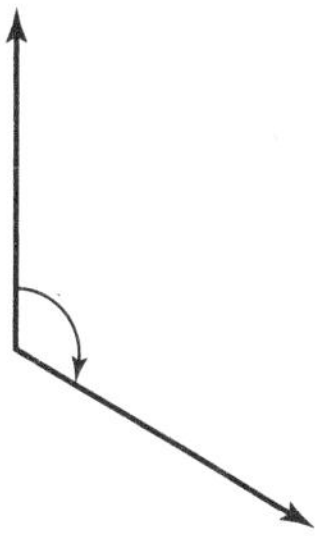

d. 360°

e. 30°

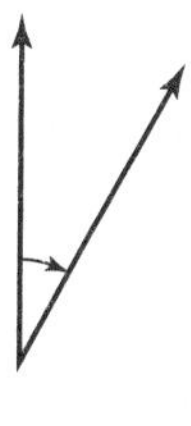

f. 540°

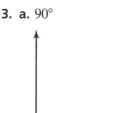

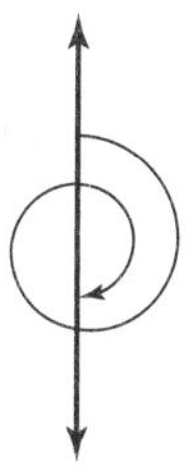

4. a. 180° **b.** 90° **c.** 150° **d.** 60°
e. 270° **f.** 345° **g.** 120° **h.** 30°

5. a. straight **b.** right
c. obtuse **d.** acute
e. none of these **f.** none of these
g. obtuse **h.** acute

Note: (e) and (f) are called reflex angles. Reflex angles are angles that are greater than 180° and less than 360°.

6. $180° - 30° = 150°$

7. $180° - 125° = 55°$

8. $90° - 27° = 63°$

9. $360° - 35° = 325°$

10. approximately 30°

11. approximately 45°

12. approximately 135°

13. approximately 90°

14. a.

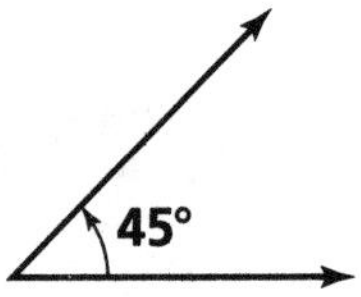

b.

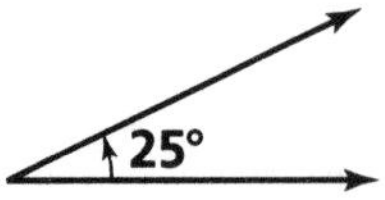

c.

d.

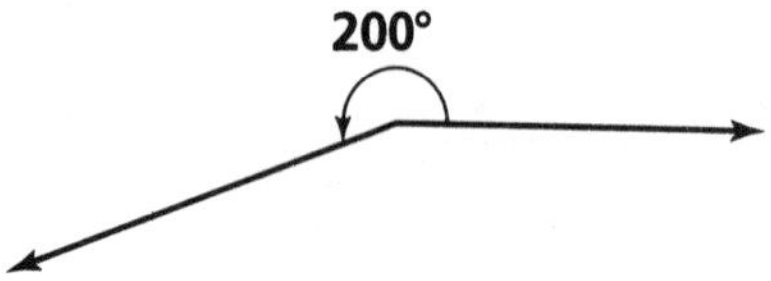

15. a. Angle 1 is larger. Angle 1 is 60° and angle 2 is 30°.

    b. The angles are the same size, 135°.

    c. Angle 1 is larger. Angle 1 is 90° and angle 2 is 45°.

16. Estimates may vary:

    a. 50° b. 135° c. 20° d. 210°

    e. 170°

17. a. 60°, 80°, 40° b. 120°, 120°, 60°, 60°

18. It seems that 1° would not make a difference. However, how far off the bee was would depend on the actual distance from the hive to the flower since the distance between two rays increases as the length of the rays increase.

19. The bee traveled 25° off course.

20. Big Bee did not hit the patch of flowers because she started farther away from the patch. Even though the angles were the same, the distance between the rays becomes greater as you move away from the vertex.

21. $m\angle a = 60°, m\angle b = 120°, m\angle d = 60°, m\angle e = 60°, m\angle f = 120°, m\angle g = 120°, m\angle h = 60°$

22. a. Lines L_1 and L_2 are parallel because the measure of the opposite interior angles formed by the parallel lines and the transversal are equal. In this case they are both 106°.

    b. The lines are not parallel, because the measure of the alternate interior angles formed by the parallel lines and the transversal are not equal.

    c. The lines are not parallel, because the measure of the alternate interior angles formed by the parallel lines and the transversal are not equal.

23. a. Answers will vary.

    b. When two intersecting lines make four angles, the angles across from each other (which do not share a side) have the same measure. (Note: We can show that vertical angles are always the same measure. Consider angles 1 and 3 above. Write the measure of angle 1 as $m\angle 1$. Then

$$m\angle 1 + m\angle 2 = 180° \textit{ and}$$
$$m\angle 2 + m\angle 3 = 180°$$

Since both left-hand sides equal 180, they must equal each other. So

$$m\angle 1 + m\angle 2 = m\angle 2 + m\angle 3.$$

Subtracting $m\angle 2$ from both sides gives that $m\angle 1 = m\angle 3$. So vertical angles are the same measure.)

    c. Student drawings and angle measures may vary. However, the patterns they observe should be the same as in part (b).

24. A

25. The opposite angles are of equal measure.

26. Liang is incorrect. The 90° angles in the picture he drew are not included in any of the angles of the equilateral triangle. He would have to subtract their measure from the total measure of the two triangles to find the angle sum of the equilateral triangle: $360° - 90° - 90° = 180°$.

Connections

27. True. For convex polygons (a polygon whose interior angles are less than or equal to 180°) you can draw diagonals from a vertex to the other vertices (except for the adjacent ones), in order to triangulate the polygon. For concave polygons (a polygon which has at least one angle greater than 180°), however, the method is less systematic.

28. **a.** There are 24 factors of 360: 1, 2, 3, 4, 5, 6, 8, 9, 10, 12, 15, 18, 20, 24, 30, 36, 40, 45, 60, 72, 90, 120, 180, 360

b. The prime factorization of 360 is $2^3 \times 3^2 \times 5$.

29. **a.** A third of a right angle is a third of 90° or 30°.

b. Two times a quarter rotation is two times 90° or 180°.

c. Two and a third times a quarter is 180° plus 30° or 210°. Later, students can write this as $2\frac{1}{3}$ times one fourth and get $\frac{7}{12}$ or $\frac{7}{12}$ of 360 or 210°.

30. 180

31. 360

32. 9

33. 1

34. **a.** one fourth

b. three fourths

c. two turns

d. 25°

35. **a.** $\frac{1}{6}$ of 60 min is 10 min

b. $\frac{1}{6}$ of 30 min is 5 min

c. Students might think in terms of fractions throughout. $\frac{1}{6}$ of a half is $\frac{1}{12}$. Or they might think in terms of minutes to get started. The answer in part (b) is 5 min. 5 min is $\frac{1}{12}$ of an hour.

d. The minute hand has moved through $\frac{1}{12}$ of a complete rotation, $\frac{1}{12}$ of 360° = 30°.

36. **a.** 45°; (8 wedges)

b. 60°; (6 wedges)

c. 120°; (3 wedges)

d. The number of equal wedges is determined by the numbers that 360 is divisible by: for example 1, 2, 3, 4, 5, 6, 8, 9, 10, etc. See the table below for more examples and central angle measures.

Number of Wedges	Central Angle Measure
1	360°
2	180°
4	90°
5	72°
9	40°
10	36°
12	30°
15	24°
18	20°
20	18°
24	15°
30	12°
36	10°
40	9°
45	8°
60	6°
72	5°
90	4°
120	3°
180	2°
360	1°

37. **a.** Angle rulers measure in degrees and rulers measure in units of length, such as in. or cm.

b. The methods are similar in that there is a starting place and an ending place to both measurements. The starting place is usually 0 with both, as well. The measurements are very different, however, in that an angle ruler measures an angle and a ruler measures a segment. Measuring angles involves the wedge or angle of turn formed by two segments that share an endpoint.

38. **a.** Turned entirely around two times ($2 \times 360° = 720°$).

b. Turned entirely around once plus another half of a circle.

c. Turned halfway around ($\frac{360°}{2} = 180°$)

39. **a.**

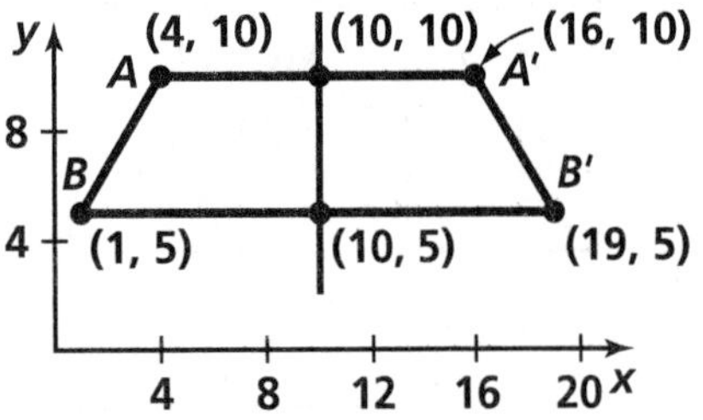

b. The point on the "new" half that corresponds to point A is (16, 10). The point on the "new" half that corresponds to point B is (19, 5).

c. It is a quadrilateral and has one pair of opposite sides parallel, and one pair of opposite sides that are equal in length. (Note: This polygon is called an isosceles trapezoid. Students may not use the word parallel, but they may describe this property.)

40. G

Extensions

41. Answers will vary.

42. The two quadrilaterals that are formed are also parallelograms. They have the same angle measures, but they have only half the height or half the base of the original parallelogram. This is because the line drawn was parallel to one of the sides of the original parallelogram.

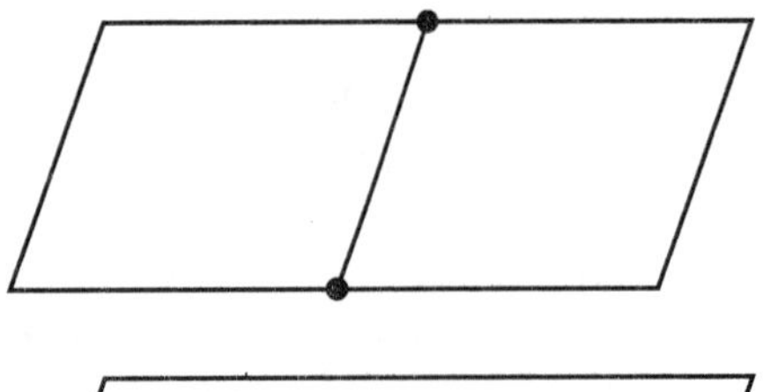

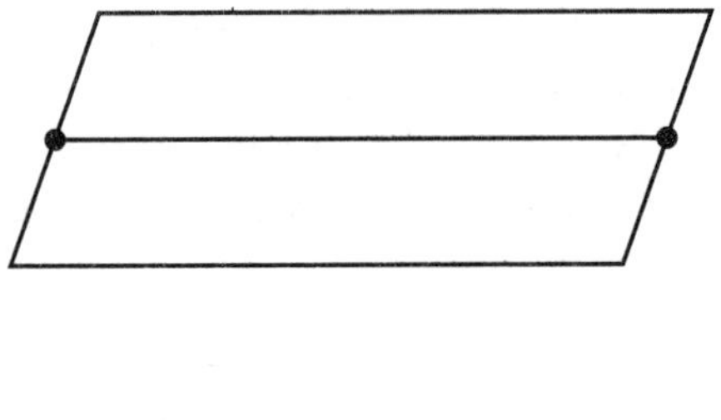

43. **a.** It is one half the length of the third side, and it does appear to be parallel to the third side. (Though it is not necessary to prove at this level, the third side is in fact parallel. One proof uses the properties of equilateral triangles and trapezoids having one pair of parallel sides.)

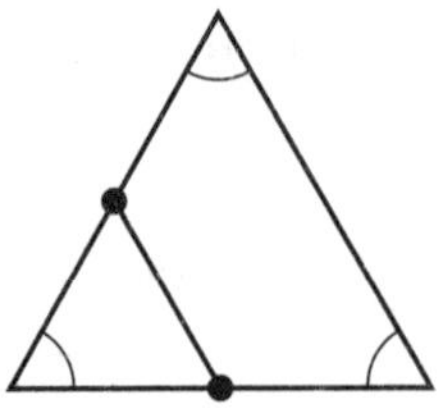

b. Yes, the observations for the equilateral triangle also apply to the isosceles triangle. The lengths of the line segments are half the length of the opposite side of the triangle. These line segments also appear parallel to the opposite side of the triangle. (Though it is not necessary to prove at this level, the third side is in fact parallel.)

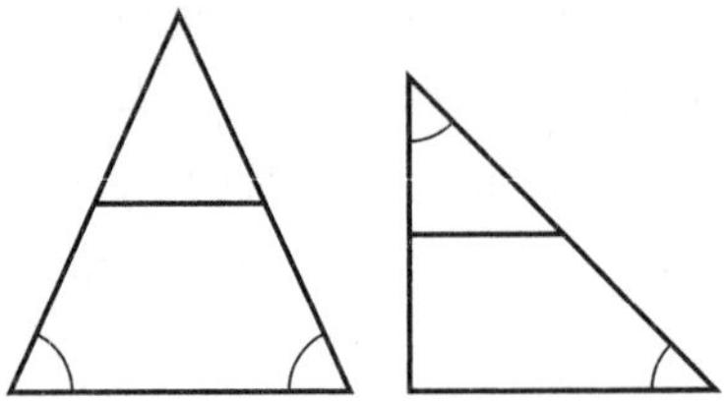

c. Yes, the observations for both the equilateral and the isosceles triangles noted in parts (a) and (b) hold true for the scalene triangle as well.

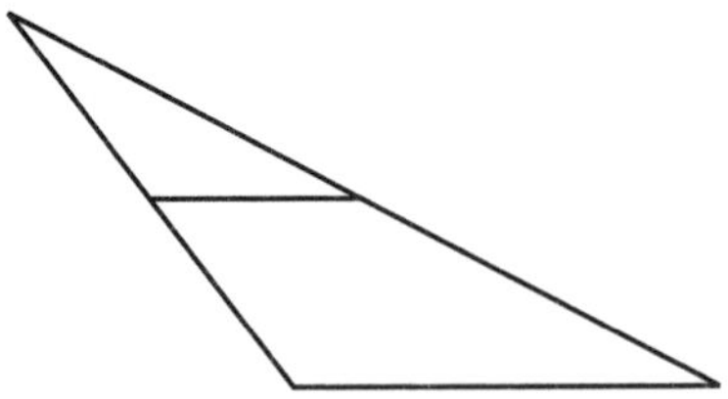

44. True. If the transversal forms a 90° angle with one of the parallel lines, the angle it forms with the other parallel line is $180° - 90° = 90°$, so it is perpendicular to this line also.

Possible Answers to Mathematical Reflections

1. a. The measure of an angle means the size of a turn or wedge. For example, an angle of 1° is a very small turn, or a very narrow wedge.

   b. There are several tools to measure angles. One of the easiest ones to use is the angle ruler. (See directions for using angle rulers in Problem 2.3.)

2. Angle measures can be estimated by using benchmarks. Benchmark angles are important in estimating. They allow us to quickly decide which two benchmarks an angle is between. Then we can estimate a value for the angle measurement. 30°, 45°, 60°, 90°, 180°, and 270° angles are good reference angles.

3. a. Parallel lines are straight lines that never meet, no matter how far they are extended.

   b. Some possible patterns:

   - The sum of two angles that share a side and whose two other sides form a straight line is 180°. (They are supplementary angles.)
   - The sum of the angles that are above the top parallel line is 180°. They form a straight line. (They are supplementary angles.)
   - The sum of the angles that are below the top parallel line is 180°. They form a straight line. (They are supplementary angles.)
   - The angle measures formed by the intersection of one of the parallel lines and the transversal have identical measures to the corresponding angles formed by the other parallel line and the transversal. (They are called corresponding angles.)
   - The two angles that are on the inside or interior part of the parallel lines, and are on the opposite side of the transversal, have equal measure. (They are alternate interior angles.)
   - The two angles that are on the inside or interior of the parallel lines, and are on the same side of the transversal have angle measures whose sum is 180°. (They are supplementary angles.)

Investigation 3 Polygon Properties and Tiling

Mathematical and Problem-Solving Goals

- Find angle sums of polygons
- Determine relationships between the number of sides and the angle sum of a regular polygon
- Form conjectures about the relationship between the number of sides and the angle sum of any polygon
- Decide which regular polygons will tile by themselves or in combinations using information about interior angles
- Explore the sum of the exterior angles of a polygon

Summary of Problems

Problem 3.1 Angle Sums of Regular Polygons

Students find angle sums and then form conjectures about the relationship between the number of sides and the angle sum of a regular polygon.

Problem 3.2 Angle Sums of Any Polygon

Students find angle sums and then form conjectures about the relationship between the number of sides and the angle sum of any polygon.

Problem 3.3 Back to the Bees!

Students look at *regular* polygons and figure out which regular polygons will tile a plane by themselves or in combinations by using information about the corner angle.

Problem 3.4 Exterior Angles of Polygons

Students explore the sum of the exterior angles of a polygon.

	Suggested Pacing	Materials for Students	Materials for Teachers	ACE Assignments
All	$4\frac{1}{2}$ days	Calculators, Shapes Sets (1 per group), angle rulers, student notebooks, blank transparencies for displaying answers, angle rulers	Overhead Shapes Set (Transparency 1.1E) , blank transparencies, overhead markers	
3.1	1 day	Student data from Problem 2.3	Transparencies 3.1A and 3.1B	1, 2, 15, 16, 21
3.2	1 day	Labsheet 3.2, construction paper, scissors	Transparency 3.2	3–10, 17, 22–24
3.3	1 day			11, 12, 18, 19, 25
3.4	1 day			13, 14, 20
All	$\frac{1}{2}$ day			

3.1 Angle Sums of Regular Polygons

Goals

- Find angle sums of regular polygons
- Determine relationships between the number of sides and the angle sum of a regular polygon

Launch 3.1

Remind students what a regular polygon is.

- *In Investigation 1, you experimented with the six regular polygons shown in your books. Someone remind us what a regular polygon is.* (A regular polygon is one in which all sides are the same size and all angles are the same size.)

Take a few suggestions, and clarify them until their definition is correct.

- *In Investigation 1, you were trying to find out which of these shapes would fit together nicely like tiles on a floor. You want to continue to think about these regular polygons by investigating the size of their angles and what happens to the measures of the angles as the number of sides increases. The sum of the angles of a polygon is called the "angle sum."*

Students should naturally understand that the angles being discussed are the angles "inside" the polygon, or interior angles. Interior angle is a term that is not necessary at this point and will formally be introduced in Problem 3.4.

Suggested Questions Put up Transparency 3.1A or refer to the textbook.

- *Which polygon has angles that appear to be the smallest?*
- *Which polygon has angles that appear to be the largest?*

These questions are asking students to make informal observations about the sizes of the interior angles without using measuring tools. They should be able to answer these questions from their exploration in Problem 2.3. At this point, students should be able to see that the size of the interior angles increases as the number of sides increases. One way to help struggling students see this is to demonstrate at the overhead projector how the sizes of the angles compare by placing one shape on top of another.

Arrange the students in groups of 2 and 3.

Explore 3.1

During this time, students can begin by entering the data they collected in Problem 2.3. They should continue measuring and recording measurements of a regular pentagon and octagon.

For students who see the patterns quickly, ask them to make a general rule. Some may even be ready to use symbols. Have the students use their rule to find the angle sums for a polygon with seven, nine, and ten sides.

Summarize 3.1

Display Transparency 3.1B. With input from the class, fill in the missing information. Accept, record, and then discuss all answers.

For example, many students will have angle measures that are close to the actual measures but not exact. Some students may disagree with the measurements others give.

Classroom Dialogue Model

One teacher handled the disagreement on angle measures in the following manner:

Teacher *I have listed the names of the five regular polygons you had to measure. For the triangle, what numbers do you have to fill in the next three columns? Does anyone have anything different?*

When a group answered yes, the teacher also recorded its numbers in the appropriate columns. For example, one group said the pentagon has five sides and each angle measures 100°, for a total of 500°. Another group said that the pentagon has five sides and each angle measures 108° for a total of 540°. The teacher listed both of these groups' answers and continued to collect information on

INVESTIGATION 3

the remaining polygons. When the chart was complete, she started to question the data.

Teacher *Why do we have different answers when we all measured the same angles? Does anyone have a suggestion for how we might resolve the angle measures we disagree on?*

In this class, many students suggested measuring the interior angles again. This resulted in some of the measures being eliminated from the chart. However, some students had given smaller angle measurements for octagons than hexagons.

Teacher *Look at all the answers that are now recorded on the chart. Are there any that don't seem reasonable?*

Students argued for elimination of some of the measures. The teacher only removed numbers from the chart when students had given a mathematical reason for eliminating them.

Teacher *What patterns do you notice in the way the size of the angles is increasing? What patterns do you notice in the way the size of the angle sum is increasing?*

Some students noticed that the angle sum seemed to be increasing by about 180° with each additional side. As a result, more numbers were eliminated from the chart because they did not fit the pattern. The teacher continued with the discussion until the class had arrived at the correct measurements. See Figure 1 below.

The teacher then tried to extend their thinking by asking *if-then* questions:

Teacher *If a regular polygon has twenty sides, what will be the sum of all the angles in that polygon? Explain why your answer makes sense.*
If a regular polygon has twenty sides, each angle must have how many degrees? Explain.

If you gently encourage students to make observations about patterns in the chart, some may look at the angle sums and observe the relationship to the triangle's 180° angle sum. You may have a student who extends this relationship by noticing that a square contains two triangles (by drawing one diagonal, $180° \cdot 2 = 360°$), a pentagon contains three triangles (by drawing two diagonals from one vertex, $180° \cdot 3 = 540°$), and so on. This will be useful for the Launch to Problem 3.2. If students are not ready, it's not necessary to force the issue now.

Question B tries to expand the ideas students have just developed. Students are asked to consider what happens to the angles of regular polygons when the lengths of the sides change. They measure the angles of the set of regular triangles and regular quadrilaterals and observe that they remain the same regardless of side length. The larger figures are *similar* to the smaller figures. In similar figures, angles are the same. These ideas are developed more fully in *Stretching and Shrinking.*

This is a good time to reinforce that changing a side length does not affect the size of an angle. An equilateral triangle is the easiest to use. Put three different ones on the overhead and ask about their angle measures and side lengths. Repeat this for one or two other polygons. Point out that two polygons with the same number of sides and equal corresponding angles are not necessarily *congruent* (same shape, same size).

Figure 1

Polygon	Number of Sides	Measure of an Angle	Angle Sum
Triangle	3	60°	180°
Square	4	90°	360°
Pentagon	5	108°	540°
Hexagon	6	120°	720°
Heptagon	7	128.6°	900°
Octagon	8	135°	1,080°
Nonagon	9	140°	1,260°
Decagon	10	144°	1,440°

3.1 Angle Sums of Regular Polygons

At a Glance

PACING 1 day

Mathematical Goals

- Find angle sums of regular polygons
- Determine relationships between the number of sides and the angle sum of a regular polygon

Launch

Remind students what a regular polygon is.

- *We call the sum of the interior angles of a polygon the "angle sum."*

Arrange six regular polygons on the overhead or refer to the textbook.

- *Which polygon has angles that appear to be the smallest?*
- *Which polygon has angles that appear to be the largest?*

Make sure that students see that the size of the interior angles increases as the number of sides increases. Demonstrate at the overhead projector how the sizes of the angles compare by placing one shape on top of another. Arrange students in groups of 2 and 3.

Materials

- Transparency 3.1A
- Overhead Shapes Set (Transparency 1.1E)
- Blank transparencies
- Overhead markers

Vocablulary

- angle sum

Explore

During this time, students begin by organizing the data they collected in Problem 2.3. They should continue measuring and recording measurements of a regular pentagon and octagon.

For students who see the patterns quickly, ask them to make a general rule. Some may even be ready to use symbols. Have the students use their rule to find the angle sums for a polygon with seven, nine, and ten sides.

Materials

- Student data from Problem 2.3
- Angle rulers
- Shapes Sets (1 per group)

Summarize

Display Transparency 3.1B. Accept and record all student answers on the chart. Some students may disagree with the measurements others give. When the chart is complete, you may want to question the data.

- *Why do we have different answers when we all measured the same angles? How might we resolve the angle measures we disagree on?*
- *Look at all the answers that are now recorded on the chart. Are there any that don't seem reasonable?*

Remove numbers from the chart when students have given a mathematical reason for eliminating them.

- *What patterns do you notice in the way the size of the angles is increasing? What patterns do you notice in the way the size of the angle sum is increasing?*

Continue with the discussion until the class arrives at the correct measurements. See the extended Summarize for more details and questions.

Materials

- Student notebooks
- Transparency 3.1B

continued on next page

Summarize

continued

Put three different-sized equilateral triangles on the overhead and ask about their angle measures and then about the side lengths. Repeat this for one or two other polygons. Point out that two polygons with the same number of sides and equal corresponding angles are not necessarily identical.

ACE Assignment Guide for Problem 3.1

Differentiated Instruction
Solutions for All Learners

Core 1–2

Other *Connections* 15–16 (angle ruler needed for 15), *Extensions* 21

Adapted For suggestions about adapting Exercise 2 and other ACE exercises, see the CMP *Special Needs Handbook.*

Answers to Problem 3.1

A. **1. and 3.** After part (3), the completed table should look like Figure 2.

2. Students should notice that the measure of the interior angles increases with the number of sides. They should also notice that, starting from the triangle, the angle sum increases by 180° with each additional side. The angle measure increases by less as the number of sides goes up.

B. Students should conclude that the length of the sides in the sets of similar polygons has no effect on the angle sum or the measure of the interior angles.

C. If the number of sides is N, then the angle sum of the polygon is $N - 2$ times 180°. Or: Angle Sum $= 180°(N - 2)$.

Figure 2

Polygon	Number of Sides	Measure of an Angle	Angle Sum
Triangle	3	60°	180°
Square	4	90°	360°
Pentagon	5	108°	540°
Hexagon	6	120°	720°
Heptagon	7	128.6°	900°
Octagon	8	135°	1,080°
Nonagon	9	140°	1,260°
Decagon	10	144°	1,440°

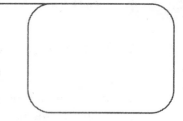

3.2 Angle Sums of Any Polygon

Goals

- Develop informal arguments for conjectures about the relationship between the number of sides and the angle sum of any polygon
- Find angle sums of any polygon

Students use their knowledge of 180° and 360° to find the sum of the angles of a polygon. In the Getting Ready for Problem 3.2, we start with a triangle and determine that any triangle has an angle sum of 180°. We then look at a quadrilateral and determine that any quadrilateral has an angle sum of 360°. Then they use what they know about the angle sum of a triangle to find the angle sum of other polygons by subdividing the polygon into non-overlapping triangles.

Launch 3.2

Suggested Questions Begin by asking students whether or not they think the angle sum formula or pattern for regular polygons they developed in Problem 3.1 will hold for polygons in general.

- *Do you think the angle sum of any triangle is 180°? How can you check?*

Draw a triangle on a sheet of paper or a transparency and label each angle 1, 2, and 3. After cutting out the triangle, tear (or cut) off all three angles and arrange the angles around a point on another sheet of paper or on the overhead.

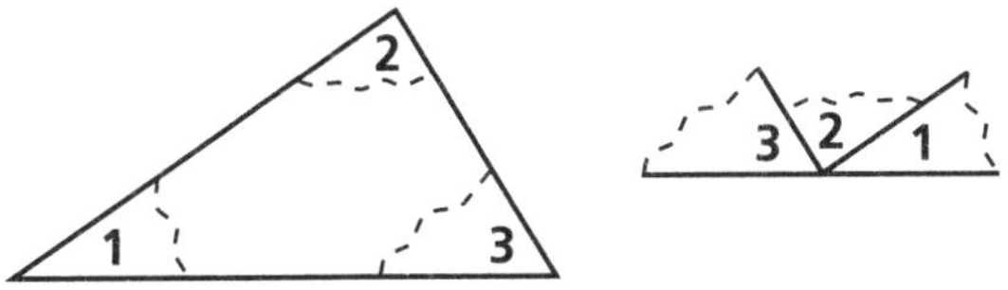

- *What do you observe about the sum of the angles of the triangle?* (Since the three angles form a straight line, the sum of the angles is 180°.)

Repeat the experiment with different shaped triangles.

- *Based on your experiments, what is the angle sum of any triangle?* (180°)
- *What if this experiment were repeated for a quadrilateral? Can you predict the sum of the angles of the quadrilateral?*

Draw a quadrilateral on a sheet of paper or a transparency and label each angle 1, 2, 3, and 4. After cutting out the quadrilateral, tear (or cut) off all four angles and arrange the angles around a point on another sheet of paper or on the overhead.

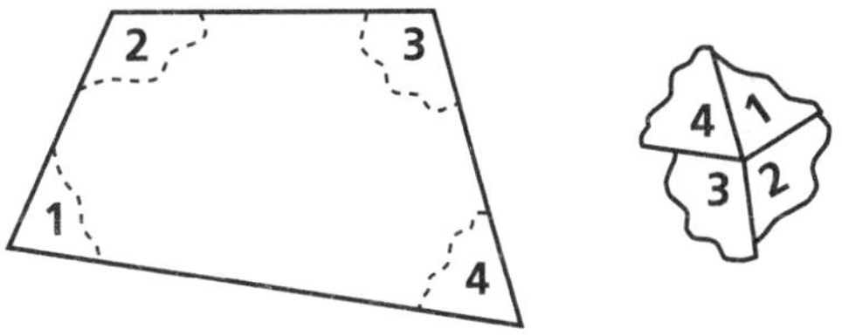

- *Based on the picture, what is the sum of angles 1, 2, 3, and 4? How do you know?* (360°, because the angles fit around a point.)
- *Make a conjecture about the angle sum of any quadrilateral.* (The angle sum of any quadrilateral is 360°.)
- *Do similar patterns hold for other polygons?* (Students may predict that the angle sums match the results they got in Problem 3.1.)

Some students may need to be reminded that the sum of the angles around a point is 360°.

- Now describe both Tia's and Cody's method for finding the sum of the angles of a polygon with sides greater than three. You could have half the students analyze one method and the others analyze the other method. In summary, a person from each group would present the argument for the reasoning in the method they explored. You could also assign one for the class to work on in class and then assign the other for homework.

Arrange the students into groups of 2 and 3.

Explore 3.2

Students should begin exploring Tia's method. If they are having trouble understanding Tia's drawings, remind them that the angle sum of every triangle is 180°.

For students having a hard time seeing that the sum of the angles of a polygon is equal to the sum of the angles in the $(N - 2)$ triangles, you can suggest numbering the angles of the triangles in Tia's method.

A similar numbering method may also help with Cody's method. Some students may need to be reminded that the sum of the angles around a point is 360°.

For students who see the patterns quickly, ask them to make a general rule. Ask how their answers compare to their answers to Problem 3.1.

Summarize 3.2

Have someone explain each method. Be sure the class understands the explanations. Let them ask questions.

Suggested Questions

- *Are the angle sums of these polygons the same as the angle sums for regular polygons with the same number of sides?* (Yes.)
- *What about the measure of each interior angle?*
  (No, because in a regular polygon each interior angle has the same size, and in these polygons, the angles are not necessarily the same size.)

Suggested Questions Ask the class:

- *What is the angle sum of a 12-sided polygon? A 100-sided polygon?*
  (A 12-sided polygon has an angle sum of 1,800° and a 100-sided polygon has an angle sum of 17,640°.)
- *What is the angle sum of any polygon with N sides?* $(180° \times (N - 2))$
- *Use the rule to find the angle sum of a polygons with 50 sides.* (8,640°)

Here is an example:

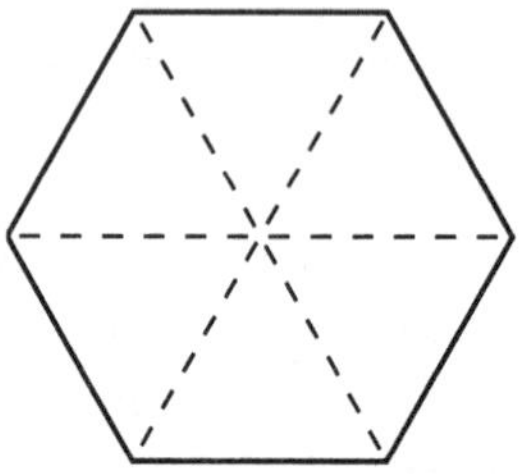

For each shape you can use either method. For the hexagon using Cody's method:
$180° \times 6 - 360° = 1{,}080° - 360° = 720°$.

For the pentagon using Tia's method:
$(N - 2) \times 180° = (5 - 2) \times 180° = 540°$, where N is the number of sides.

You can modify the chart in Problem 3.1 so that students see that the angle sum of any polyhedron is $180° \times (N - 2)$. Use this chart to launch the next problem.

At a Glance

3.2 Angle Sums of Any Polygon

PACING 1 day

Mathematical Goals

- Develop informal arguments for conjectures about the relationship between the number of sides and the angle sum of any polygon
- Find angle sums of any polygon

Launch

Ask students whether or not they think the angle sum formula or pattern for regular polygons will hold for polygons in general.

- *Do you think the angle sum of any triangle is 180°? How can we check?*

Draw a triangle on a sheet of paper or a transparency and label each angle 1, 2, and 3. After cutting out the triangle, tear (or cut) off all three angles and arrange the angles around a point on another sheet of paper or on the overhead.

- *What do you observe about the sum of the angles of the triangle?*

Repeat the experiment with different shaped triangles.

- *Based on your experiments, what is the angle sum of any triangle?*
- *What if this experiment was repeated for a quadrilateral?*
- *Can you predict the sum of the angles of the quadrilateral?*

Draw a quadrilateral on a sheet of paper or a transparency and label each angle 1, 2, 3, and 4. After cutting out the quadrilateral, tear (or cut) off all four angles and arrange the angles around a point or on the overhead.

- *Based on the picture, what is the sum of angles 1, 2, 3, and 4? How do you know?*
- *Make a conjecture about the angle sum of any quadrilateral.*
- *Can you predict the sum of the angles of a pentagon? A hexagon? Any* N*-sided polygon?*

Describe Cody and Tia's methods for finding the angle sum of a polygon. Arrange the students into groups of 2 and 3.

Materials

- Transparency 3.2
- Overhead Shapes Set (Transparency 1.1E)
- Construction paper and scissors

Explore

Students should begin exploring Tia's method. You may need to remind students that the angle sum of every triangle is 180°, and that the sum of the angles around a point is 360°. For students having a hard time seeing that the sum of the angles of a polygon are equal to the sum of the angles in the $(N - 2)$ triangles, you can suggest numbering the angles of the triangles in Tia's method. For students who see the patterns quickly, ask them to make a general rule. Ask how their answers compare to their answers to Problem 3.1.

Materials

- Labsheet 3.2
- Shapes Sets (1 per group)

continued on next page

Summarize *continued*

Have someone explain each method.

- *Are the angle sums of these polygons the same as the angle sums for regular polygons with the same number of sides?*
- *What about the measure of each interior angle?*

Ask the class:

- *What is the angle sum of a 12-sided polygon? A 100-sided polygon? What is the angle sum of any polygon with* N *sides?*

Materials

- Student notebooks

ACE Assignment Guide for Problem 3.2

Differentiated Instruction
Solutions for All Learners

Core 3–6, 9

Other *Applications* 7, 8, 10; *Connections* 17; *Extensions* 22–24; unassigned choices from previous problems

Adapted For suggestions about adapting ACE exercises, see the CMP *Special Needs Handbook.*

Answers to Problem 3.2

A. 1. By drawing diagonals from a vertex of the polygon, Tia sectioned off triangles inside the polygon. The number of triangles created inside the polygon is always two less than the number of sides of the polygon. Since the sum of the angles of a triangle equals 180°, the sum of the angles of a polygon is the number of triangles drawn inside times 180°, or (two less than the number of sides) times 180°.

2. The angle sum of the pentagon is 540°, the angle sum of the quadrilateral is 360°, and the angle sum of the octagon is 1,080°.

3. Yes. When you draw diagonals from a vertex of a polygon you get triangles, whose angles sum to 180° times the number of triangles. If you use this mathematical statement:
(Number of sides of polygon $-$ 2) $\times$ 180°,
you will get the angle sum of the polygon. This is consistent with what we learned about regular polygons.

B. 1. Cody drew line segments from a point inside of each polygon to all of its vertices, thereby forming triangles inside the polygon. He then discovered that if you multiplied the number of triangles by 180° (finding the total angle measurements of all the triangles created), and subtracted 360° from this sum (for the angles around the interior point that are not part of the polygon's angles), the result is the sum of the interior angles of the original polygon.

2. The angle sum of the pentagon is 540°, the angle sum of the quadrilateral is 360°, and the angle sum of the octagon is 1,080°.

3. Yes. We could use this mathematical statement:
(Number of triangles) $\times$ 180° $-$ 360° to get the angle sum of the polygons.

C. Yes. The angle sum of a regular polygon with *N* sides is the same as the angle sum of any polygon with *N* sides.

3.3 Back to the Bees!

Goal

- Decide which regular polygons will tile by themselves or in combinations using information about interior angles

Launch 3.3

By now students should have an idea of which regular polygons will tile and which will not. If needed, remind them about the discussion that began in Investigation 1 about which shapes will tile a surface and which will not.

Suggested Questions

- *Which of the regular polygon shapes (Shapes A–F) did we learn would tile a surface (fit together so that there are no gaps or overlaps) by themselves?* (Students should recall that the triangle, square, and hexagon all fit that requirement.)
- *How can we tell for sure that a shape, like these hexagons, fits exactly around each point in a tiling? We know the fit looks good, but how can we use mathematics to tell for sure?* (Students may notice that if the measure of one angle of a regular polygon is a factor of 360°, the polygon will tile. You can also leave this as an open question for them to think about as they explore.)

Have students work together in groups of 2–4.

Explore 3.3

Suggested Questions As you move from group to group, ask questions about angles to help students focus on them as a consideration in forming a tiling.

- *How much turn must there be to completely surround a vertex point?* (360°)
- *How many degrees are in the angles of the polygon you are investigating?*
- *How many degrees are in all of the angles around this vertex point?* (360°)
- *What would we expect the angle sum around a vertex to be?* (360°)

When students have completed the exploration of the regular polygons, they should move to the combinations of regular polygons.

Going Further

You can ask students to explore whether any quadrilateral or triangle will tile. Be sure they draw pictures to illustrate their answer. The answer is yes. Use four copies of a quadrilateral to arrange them around a point. The sum of the angles is 360° so they will fit exactly around a point. Any triangle will also tile. You will need six copies of the triangle to fit around a point. The following are two examples of a non-regular quadrilateral and triangle that tile.

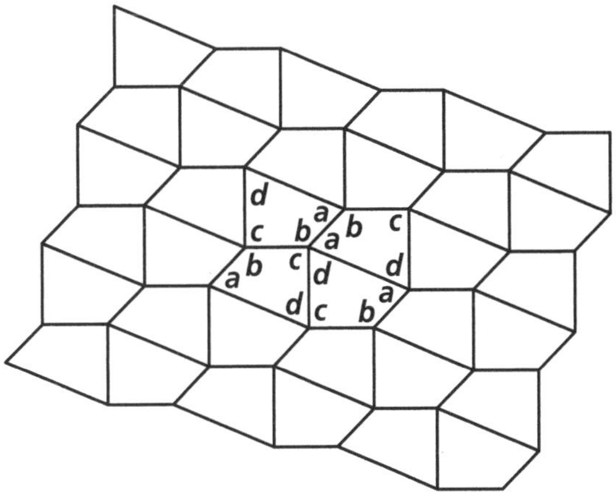

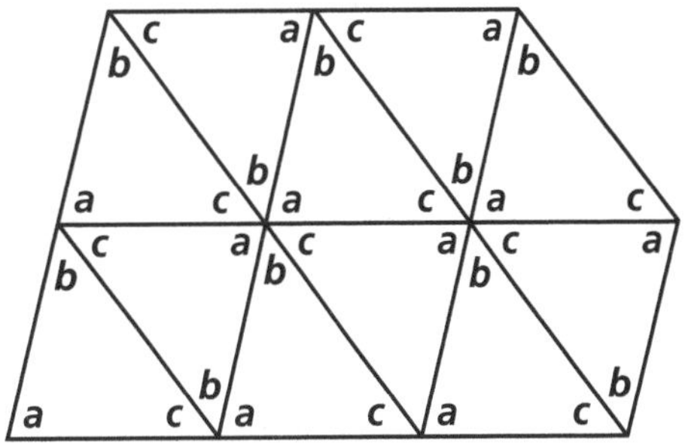

Summarize 3.3

Students should be able to explain why there are only three regular polygons that tile using angle measure as part of their argument. They should also be able to explain why certain combinations of regular polygons work using angle measures. Be sure to ask them to show why they think their design forms a tiling with no gaps or overlaps. One simple example is octagons and squares: the interior angle in a regular octagon is 135°, two octagons would be 270°, and adding an angle from the square would make the necessary 360°.

There are eight combinations of regular polygons that will tile so that each vertex has exactly the same pattern of polygons. These are sometimes called semi-regular or Archimedean tessellations. Note the numbers in parentheses refer to the polygon by side number (8 means a regular octagon, 6 means a regular hexagon, etc.) and the order they appear around a vertex of the tiling.

- 2 octagons and 1 square (8-8-4)
- 1 square, 1 hexagon, and 1 dodecagon (4-6-12)
- 4 triangles and 1 hexagon (3-3-3-3-6)
- 3 triangles and 2 squares (4-3-4-3-3)
- 1 triangle, 2 squares, and 1 hexagon (4-3-4-6)
- 1 triangle and 2 dodecagons (3-12-12)
- 3 triangles and 2 squares (4-3-3-3-4)
- 2 triangles and 2 hexagons (3-6-3-6)

Note there are two arrangements with triangles and squares, but depending on the arrangement they produce different tile patterns.

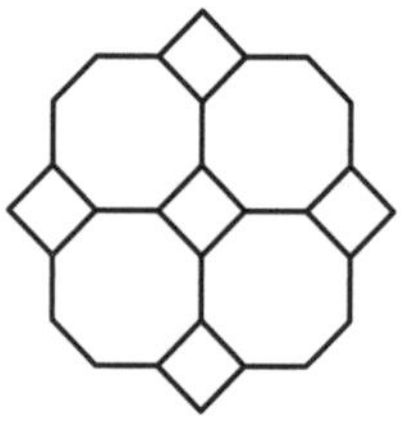

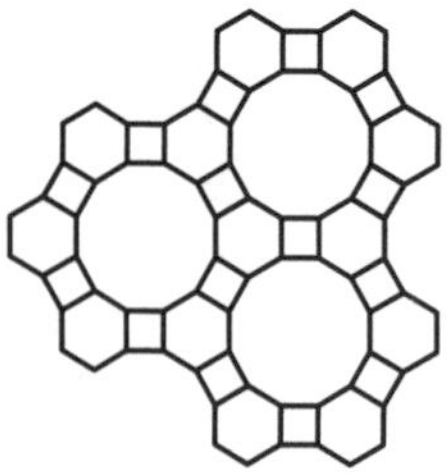

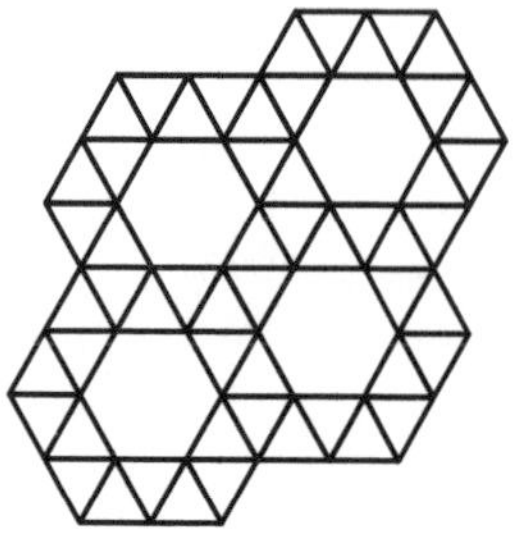

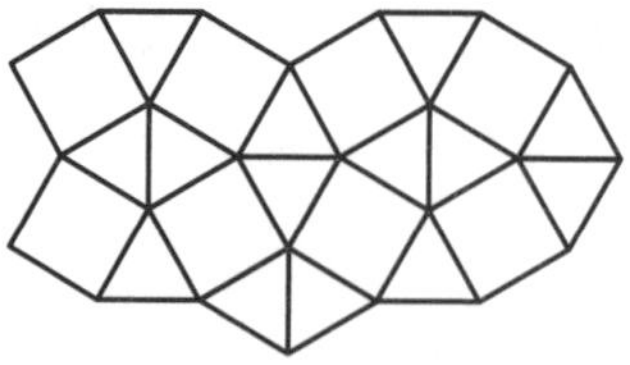

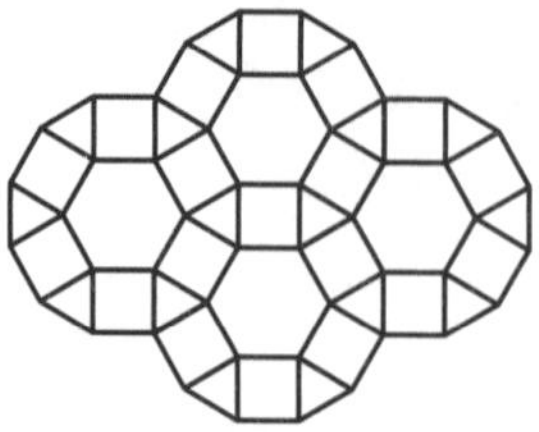

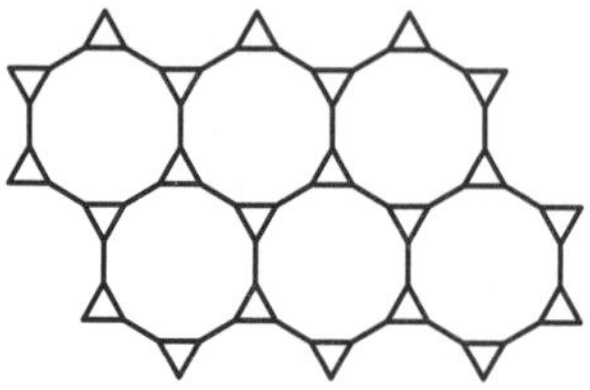

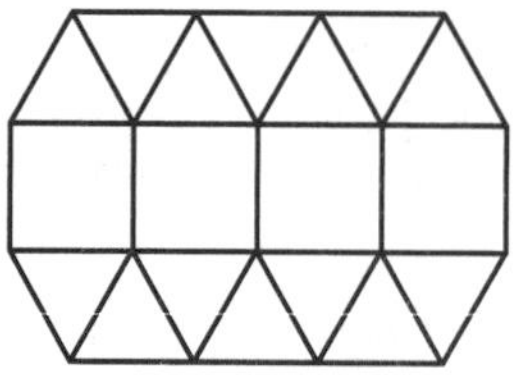

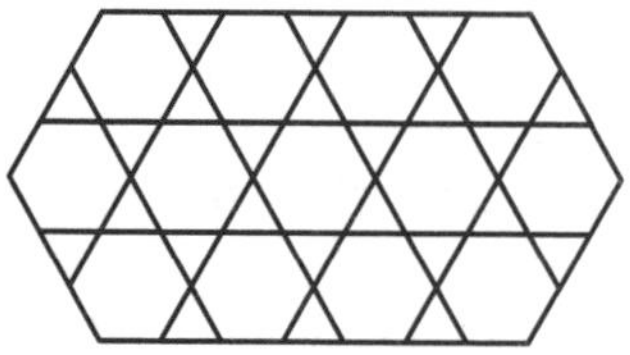

If you allow the pattern to vary from vertex to vertex, you can make at least two more tilings.

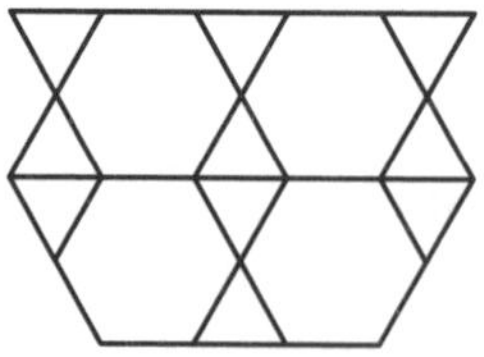

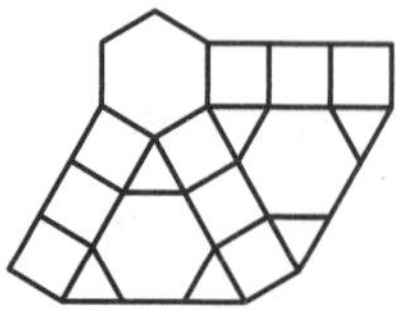

3.3 Back to the Bees!

At a Glance

PACING 1 day

Mathematical Goal

- Decide which regular polygons will tile by themselves or in combinations using information about interior angles

Launch

Students should have an idea about which regular polygons will tile and which will not. If needed, remind them about the discussions from Investigation 1.

- *Which of the regular polygon shapes (Shapes A–F) did we learn would tile a surface—fit together so that there are no gaps or overlaps—by themselves?*

Students should recall that the triangle, square, and hexagon all tile.

- *How can we tell for sure that a shape, like these hexagons, fits exactly around each point in a tiling? We know the fit looks good, but how can we use mathematics to tell for sure?*

Have students work together in groups of 2–4.

Materials

- Overhead Shapes Set (Transparency 1.1E)

Explore

As you move from group to group, ask questions about angles to help students focus on them as a consideration in forming a tiling.

- *How much turn must there be to completely surround a vertex point?*
- *How many degrees are in the angles of the polygon you are investigating?*
- *What would we expect the angle sum around a point to be?*

When students have completed the exploration of the regular polygons, they should move to the combinations of regular polygons.

Going Further

Ask students to explore whether any quadrilateral will tile.

Materials

- Shapes Sets (1 per group)

Summarize

Students should be able to explain why there are only three regular polygons that tile using angle measure as part of their argument. They should also be able to explain why certain combinations of regular polygons work using angle measures.

- *Why do you think your design forms a tiling with no gaps or overlaps?*

Materials

- Student notebooks

continued on next page

Summarize *continued*

There are eight combinations of regular polygons that will tile so that each vertex has exactly the same pattern of polygons. (note the numbers in parentheses refer to the polygon by side number):

2 octagons and 1 square (8-8-4)
1 square, 1 hexagon, and 1 dodecagon (4-6-12)
4 triangles and 1 hexagon (3-3-3-3-6)
3 triangles and 2 squares (4-3-4-3-3)
1 triangle, 2 squares, and 1 hexagon (4-3-4-6)
1 triangle and 2 dodecagons (3-12-12)
3 triangles and 2 squares (4-3-3-3-4)
2 triangles and 2 hexagons (3-6-3-6)

Note there are two arrangements with triangles and squares, but depending on the arrangement they produce different patterns.

ACE Assignment Guide for Problem 3.3

Differentiated Instruction
Solutions for All Learners

Core 11, 12
Other *Connections* 18, 19; *Extensions* 25; unassigned choices from previous problems

Adapted For suggestions about adapting ACE exercises, see the CMP *Special Needs Handbook.*

Answers to Problem 3.3

A. 1.

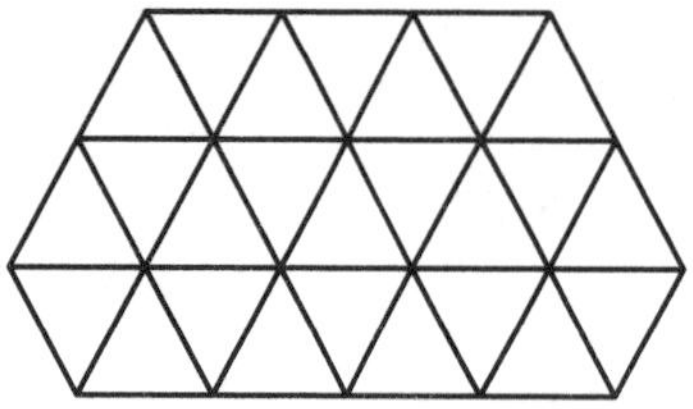

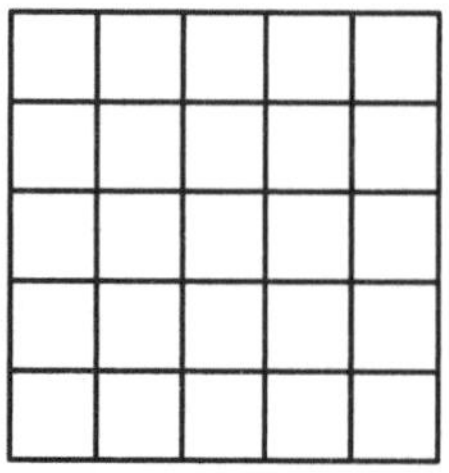

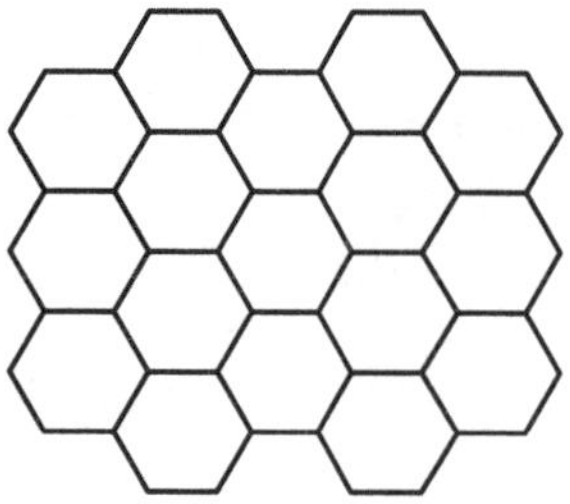

2. Equilateral triangles, squares, and hexagons tile because the measure of an interior angle for each (60°, 90°, 120°) divides evenly into 360°.

B. A regular polygon will form a tiling only if its angle measurement is a factor of 360°, and the angle measurements of pentagons, heptagons, and octagons are not factors of 360°.

C. 1. Answers and sketches will vary. Example:

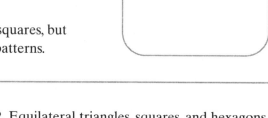

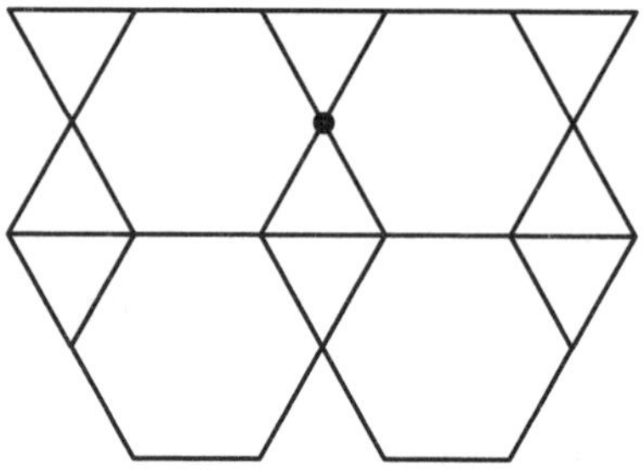

There are eight tilings using combinations of regular polygons. See Summarize above.

2. The sum of the angles that meet at a point in the tiling is always 360°.

3.4 Exterior Angles of Polygons

Goal

- Explore the sum of the exterior angles of a polygon

An interesting fact emerges—the sum of the exterior angles of a polygon is always 360°. Intuitively, this may not be surprising. That is, if you start at one vertex and walk completely around the polygon to the starting vertex, you have in essence done a 360-degree rotation.

Launch 3.4

Put up several regular polygons on the overhead.

Suggested Questions

- *What pattern do you see in the sizes of the interior angles as the number of sides increases?* (The sizes of the angles are increasing. They are getting closer and closer to 180°.)
- *Will they ever be equal to or greater than 180°?* (No. If they are equal to 180°, then the angles would all lie on a straight line and there would be no polygon. Since the polygon is regular, if one angle is greater than 180°, all of the angles are greater than 180°. In this case there would be no way to connect the sides to form a polygon.)
- *What happens to the shape of the polygon as the interior angle measures increase?* (It becomes more and more like a circle.)

Show the class an example of an exterior and interior angle of a polygon. These two angles come in pairs. Students might note that the sum of their measures is 180°.

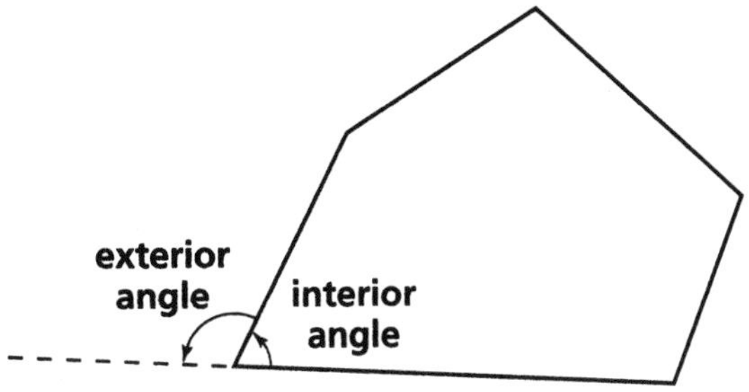

Tell the class that there are two sets of exterior angles depending on how you extend the sides of a polygon. The important thing is that the sides have to be extended in the same direction—either all clockwise or all counterclockwise.

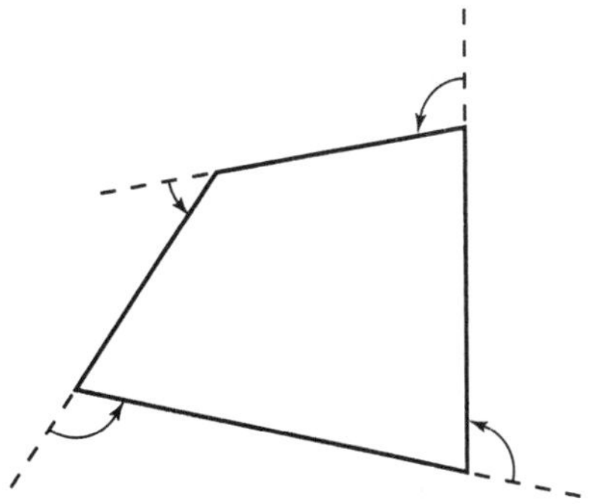

One set of exterior angles (counter clockwise)

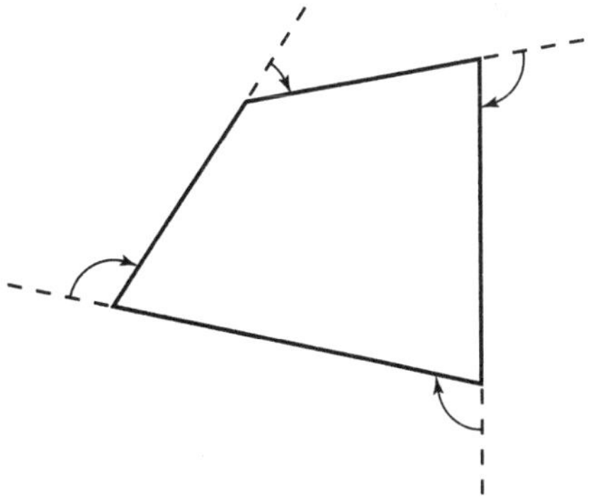

The other set of exterior angles (clockwise)

Ask the class if any of them have done any skateboarding. You might ask them how angles or the language of angles is used in skateboarding.

Tell the class about the skateboarder who is skating around a park in the shape of a polygon. You might demonstrate this with a polygon.

Suggested Question

- *As she turns the first corner, what angle of turn does she make?*

Tell the class that their challenge is to find how many degrees the skateboarder skates through as she skates once around a park shaped like a polygon. Tell the class that the skateboarder is going counterclockwise around the park. See the top figure in this column.

Students can work in groups of 2–4.

Explore 3.4

Be sure that students have a consistent set of exterior angles. For those students that finish early, you can ask them to explore the sum of the exterior angles if the skateboarder skates in the opposite direction. There is no difference in the sum.

Going Further

Suggest that students try a square or another regular polygon. Some might want to draw an irregular polygon and measure the exterior angles.

Summarize 3.4

Go over the answers. Ask the class to explain why the sum of 360° makes sense.

Put up some regular polygons. Ask for the measure of each interior angle. Then ask for the sum of the exterior angles. Ask for the measure of each exterior angle and mark them on the polygon.

- *Make a conjecture about the sum of the exterior angles of a polygon.* (The sum is always 360°.)

Put up an irregular polygon and label the measures of each interior angle. Ask for the sum of the exterior angles.

Repeat the above activities for the other set of exterior angles.

Mathematics Background

For background on exterior angles, see page 10.

Going Further

Challenge the class to find a reason why the angle sum of the interior angles of a polygon is 360°.

Students might use an arithmetic argument. They will note that the sum of an interior angle and its exterior angle is 180°. In an N-sided polygon, the sum of all these pairs of angles is N(180). This sum includes the sum of the interior angles. So, subtract the sum of the interior angles.

$$N(180) - (N - 2)180$$

Students will use specific cases for N to show that the sum is always 360°.

3.4 Exterior Angles of Polygons

At a Glance

PACING 1 day

Mathematical Goal

- Explore the sum of the exterior angles of a polygon

Launch

Put up several regular polygons on the overhead.

- *What pattern do you see in the sizes of the interior angles as the number of sides increases?*
- *Will they ever equal or be greater than 180°?*
- *What happens to the shape of the polygon as the interior angle measures increase?*

Show the class an example of an exterior and interior angle of a polygon. These two angles come in pairs. Students might note that the sum of their measures is 180°.

Remind the class that there are two sets of exterior angles depending on how you extend the sides of a polygon. The important thing is that the sides have to be extended in the same direction—either all clockwise or all counterclockwise.

Ask the class if any of them have done any skateboarding. You might ask them how angles or the language of angles is used in skateboarding. Tell the class about the skateboarder who is skating around a park in the shape of a polygon. You might demonstrate this with a polygon.

- *As she turns the first corner, what angle of turn does she make?*
- *Your challenge is to find how many degrees the skateboarder skates through as she skates around a park shaped like a polygon once. The skateboarder is going counterclockwise around the park.*

Students can work in groups of 2–4.

Materials

- Overhead Shapes Set (Transparency 1.1E)

Vocabulary

- interior angle
- exterior angle

Explore

Be sure that students have a consistent set of exterior angles. For those students that finish early, you can ask them to explore the sum of the exterior angles if the skateboarder skates in the opposite direction. There is no difference in the sum.

Going Further

Suggest that students try a square or another regular polygon. Some might want to draw an irregular polygon and measure the exterior angles.

Materials

- Shapes Sets (1 per group)
- Angle rulers

continued on next page

Summarize

continued

Go over the answers. Ask the class to explain why the sum of 360° makes sense.

Put up some regular polygons. Ask for the measure of each interior angle. Then ask for the sum of the exterior angles.

Put up an irregular polygon and label the measures of each interior angle. Ask for the sum of the exterior angles.

Repeat the above activities for the other set of exterior angles.

Materials

- Student notebooks

ACE Assignment Guide for Problem 3.4

Differentiated Instruction
Solutions for All Learners

Core 13, 14

Other *Connections* 20; unassigned choices from previous problems

Adapted For suggestions about adapting ACE exercises, see the CMP *Special Needs Handbook.*

Answers to Problem 3.4

A. 1. The interior angles are 50°, 95°, and 35°. The sum of the three angles of a triangle is 180°, and to find the missing angle measure for this triangle you could solve: $50° + 95° + x = 180°$, and find that $x = 35°$.

2. Angle 1 measures 145°. Since angle 1 and the unknown angle form a straight line, the sum of their angle measures is 180° (they are supplementary). Therefore to find the measure of angle 1, you would subtract 35° from 180° to get 145°.

3. Angle 2 measures 85°, (180° − 95°); angle 3 measures 130°, (180° − 50°).

B. Starting with exterior angle 1, the sum of the angles for which she turns are 85° + 145° + 130° = 360°.

C. 1. Answers will vary. One possibility is:

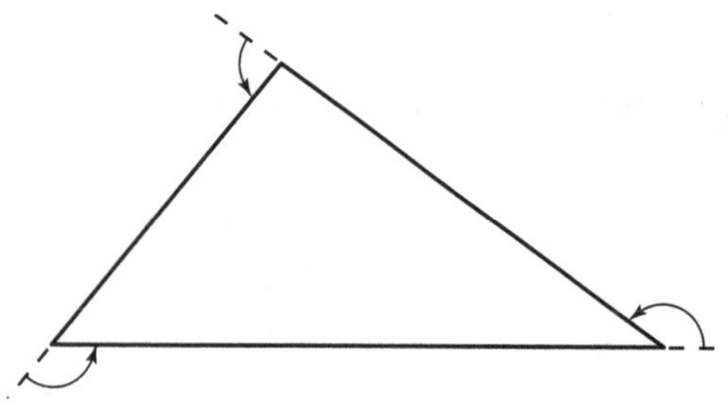

2. The exterior angles for this example are 145°, 130°, and 85°. The sum of the exterior angles is 360°.

3. The sum of the exterior angles is the same.

4. Yes, because measuring the exterior angles in one direction is like moving "all the way" around a point, which is 360°, by starting at a certain point and returning to that point facing in the same direction. Students may choose to draw another triangle to check their thinking.

The student edition pages for this investigation begin on the next page.

STUDENT PAGE

Notes

Investigation 3

Polygon Properties and Tiling

You learned about angles and angle measure in Investigations 1 and 2. What you learned can help you figure out some useful properties of the angles of a polygon. Let's start with the sum of the measures of all the inside angles at the vertices of a polygon. This sum is called the **angle sum** of a polygon.

3.1 Angle Sums of Regular Polygons

Below are six regular polygons that are already familiar to you.

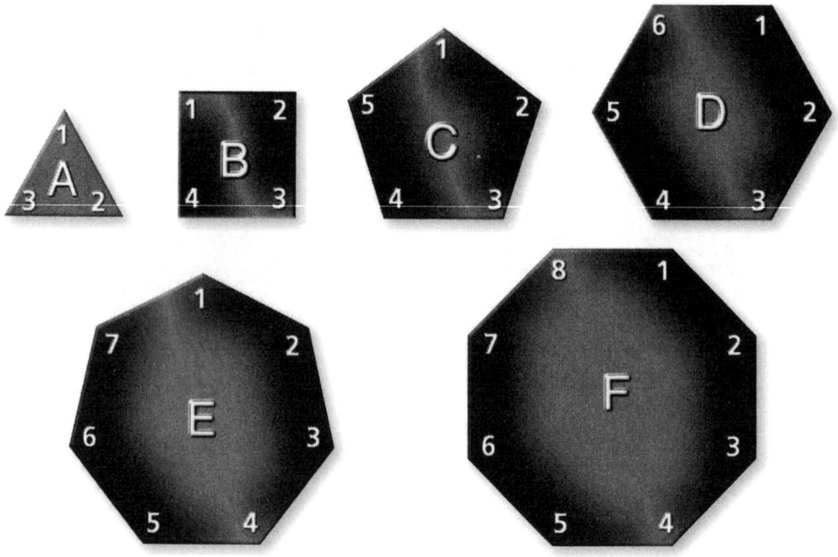

What is the angle sum of each figure?

Do you see a pattern relating the number of sides to the angle sum?

Notes

Problem 3.1 Angle Sums of Regular Polygons

A. 1. In Problem 2.3, you measured the angles of some regular polygons—triangles, squares, and hexagons. Record the number of sides, the angle measures, and the angle sum of a triangle, square, and hexagon in a table like the one below.

active math online
For: Angle Sum Activity
Visit: PHSchool.com
Web Code: amd-3301

Polygon	Number of Sides	Measure of an Angle	Angle Sum
Triangle	■	■	■
Square	■	■	■
Pentagon	■	■	■
Hexagon	■	■	■
Heptagon	■	■	■
Octagon	■	■	■
Nonagon	■	■	■
Decagon	■	■	■

2. Measure an angle of the regular pentagon and regular octagon from your Shapes Set. Record the measures of the angles and the angle sums in your table. What patterns do you see?

3. Use your patterns to fill in the table for a regular polygon with seven, nine, and ten sides.

B. Below are two sets of regular polygons of different sizes. Do the same patterns relating the number of sides, the measures of the angles, and the angle sums apply to these shapes? Explain.

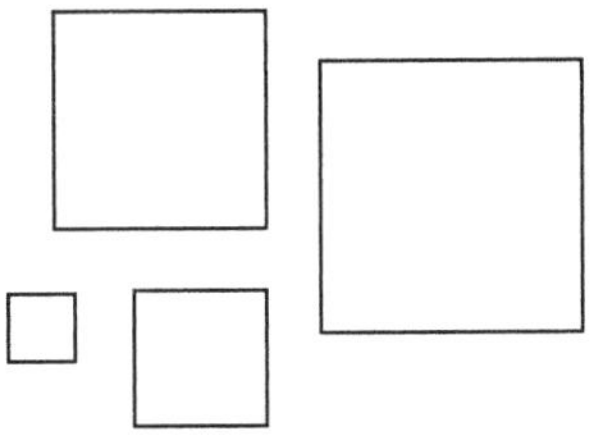

C. Describe how you could find the angle sum of a regular polygon that has N sides.

ACE **Homework starts on page 62.**

STUDENT PAGE

STUDENT PAGE

Notes

3.2 Angle Sums of Any Polygon

Do the patterns that you observed for the angle sum of regular polygons apply to all polygons?

Getting Ready for Problem 3.2

Suppose you tear the three corners off of a triangle. You can arrange them this way:

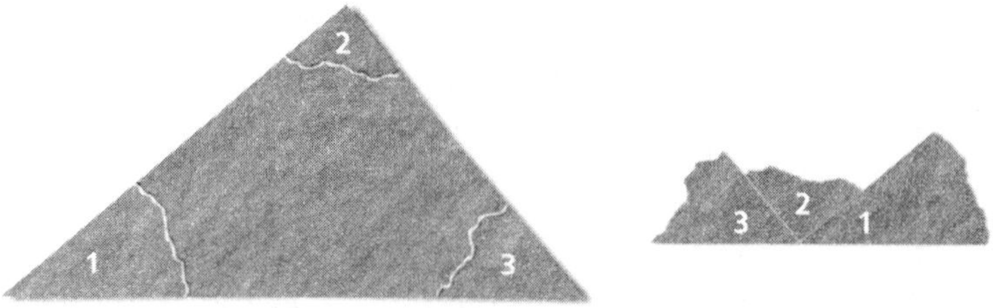

- Based on the picture, what is the sum of angles 1, 2, and 3? How do you know?
- Make a conjecture about the angle sum of any triangle.

You could do the same thing with a quadrilateral.

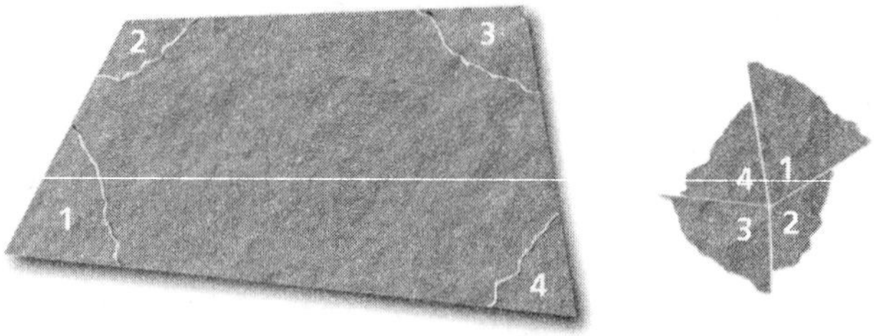

- Based on the picture, what is the sum of angles 1, 2, 3, and 4? How do you know?
- Make a conjecture about the angle sum of any quadrilateral.
- Do similar patterns hold for other polygons?

Problem 3.2 Angle Sums of Any Polygon

Tia and Cody claim that the angle sum of any polygon is the same as the angle sum of a regular polygon with the same number of sides. They use diagrams to illustrate their reasoning.

Notes

A. Tia divides polygons into triangles by drawing all the *diagonals* of the polygons from one vertex, as in the diagrams below:

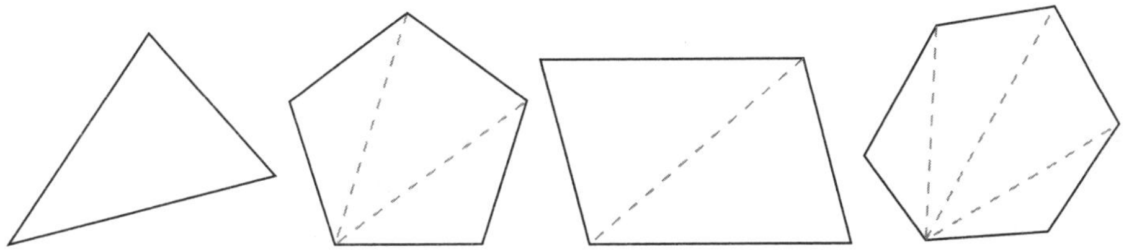

1. Study Tia's drawings. How can you use Tia's method to find the angle sum of each polygon?
2. Copy these three polygons. Use Tia's method to find the angle sum of each polygon.

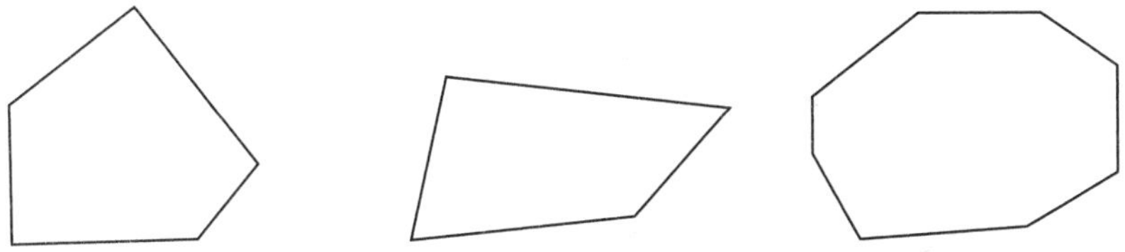

3. Does Tia's method work for any polygon? Explain.

B. Cody also discovered a method for finding the angle sum of any polygon. He starts by drawing line segments from a point within the polygon to each vertex.

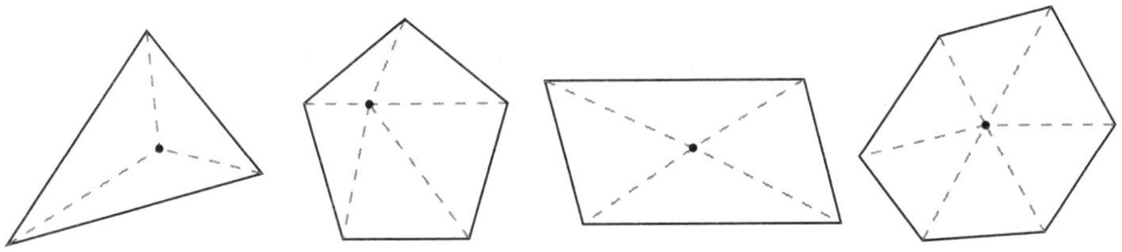

1. Study Cody's drawings. How can you use Cody's method to find the angle sum of each polygon?
2. Copy the three polygons from Question A part (2). Use Cody's method to find the angle sum of each polygon.
3. Does Cody's method work for any polygon? Explain.

C. In Problem 3.1, you found a pattern relating the number of sides of a regular polygon to the angle sum. Does the same pattern hold for any polygon? Explain.

ACE **Homework starts on page 62.**

Notes

3.3 Back to the Bees!

When the honeybees make a honeycomb, they build tubes. As the tubes press together, they become hexagonal in shape. So, the surface of a honeycomb looks like it is covered with hexagons. We can't ask honeybees why their honeycomb construction results in hexagons. However, there are some mathematical properties of hexagons that may offer explanations.

Below is a tiling of regular hexagons. Notice that three angles fit together exactly around any point in the tiling.

Why do these regular hexagons fit together so neatly?

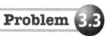

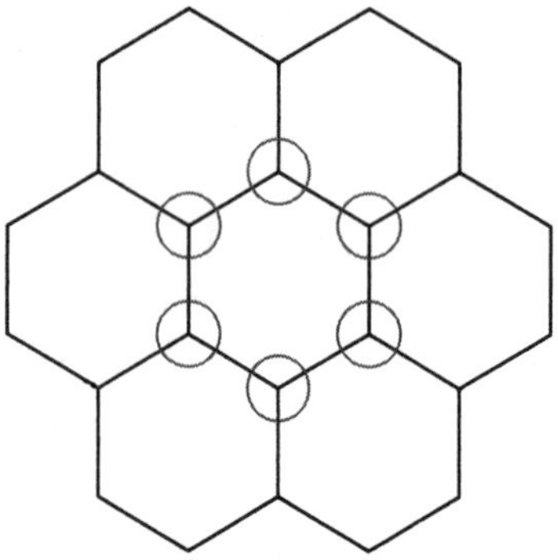

In Problem 1.3, you experimented to find which regular polygons could tile a surface.

What are the properties of these shapes that allow them to fit together so neatly around a point?

Problem 3.3 Angles in Tilings

A. In Problem 1.3, you explored tilings made from a single type of regular polygon. You found that only equilateral triangles, squares, and regular hexagons could be used to tile a surface.

1. For each of these shapes, make a tiling and sketch the results.
2. In each case, explain why copies of the shape fit neatly around a point.

B. In Problem 1.3, you also found that regular pentagons, regular heptagons, and regular octagons could not be used to tile a surface. Explain why copies of these polygons do not fit neatly around a point.

STUDENT PAGE

Notes

C. 1. Find tilings using combinations of two or more shapes from your Shapes Set. Sketch your results.

2. What do you observe about the angles that meet at a point in the tiling?

ACE Homework starts on page 62.

Did You Know?

One of the leading golf ball manufacturers developed a pattern using hexagons for golf balls. They claim it is the first design to cover 100% of the surface area of a golf ball. This pattern of mostly hexagons almost eliminates flat spots found on typical golf balls, which interfere with their performance. This new design produces a longer, better flight for the golf ball.

Go Online PHSchool.com **For:** Information about golf **Web Code:** ame-9031

Notes

3.4 Exterior Angles of Polygons

An angle *inside* a polygon, formed by the polygon's sides, is an **interior angle.** By extending a side of a polygon, you can make an **exterior angle,** which is *outside* the polygon. Extending a side of the polygon forms one ray of the exterior angle.

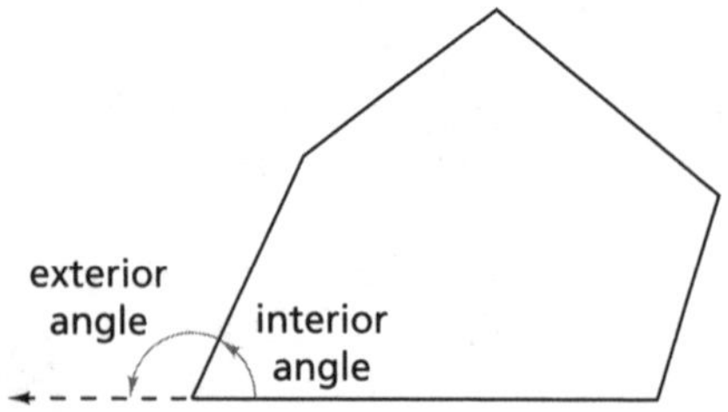

Figure 1 shows the exterior angles made by extending sides as you move counterclockwise around the polygon. Figure 2 shows the exterior angles formed by extending sides as you move clockwise around the polygon.

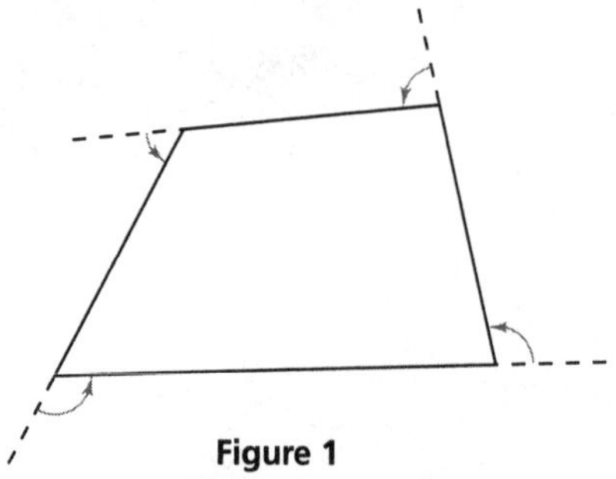

Figure 1
Exterior angles as you move counterclockwise.

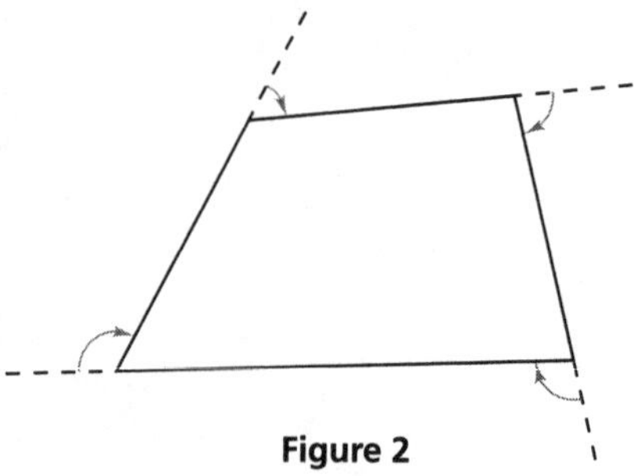

Figure 2
Exterior angles as you move clockwise.

STUDENT PAGE

Notes

Problem 3.4 Exterior Angles of Polygons

A skateboarder is skating on a triangular path around a park. In the diagram below, each segment of the path has been extended to show the angle of turn the in-line skater makes as she turns the corner. Each of these angles is an exterior angle of the triangle.

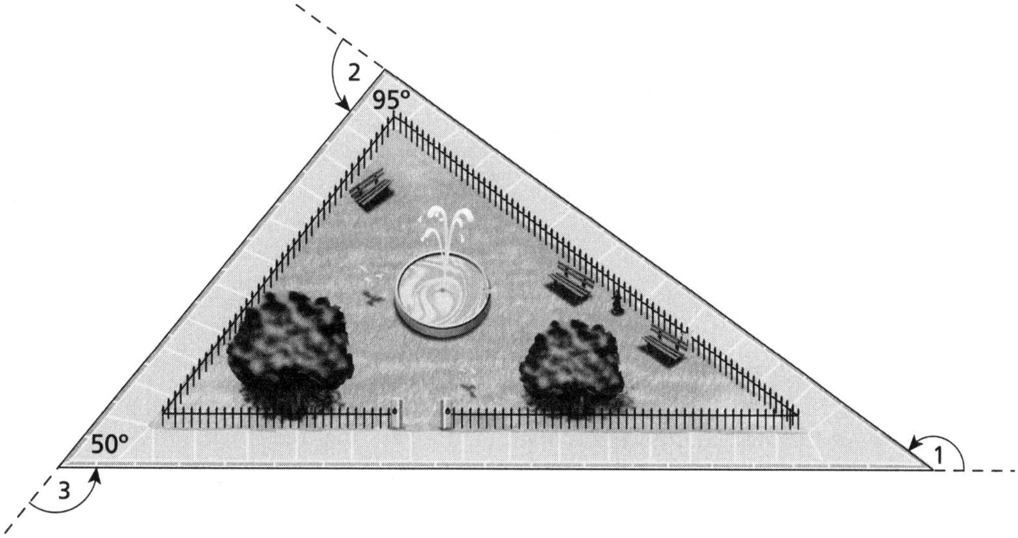

A. 1. What are the measures of the interior angles of the triangle?

2. What is the measure of angle 1?

3. What are the measures of angle 2 and angle 3?

B. Suppose the skateboarder skates once around the park counterclockwise, turning each corner exactly once. What is the sum of the angles through which she turns?

C. 1. Draw another triangle and mark the exterior angles going in one direction around the triangle.

2. Measure the exterior angles and find the sum.

3. Compare the exterior angle sum of your triangle to the sum you found for the triangle in Question B.

4. Can you predict the exterior angle sum for another triangle? Explain.

ACE **Homework starts on page 62.**

STUDENT PAGE

STUDENT PAGE

Notes

Applications

1. Without measuring, find the measures of the angle labeled x in each regular polygon.

a.

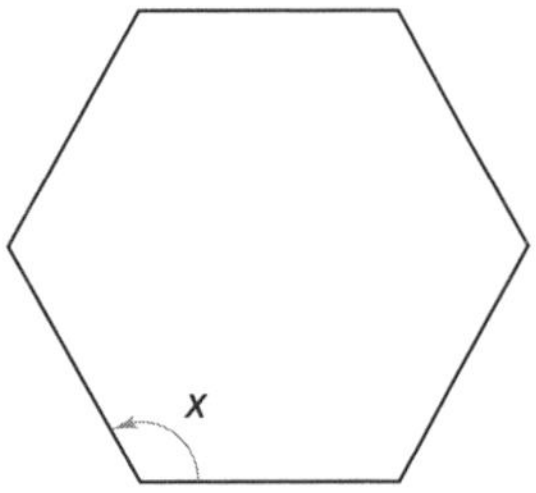

b.

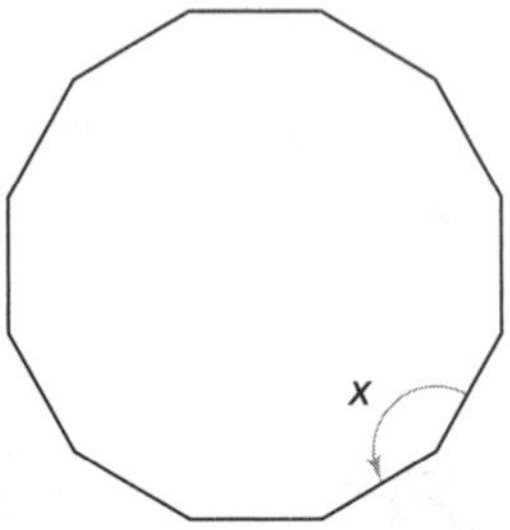

2. Below are sets of regular polygons of different sizes. Does the length of a side of a regular polygon affect the sum of the interior angle measures? Explain.

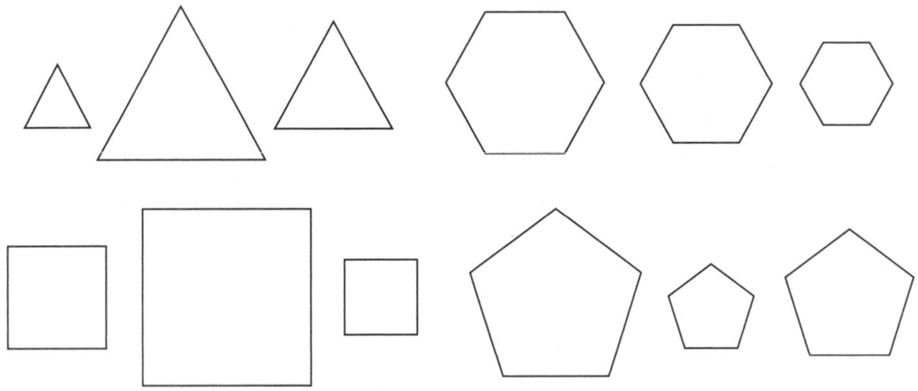

Notes

Applications

For Exercises 3–9, find the measure of each angle labeled *x*.

3.

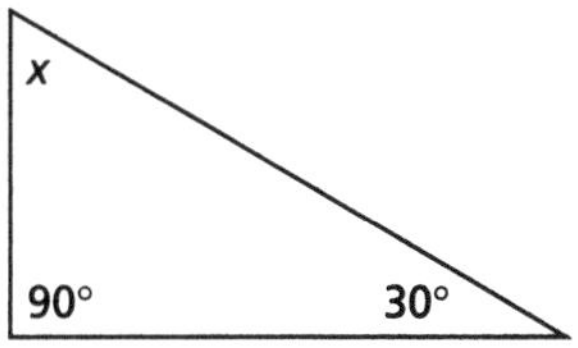

4.

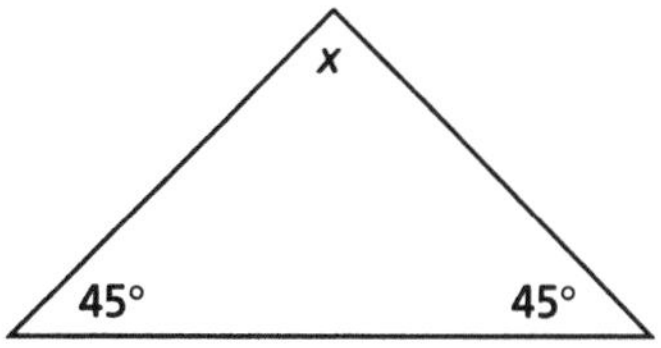

5.

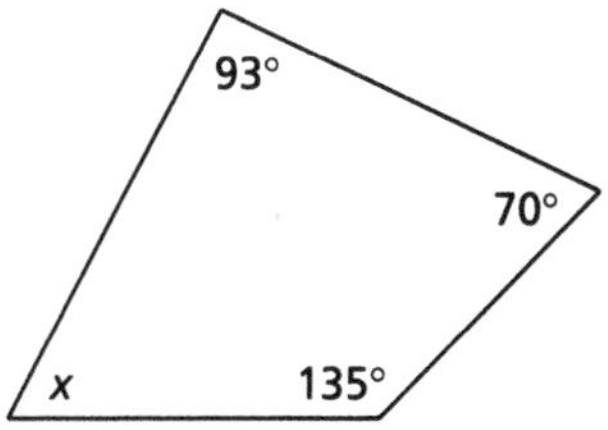

6. This figure is a parallelogram.

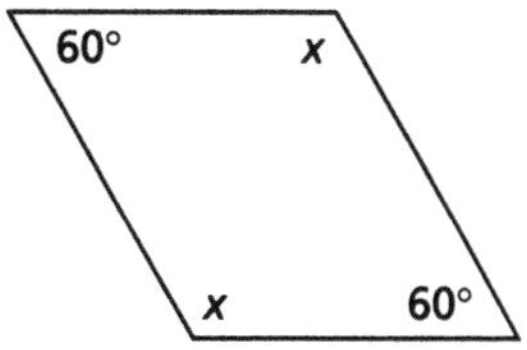

7.

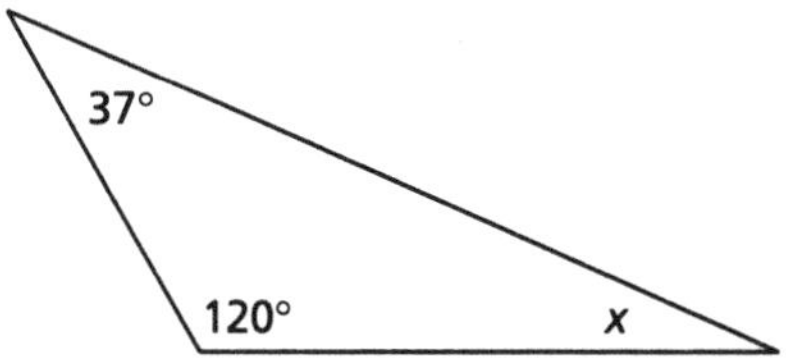

Homework Help Online
PHSchool.com
For: Help with Exercise 7
Web Code: ame-3307

8. This figure is a regular hexagon.

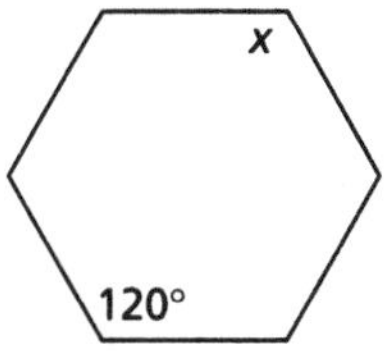

9. This figure is a parallelogram.

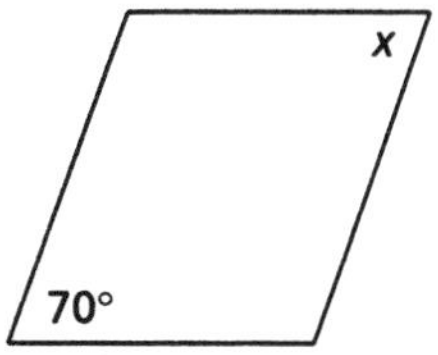

10. A **right triangle** has one right angle and two acute angles. Without measuring, find the sum of the measures of the two acute angles. Explain.

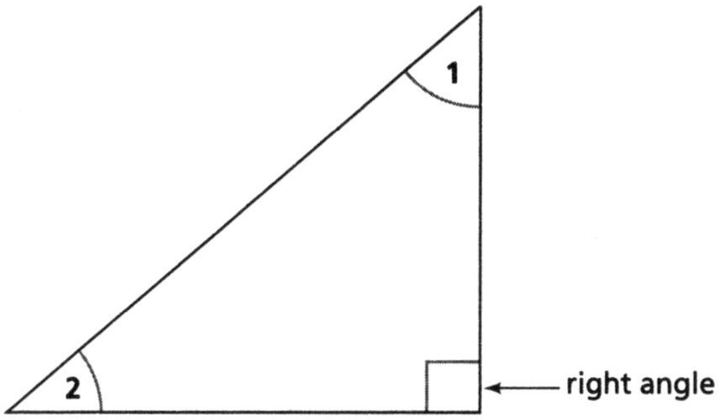

STUDENT PAGE

Notes

11. This figure is a regular dodecagon. A dodecagon has 12 sides.

a. What is the sum of the measures of the angles of this polygon?

b. What is the measure of each angle?

c. Can copies of this polygon be used to tile a surface? Explain.

Go Online PHSchool.com
For: Multiple-Choice Skills Practice
Web Code: ama-3354

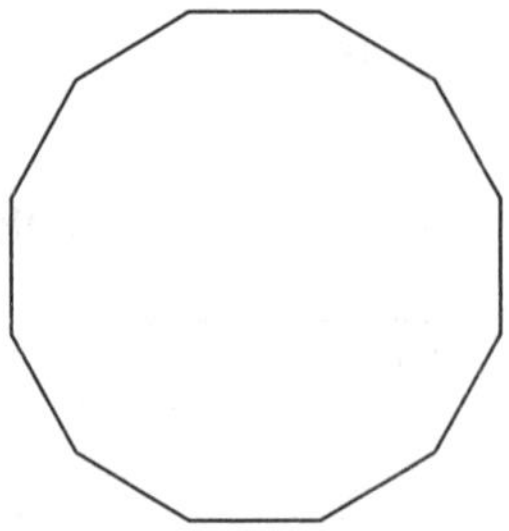

12. **Multiple Choice** Which of the following will tile a plane?

A. regular heptagon and equilateral triangle

B. square and regular octagon

C. regular pentagon and regular hexagon

D. regular hexagon and square

13. Suppose an in-line skater skates around a park that has the shape of a quadrilateral. Suppose he skates once around the quadrilateral, turning each corner exactly once. What is the sum of the angles through which he turns?

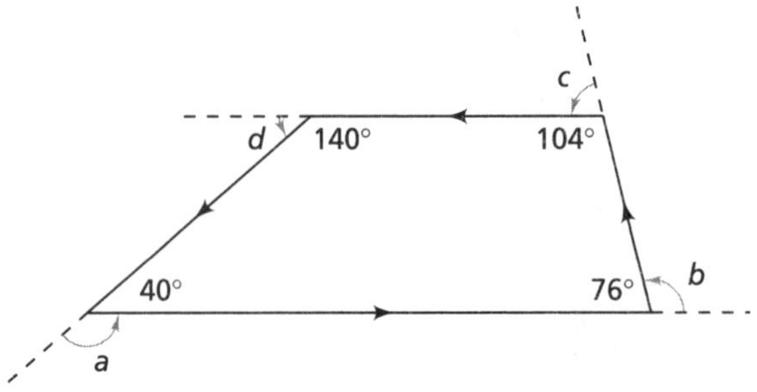

Notes

14. **a.** Suppose an in-line skater skates around a park that has the shape of a regular pentagon. If he skates once around the pentagon, turning each corner exactly once, what is the sum of the angles through which he turns?

b. How many degrees will the skater turn if he skates once around a regular hexagon? A regular octagon? A regular polygon with N sides? Explain.

Connections

15. A regular decagon and a star are shown below. Measure the angles inside the star to find the angle sum of the star. Compare your results to the angle sum for a regular decagon.

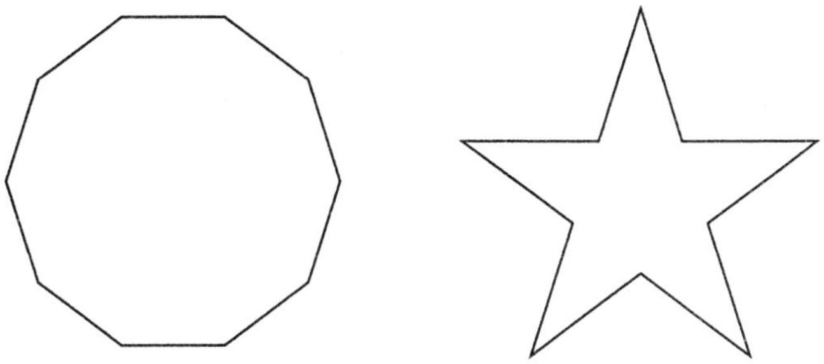

16. In the diagram below, the dashed line is a line of symmetry for the equilateral triangle. Examine the two smaller triangles that are formed by the dashed line. What do you know about the angles and the line segments of triangles ABD and ACD? Give reasons to support the relationships you find.

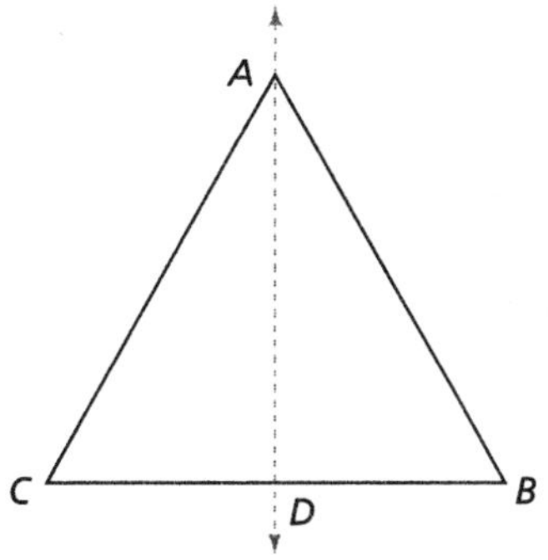

Notes

17. Multiple Choice Figure $QSTV$ is a rectangle. The lengths QR and QV are equal. What is the measure of angle x?

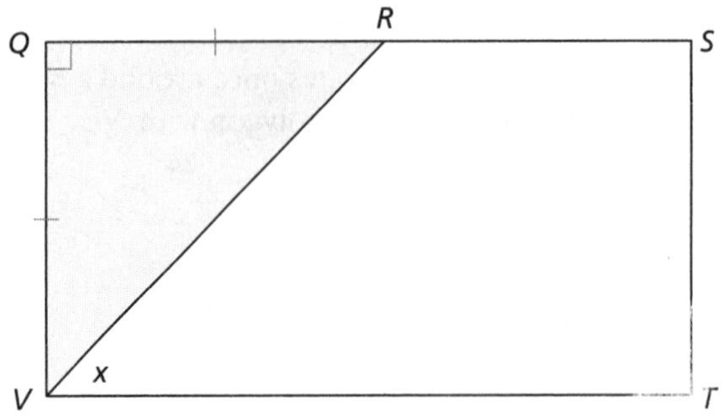

F. 20° **G.** 45°

H. 90° **J.** 120°

18. Choose a non-rectangular parallelogram from your Shapes Set or draw one of your own. Try to fit copies of the parallelogram exactly around a point. Sketch a picture to help explain what you found.

19. Choose a scalene triangle from your Shapes Set or draw one of your own. Try to fit copies of your triangle exactly around a point. Sketch a picture to help explain what you found.

STUDENT PAGE

STUDENT PAGE

Notes

20. In the diagram below, two parallel lines are cut by a transversal. Use what you learned in Investigation 2 to find the missing angle measures.

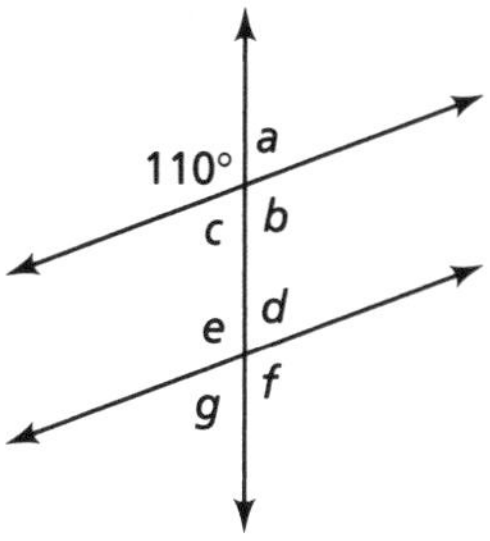

Extensions

21. a. Complete this table about regular polygons and look for a pattern.

Regular Polygons

Number of Sides	Measure of Interior Angle
4	$\frac{1}{2}$ of 180°
6	$\frac{2}{3}$ of 180°
8	$\frac{3}{4}$ of 180°
10	■

b. Does this pattern continue? Explain.

c. Is there a similar pattern for regular polygons with odd numbers of sides?

22. Kele claims that the angle sum of a polygon that he has drawn is 1,660°. Can he be correct? Explain.

23. Look at the polygons below. Does Tia's method of finding the angle sum (Problem 3.2) still work? Does Cody's method also still work? Can you still find the angle sum of the interior angles without measuring? Explain.

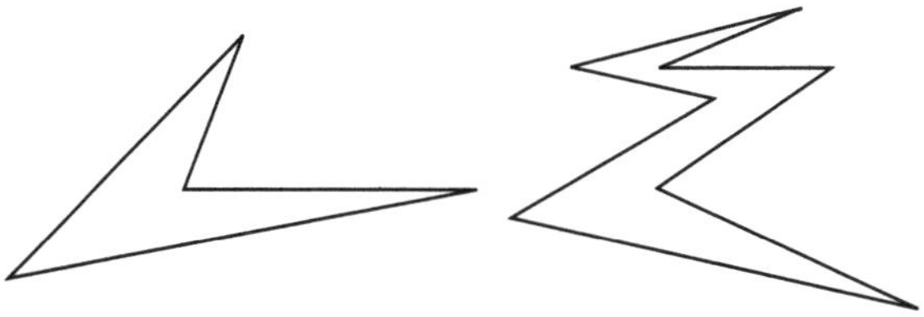

Connections Extensions

STUDENT PAGE

STUDENT PAGE

Notes

24. Below are a quadrilateral and a pentagon with the diagonals drawn from all the vertices.

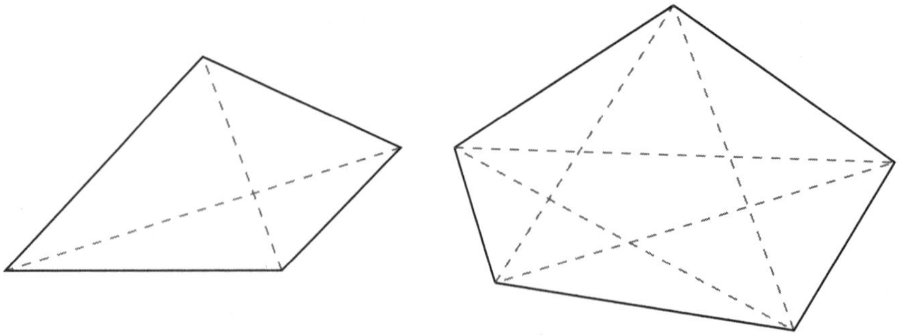

a. How many diagonals does the quadrilateral have? How many diagonals does the pentagon have?

b. Find the total number of diagonals for a hexagon and for a heptagon.

c. Copy the table below and record your results from parts (a) and (b). Look for a pattern relating the number of sides and the number of diagonals to complete the table.

Number of Sides	4	5	6	7	8	9	10	11	12
Number of Diagonals	■	■	■	■	■	■	■	■	■

d. Write a rule for finding the number of diagonals for a polygon with N sides.

25. Would a quadrilateral like the one below tile a plane? Explain.

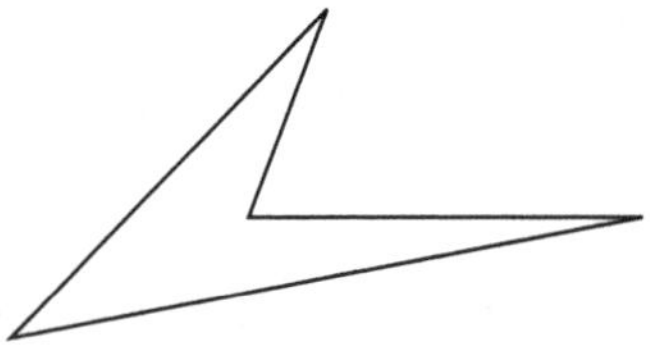

Notes

Mathematical Reflections 3

In this investigation, you explored patterns for angle sums of polygons. You also investigated how the interior angle measures of a polygon determine whether copies of the polygon will fit exactly around a point. The questions below will help you summarize what you have learned.

Think about your answers to these questions, and discuss your ideas with other students and your teacher. Then write a summary of your findings in your notebook.

1. a. What is the angle sum of a triangle? A quadrilateral? A hexagon? A polygon with N sides?

b. Describe how you can find the measure of each interior angle of a regular polygon.

c. As the number of sides in a regular polygon increases, what happens to the measure of an interior angle?

2. Describe how you can find the sum of the measures of the exterior angles of a polygon.

Unit Project What's Next?

What information about shapes can you add to your *Shapes and Designs* project?

STUDENT PAGE

Notes

Investigation 3

ACE Assignment Choices

Differentiated Instruction
Solutions for All Learners

Problem 3.1

Core 1–2
Other *Connections* 15–16; *Extensions* 21

Problem 3.2

Core 3–6, 9
Other *Applications* 7, 8, 10; *Connections* 17; *Extensions* 22–24; unassigned choices from previous problems

Problem 3.3

Core 11, 12
Other *Connections* 18, 19; *Extensions* 25; unassigned choices from previous problems

Problem 3.4

Core 13, 14
Other *Connections* 20; unassigned choices from previous problems

Adapted For suggestions about adapting Exercise 2 and other ACE exercises, see the CMP *Special Needs Handbook.*

Applications

1. **a.** $x = 120°$ **b.** $x = 150°$
2. No, because the sum of the interior angles of a regular polygon are the same for any regular polygon with the same number of sides. For example, any regular triangle (equilateral triangle) has angle sum 180° and any regular quadrilateral (square) has angle sum 360°.
3. 60°   4. 90°   5. 62°
6. 120°, 120°
7. 23°   8. 120°   9. 70°
10. They must sum to 90° since a triangle's angle sum is 180° and one of the angles is 90°.
11. **a.** $180°(12 - 2) = 1{,}800°$

    b. $\frac{1{,}800}{12} = 150°$

    c. No. Multiples of 150° are 300° and 450°, not 360°.
12. B
13. 360°, because it is the sum of all his turns: 140° at angle *a*, 104° at angle *b*, 76° at angle *c*, and 40° at angle *d*. Also, as he turns around the angles of his quadrilateral he is making a complete 360° turn.
14. **a.** $72° \times 5 = 360°$.

    b. If he turns around a regular hexagon, he will go $60° \times 6 = 360°$. For an octagon, he would go $45° \times 8 = 360°$. No matter which polygonal shape the garden is, he will make a complete 360° turn because he will arrive back at the same vertex facing the same direction from where he started.

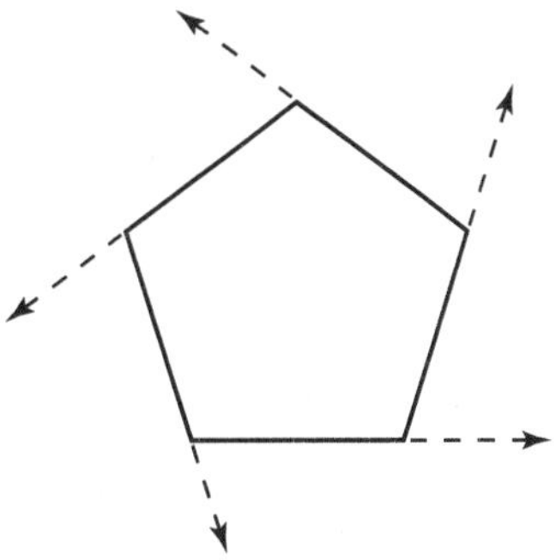

Connections

15. The star has five interior angles that are 35° and five that are 253°. Adding one of each of those gives 288°, which is the same as adding two of the regular decagon's angles (144° + 144°). The star has the same angle sum as the regular decagon.

ACE ANSWERS 3

16. Some possible answers are: Triangle *ABD* is identical to triangle *ACD* because the line of symmetry cuts triangle *ABC* into two identical triangles; $\angle ADB$ is identical to $\angle ADC$ and $\angle B$ is identical to $\angle C$ because they are corresponding angles of triangles *ABD* and *ACD*; $\angle ADC$ and $\angle ADB$ are right angles because the line of symmetry is perpendicular to the base of triangle; $\angle BAD$ is identical to $\angle DAC$ because the line of symmetry cuts $\angle BAC$ in half.

17. G (45°). Since triangle *QRV* is an isosceles right triangle, then $\angle QVR$ is 45°. $\angle QVT$ is a right angle since figure *QSTV* is a rectangle. So, $\angle x$ is equal to 90° − 45°, or 45°.

18. It works! The tiling will require 4 copies of the parallelogram around each point. Sketches will vary. Example:

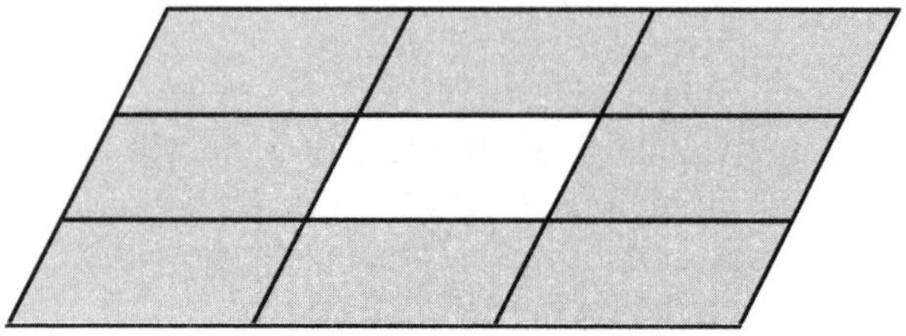

19. It works! There will be 6 copies of the triangle at each vertex, with two of each distinct angle at the vertex. Sketches will vary. Example:

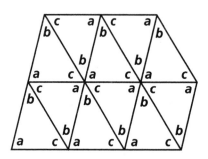

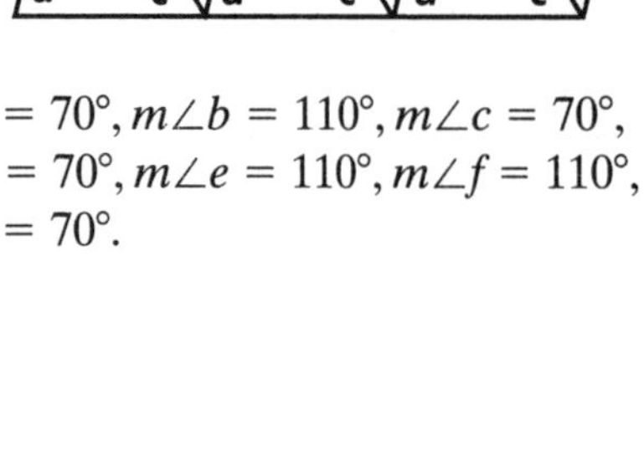

20. $m\angle a = 70°, m\angle b = 110°, m\angle c = 70°, m\angle d = 70°, m\angle e = 110°, m\angle f = 110°$, and $m\angle g = 70°$.

Extensions

21. a. A regular decagon will have interior angles measuring $\frac{4}{5}$ of 180°.

b. This pattern will continue. The easiest way to see this is algebraically: the angle sum of a polygon with N sides is $180(N - 2)$. Then each angle has measure $\frac{180(N-2)}{N}$. If N is even, N is twice some integer, say b. Then $\frac{180(N-2)}{N} = \frac{180(2b-2)}{2b} = \frac{180(b-1)}{b}$, leading to this pattern. Here students will probably check that the pattern works for other polygons.

c. There is a similar pattern for odd numbers:

Regular Polygons

Number of Sides	Measure of Interior Angle
3	$\frac{1}{3}$ of 180°
5	$\frac{3}{5}$ of 180°
7	$\frac{5}{7}$ of 180°
9	$\frac{7}{9}$ of 180°

This pattern will also continue. The algebraic reason is similar to part (b). The easiest way to see this is algebraically: the angle sum of a polygon with N sides is 180(N − 2). Then each angle has measure $\frac{180(N-2)}{N}$. If N is odd, $N = 2c + 1$ for some integer c. Then $\frac{180(N-2)}{N} = \frac{180(2c+1-2)}{2c+1} = \frac{180(2c-1)}{2c+1}$, leading to this pattern.

22. No, because 180 is not a factor of 1,660.

23. Although the methods yield weird results for these shapes, you can still find the angle sum without measuring. You can divide the first shape into two triangles and add the angle sums of each triangle, so the first figure has 360°, consistent with what you know about quadrilaterals. You can divide the second into two triangles and two quadrilaterals (or some other combination) and get that the angle sum is 1,080°, consistent with what you know about 8-sided polygons.

24. a. The quadrilateral has 2 diagonals and the pentagon has 5 diagonals.

b. The total number of diagonals for the hexagon is 9, and a heptagon is 14.

c. (Figure 3)

d. The rule is: *Subtract 3 from the number of sides of the polygon, multiply that difference by the number of sides and divide that product by 2.* There may be other ways of saying this. Use the formula $\frac{N(N-3)}{2}$, where N is the number of sides.

25. Yes, any quadrilateral tiles a plane.

Possible Answers to Mathematical Reflections

1. a. The angle sum of a triangle is 180°, a quadrilateral is 360°, a hexagon is 720°, and a polygon with N sides is $(N - 2)180°$.

b. To get the size of each interior angle of a *regular* polygon, divide the sum from part (a) by the number of sides.

c. As the number of sides increases in regular polygons, the measures of the interior angles increase.

2. It is always 360°, since by making each turn described by the exterior angles, one eventually comes back to the starting direction having made *one* complete (360°) turn.

Figure 3

Number of Sides	4	5	6	7	8	9	10	11	12
Number of Diagonals	2	5	9	14	20	27	35	44	54

Investigation 4 Building Polygons

Mathematical and Problem-Solving Goals

- Decide whether any three side lengths will make a triangle
- Find that the sum of two side lengths of a triangle must be greater than the third side length
- Decide whether any four side lengths will make a quadrilateral
- Find that the sum of three side lengths of a quadrilateral must be greater than the fourth side length.
- Use properties of quadrilaterals to make specific quadrilaterals.

Summary of Problems

Problem 4.1 Building Triangles

Students use Polystrips to build triangles given three side lengths. They observe that the sum of two side lengths of a triangle must be greater than the third side length and for three lengths that work there is exactly one triangle that can be built.

Problem 4.2 Building Quadrilaterals

Students use Polystrips to build quadrilaterals given four side lengths. They find that to make a quadrilateral, the sum of three side lengths must be greater than the fourth side length. If a quadrilateral can be built, they also learn that different combinations of the side lengths will produce different shaped quadrilaterals.

Problem 4.3 The Quadrilateral Game

Students play a game that gives them a chance to practice using what they have learned about polygons and assimilate the information of this unit.

	Suggested Pacing	Materials for Students	Materials for Teachers	ACE Assignments
All	$4\frac{1}{2}$ days	Calculators, student notebooks	Blank transparencies and transparency markers	
4.1	2 days	Polystrips (or Labsheet 4.1A) and fasteners, Labsheet 4.1B, three number cubes		1–8, 21, 29
4.2	1 day	Polystrips (or Labsheet 4.1A) and fasteners, Labsheet 4.2		9–18, 22–24, 30, 31
4.3	1 day	Rubber bands, geoboards (1 per group), number cubes (2 per group), Labsheet 4.3	Overhead geoboard or geoboards, rubber bands	19–20, 25–28, 32
MR	$\frac{1}{2}$ day			

4.1 Building Triangles

Goals

- Build triangles given three side lengths
- Decide whether any three lengths will make a triangle
- Find that the sum of two side lengths of a triangle must be greater than the third side length

Launch 4.1

Advice for Using the Polystrips

Help students to be conscientious when using the Polystrips to represent the length they want. It is the space between two holes that represents a length of one unit. We count spaces, not holes. (This is the fence-post problem. It takes three fence posts to hold up two lengths of fence. If we want to know how long the fence is, we count fence sections, not posts.) You may want to number the holes (starting with zero) on the Polystrips so students can immediately find the given length.

It is a good idea to demonstrate how to use the Polystrips and count side lengths. First, choose three numbers under 20, such as 6, 8, and 12. Build a triangle with the Polystrips using those numbers as side lengths. Then, have each group build a 6-8-12 triangle, and check to see that each group knows how to fasten the strips together to represent the lengths.

Suggested Questions Remind the class of earlier discussions they may have had about the use of triangles in buildings.

- *We know certain conditions must be true about the angles of a triangle. The sum of the angle measures of a triangle is equal to 180°.*
- *Are there special conditions for the side lengths of a triangle?*

Ask a student to roll three number cubes. Find the sum of the numbers and tell the class that this is one side length of a triangle. Write the number on the board, labeling it side length 1. Roll the three number cubes two more times to find the other two lengths and record their sums.

Side 1	Side 2	Side 3	Triangle?
■	■	■	■

Try to build a triangle with these three numbers.

Note: the random generator on a graphing calculator can be used to generate numbers for side lengths.

Challenge the class to explore the question—can a triangle be built with any three side lengths?

Let students work in groups of 2 or 3.

Explore 4.1

Make sure students are using the Polystrips correctly. The labsheet will help them to keep records and sketches of their work.

They may quickly see that if a triangle can be built from a set of numbers, then it is unique.

As groups finish, ask them if they have any special triangles among their examples (isosceles, equilateral, right triangle, etc.).

Summarize 4.1

When students have done some exploration and addressed the questions about triangles, the whole-class discussion should clarify the patterns that were revealed. Give students a chance to share their insights.

Have groups make conjectures about what lengths will and will not make a triangle and why. Here are some conjectures students have made (they may be similar to those given for quadrilaterals in Problem 4.2):

Daniella said that two short sides added together have to be more than the longest side.

Paul said that if the two short sides are less than the long side, they fall on top of each other.

Yvonne said the two short sides could not add up to the same as the long side or they won't stick up and leave any space inside.

Suggested Questions Ask students to hypothesize about how the various responses are alike and how they are different.

- *Can we come up with a summary statement that would help someone who is not here today know how to judge whether three lengths will make a triangle without actually building the triangle?*

Write the current summary statement on the board. As students add to the discussion, revise the statement as improvements are suggested. Ask questions to stretch the students' thinking until you have a rule that clearly distinguishes lengths that will work from those that won't. One good way to push their thinking in a situation like this is to make up examples to test.

Suggested Questions Give them a set of numbers and ask which ones will make a triangle and why.

4, 3, 5   8, 2, 12   8, 8, 4

- *Which ones form a triangle? Why?*
- *Do any of these triangles have special properties? Describe them.*

Ask the class if any of their data produced equilateral, isosceles, or right triangles. This is also an opportunity to review the symmetry of triangles.

Students should leave this problem with the ability to respond to the questions posed in the problem. Answers should be more than just a yes or no; continue to pose questions that ask them to explain why certain lengths work and others do not.

Some teachers take this opportunity to discuss with students how mathematicians think and how they record the results of their experimentation. You might tell them that they are not responsible for knowing the following, but that you want to show them how mathematicians would use the language of mathematics to record their generalization.

Mathematicians try to talk about ideas at a general level, rather than about a specific case. For example, they give names to the lengths of a triangle's sides rather than talking about a triangle with specific sides like 8 cm, 5 cm, and 6 cm. Instead, they call the sides of a triangle by letters, such as side a, side b, and side c. So a triangle with sides a, b, and c stands for any triangle you can make. Mathematicians would write your statement like this:

"If a and b represent the two shorter sides of a triangle and c represents the longest side, then $a + b > c$."

This is called the Triangle Inequality Property. At this point, students do not need to remember the name, but should remember the condition for side lengths.

At a Glance

4.1 Building Triangles

PACING 2 days

Mathematical Goals

- Build triangles given three side lengths
- Decide whether any three lengths will make a triangle
- Find that the sum of two side lengths of a triangle must be greater than the third side length

Launch

Demonstrate how to use the Polystrips and count side lengths. Help students use the Polystrips to represent the length they want. It is the space between two holes that represents a length of one unit. We count spaces, not holes. Choose three numbers under 20, and build a triangle with the Polystrips using those numbers as side lengths. Challenge the class to explore the question—can a triangle be built with any three side lengths?

Remind the class of earlier discussions they may have had about the use of triangles in buildings.

- *We know certain conditions must be true about the angles of a triangle. The sum of the angle measures of a triangle is equal to 180°. Are there special conditions for the side lengths of a triangle?*

Ask a student to roll three number cubes. Find the sum of the numbers and tell the class that this is one side length of a triangle. Write the number on the board, labeling it side length 1. Roll the three number cubes two more times to find the other two lengths and record their sums.

Try to build a triangle with these three numbers.

Let students work in groups of 2 or 3.

Materials

- Polystrips (or Labsheet 4.1A) and fasteners
- Three number cubes

Explore

The labsheet will help students to keep records and sketches of their work. They may quickly see that if a triangle can be built from a set of numbers, then it is unique. As groups finish, ask if they have any special triangles among their examples (isosceles, equilateral, right triangles, etc.).

Materials

- Labsheet 4.1B

Summarize

Have groups make conjectures about what lengths will and will not make a triangle and why.

- *Can we come up with a summary statement that would help someone who is not here today know how to judge whether three lengths will make a triangle without actually building the triangle?*

Materials

- Student notebooks

continued on next page

Summarize *continued*

Write the current summary statement on the board. As students add to the discussion, revise the statement as improvements are suggested. Ask questions until you have a rule that distinguishes lengths that will work from those that will not. Test some example side lengths: 4, 3, and 5; 8, 2, and 12; and 8, 8, and 4.

- *Which ones form a triangle? Why?*
- *Do any of these triangles have special properties? If so, describe them.*

ACE Assignment Guide for Problem 4.1

Differentiated Instruction
Solutions for All Learners

Core 1–5

Other *Applications* 6–8, *Connections* 21, *Extensions* 29

Adapted For suggestions about adapting Exercise 8 and other ACE exercises, see the CMP *Special Needs Handbook*.

Connecting to Prior Units 21: *Bits and Pieces I*

Answers to Problem 4.1

A. 1. Answers will vary. Possible answers: 8, 6, and 10; 3, 6, and 6

2. Answers will vary. Possible answer: 5, 9, and 16.

3. If the sum of any two side lengths is greater than the length of the third side, you can build a triangle.

4. Answers will vary. The important thing is that students understand that the sum of any two sides must be greater than the third. Possible answers: 3, 3, and 3 will make a triangle, as will 2, 6, and 7. Although 3, 3, and 7 will not make a triangle, and neither will 3, 4, and 12.

B. No, you always get the same triangle, just rotated.

C. Because any three side lengths determine only one triangle. So if someone builds a triangle with certain side lengths, that triangle will be stable The sides of the triangle will not shift to form a new triangle.

4.2 Building Quadrilaterals

Goals

- Build quadrilaterals given four side lengths
- Decide whether any four side lengths will make a quadrilateral
- Find that the sum of three side lengths of a quadrilateral must be greater than the fourth side length

Students find that to make a quadrilateral, the sum of three side lengths must be greater than the fourth side length. If a quadrilateral can be built, they also learn that different combinations of the side lengths will produce different shaped quadrilaterals. Also by pushing on the vertex of a quadrilateral, the shape will change, thus producing different shapes with the same arrangement of side lengths.

Students begin by considering the question of whether any four lengths will make a quadrilateral. Students are to choose four numbers under twenty, and then try to construct a quadrilateral from those side lengths. They keep a record of their work and return to their data to look for common and unusual quadrilaterals.

Launch 4.2

When the students understand how to manipulate the Polystrips, raise the question of the relationship among the lengths of the sides of a quadrilateral.

Suggested Questions

- *Can you make a quadrilateral using any four lengths for the sides?*

Let a student or two state their opinion.

- *We are going to conduct an experiment to gather data to help with this question. Look for relationships that will let you predict, without building, whether four line segments will make a quadrilateral. Let's record the following example as your first piece of data.*

Record the following on the board.

Side 1	Side 2	Side 3	Side 4	Make a Quadrilateral?
6	8	12	5	Yes

- *In your groups, choose four numbers to be the lengths of the sides of a quadrilateral. Use Polystrips to test the four lengths. Record exactly what your numbers are and whether or not they will make a quadrilateral. Make a sketch and label the side lengths. Then, repeat the test with four new numbers. As you select lengths for the sides, try to create interesting and different quadrilaterals.*

Explain to students that keeping an accurate record of their data is very important because it allows them to recreate examples as evidence of what they discovered. Let students work in groups of 2 or 3.

Explore 4.2

Make sure the students keep in mind the question of whether any four side lengths will make a quadrilateral. Encourage them to consider different arrangements and to record differences in the shapes that may occur. Encourage students to make sketches of their quadrilaterals. Be sure they are recording the side lengths in a table.

Suggested Question If a group is not making progress on the question of constructing more than one quadrilateral with a given set of four lengths, share something such as the following as a challenge.

- *In another class, a group said they thought they could make more than one quadrilateral with the lengths 6, 8, 10, and 12. They said, "We put the 10 between the 6 and the 8, and the quadrilateral is different from the one we get when we put the 10 between the 8 and the 12." (Demonstrate this with Polystrips.) What do you think about this group's idea?*

Summarize 4.2

Have the groups report their findings and build examples to support their conclusions. You want them to leave the experience not only able to explain what happened, but also able to design a set of lengths that will provide evidence to support their findings.

A summary of strategies for finding different quadrilaterals from a given set of side lengths should arise from the discussion. Two powerful strategies that focus on different aspects of what determines a quadrilateral are:

- Put the set of lengths together in different orders. (This technique highlights the role of side lengths in determining a shape.)
- Build a quadrilateral from Polystrips and then alter its shape by pressing on the sides or vertices of the quadrilateral. A quadrilateral with any given side lengths can form an infinite number of different quadrilaterals. (This technique highlights the role of angles in determining a shape and the lack of rigidity for quadrilaterals.)

If four lengths make a polygon, the shape is not unique. Ask for examples of this. Put them on the board or poster paper. Add others with descriptions as the discussion continues.

Students should be able to determine that a parallelogram is formed if opposite side lengths are equal. The parallelogram will become a rectangle as the vertices are pushed to form right angles. Pushing further will change the rectangle (which is a parallelogram) to a non-rectangular parallelogram.

Have several students demonstrate or share their drawings of quadrilaterals that have symmetry. Ask whether a quadrilateral is rigid. Discuss how the addition of a diagonal to a quadrilateral produces a rigid figure.

Ask students why the diagonal produces a rigid figure. Some students may bring up that it has something to do with the two triangles that are formed.

4.2 Building Quadrilaterals

At a Glance

PACING 1 day

Mathematical Goals

- Build quadrilaterals given four side lengths
- Decide whether any four side lengths will make a quadrilateral
- Find that the sum of three side lengths of a quadrilateral must be greater than the fourth side length

Launch

When the students understand how to manipulate the Polystrips, ask about the relationship among the lengths of the sides of a quadrilateral.

- *Can you make a quadrilateral using any four lengths for the sides?*
- *We are going to conduct an experiment to gather data to help with this question. Look for relationships that will let you predict, without building, whether four line segments will make a quadrilateral. Let's record the following example as your first piece of data.*

Record the following on the board:

Side 1: (6); Side 2: (8); Side 3: (12); Side 4: (5).

- *Can these side lengths form a quadrilateral?*
- *In your groups, choose four numbers to be the lengths of the sides of a quadrilateral. Use Polystrips to test the four lengths. Record exactly what your numbers are and whether or not they will make a quadrilateral. Then, repeat the test with four new numbers.*

Let students work in groups of 2 or 3.

Materials

- Polystrips (or Labsheet 4.1A) and fasteners

Explore

Encourage students to make sketches. Be sure they are recording the side lengths in a table. If a group is struggling tell them:

- *A group said they thought they could make more than one quadrilateral with the lengths 6, 8, 10, and 12. They said, "We put the 10 between the 6 and the 8, and the quadrilateral is different from the one we get when we put the 10 between the 8 and the 12." What do you think?*

Materials

- Labsheet 4.2

Summarize

Have the groups report their findings and build examples to support their conclusions. A summary of strategies for finding different quadrilaterals from a given set of side lengths should be discussed. Two powerful strategies are putting the set of lengths together in different orders or building a quadrilateral from Polystrips and altering its angles by pressing on the sides or vertices of the quadrilateral.

If four lengths do make a quadrilateral, the shape is not unique. Students should determine that a parallelogram is formed if opposite side

Materials

- Student notebooks

continued on next page

Summarize

continued

lengths are equal. The parallelogram will become a rectangle as the vertices are pushed to form right angles. Pushing further will change the rectangle to a non-rectangular parallelogram.

- *Is a quadrilateral a rigid figure?*

Discuss how the addition of a diagonal to a quadrilateral produces a rigid figure.

- *Why does the diagonal produce a rigid figure?*

ACE Assignment Guide for Problem 4.2

Differentiated Instruction
Solutions for All Learners

Core 9–13

Other *Applications* 14–18; *Connections* 22–24; *Extensions* 30–31; unassigned choices from previous problems

Adapted For suggestions about adapting ACE problems, see the CMP *Special Needs Handbook*.

Answers to Problem 4.2

A. 1. The set 3, 5, 10, and 20 does not make a quadrilateral. Possible sketches:

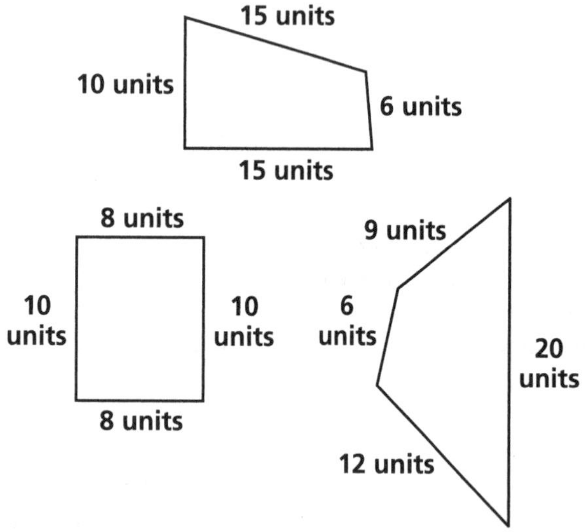

2. Answers will vary. Example: the sides 3, 5, 10, and 22 do not make a quadrilateral.

B. 1. No. For example, it would not be possible with side lengths 18, 1, 1, and 1. If the sum of any of the three of the side lengths is not greater than the fourth side length, a quadrilateral cannot be formed.

2. Yes. Putting the sides in a different order makes a different quadrilateral. For example, side lengths 8, 8, 10, and 10 could be used to make a parallelogram or a kite.

3. Rectangles and parallelograms both have two pairs of identical sides. For example, 8, 8, 10, and 10 could build a rectangle or a non-rectangular parallelogram. Squares must have all four sides the same; for example, 4, 4, 4, and 4.

C. 1. The side lengths stay the same and the angle measures change resulting in a different quadrilateral with the same side lengths.

2. The figure becomes rigid, because by putting in a diagonal you have created two triangles with specific side lengths, and pushing on the side lengths will not change the lengths or angles of the triangles, and therefore of the quadrilateral. This is because there is only one triangle that can be made with 3 specific side lengths, which means they are fixed and will not change.

D. 1. Similarity: For each case, given any side length, the sum of the other sides must be larger than the first one to be able to form the triangle or the quadrilateral. Difference: Given a set of three possible side lengths one can make at most one triangle, while given a set of four possible side lengths one could make many different quadrilaterals.

2. Using triangles guarantees stability of the constructed shape.

4.3 The Quadrilateral Game

Goal

- Use the properties of quadrilaterals to build specific quadrilaterals.

Launch 4.3

If you have a copy of a geoboard for the overhead, put it on the overhead and explain to the students what a geoboard is (a square array of 25 pegs). Otherwise, hold up a geoboard and explain its construction. Put a rubber band around the smallest square. Tell the class that this is a unit square, since each side is 1 unit long.

Describe the game. Divide the class into two teams. Let one team go first and roll two number cubes, one at a time. Give the team time to think about the clue and then ask them to suggest a strategy for forming the new quadrilateral. Ask the other team if they agree. If not, why? Then let the other team have a turn. Announce the number of points each team has after this round of play.

Once the class understands the rules and scoring let them play the game.

Let teams of two play each other.

Mathematics Background

For background on the angles of a polygon, see page 7.

Explore 4.3

Look for good discussions and strategies to share in the summary.

Summarize 4.3

Discuss interesting strategies and difficult situations.

- *Can someone give me an example of when they received zero points during a turn? What about one, two, three, or four points?*
- *What does it mean when a figure on the geoboard already matches the new description?*
- *Which sets of descriptions on the grid are equivalent?*
- *Which situations were particularly challenging or interesting?*

Going Further

You could ask the class or interested students to write a similar game for triangles or for another polygon.

In the course of the discussion, some students may observe that there is a big difference between (for instance) rolling a 5, and then 1, and rolling a 1, and then 5. One of these outcomes results in subtracting points from the player's score while one results in adding points. If students mention this, you may want to take a moment to discuss it.

- *Does everyone agree that there is a difference between 1, 5 and 5, 1?*
- *What about between 2, 6 and 6, 2?*
- *What if you had two dice? Would there still be a difference between 1, 5 and 5, 1? How would you be able to tell?*

This is not the place to master these questions, but this difference is an important one in probability and a difficult one for students to consider. This is one place to prepare them for the probability units later in the curriculum.

4.3 The Quadrilateral Game

At a Glance

PACING 1 day

Mathematical Goal

- Use the properties of quadrilaterals to build specific quadrilaterals.

Launch

If you have an overhead geoboard, place it on the overhead and explain to the students what it is (a square array of 25 pegs). Otherwise, hold up a geoboard and explain its construction. Put a rubber band around the smallest square.

Show a unit square and tell students that it is a unit square because each side is 1 unit long. Describe the game using the directions and rules in the student edition.

Divide the class into two teams. Let one team go first and roll two number cubes, one at a time. Give the team time to think about the clue and then ask them to suggest a strategy for forming the quadrilateral. Ask the other team if they agree. If not, why? Then let the other team have a turn.

Announce the number of points each team has after this round of play.

Once the class understands the rules and scoring, let them play the game.

A good strategy is to have teams of two play each other.

Materials

- Rubber bands
- Overhead geoboard or geoboard
- Labsheet 4.3

Explore

Look for good discussions and strategies to share in the summary.

Materials

- Geoboards (1 per group)
- Number cubes (2 per group)
- Rubber bands

Summarize

Discuss interesting strategies and difficult situations.

- *Can someone give me an example of when they received zero points during a turn? What about one, two, three, or four points?*
- *What does it mean when a figure on the geoboard already matches the new description?*
- *Which sets of descriptions on the grid are equivalent?*

Going Further

You could ask the class or interested students to write a similar game for triangles or for another polygon.

Materials

- Student notebooks

ACE Assignment Guide for Problem 4.3

Differentiated Instruction
Solutions for All Learners

Core 19–20, 25–28

Other *Extensions* 32 (polystrips are needed); unassigned choices from previous problems

Adapted For suggestions about adapting ACE exercises, see the CMP *Special Needs Handbook.*

Answers to Problem 4.3

A. Since this is a record of students' strategies and difficult situations while playing the game, answers will vary. One possible situation in which students do not need to move any corners on their turn is if they had a square on their geoboard, and then rolled a 4, 2: 'A quadrilateral with four right angles.'

B. Answers will vary again. For example, students may describe an isosceles trapezoid—a trapezoid with its non-parallel sides congruent. OR they may describe a concave kite—a kite with an interior angle greater than 180°.

The student edition pages for this investigation begin on the next page.

STUDENT PAGE

Notes

Investigation 4

Building Polygons

In the last two investigations, you explored the relationship between the number of sides of a polygon and the measure of its interior angles. Now you will turn your attention to the sides of a polygon.

How do the side lengths of a polygon affect its shape?

You can use polystrips and fasteners like these:

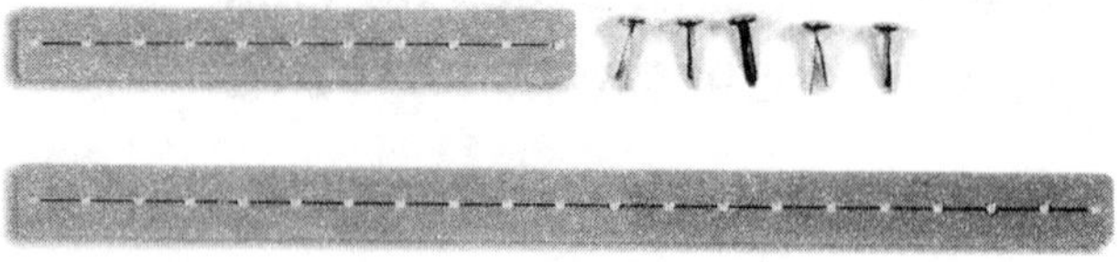

to build polygons with given side lengths and study their properties.

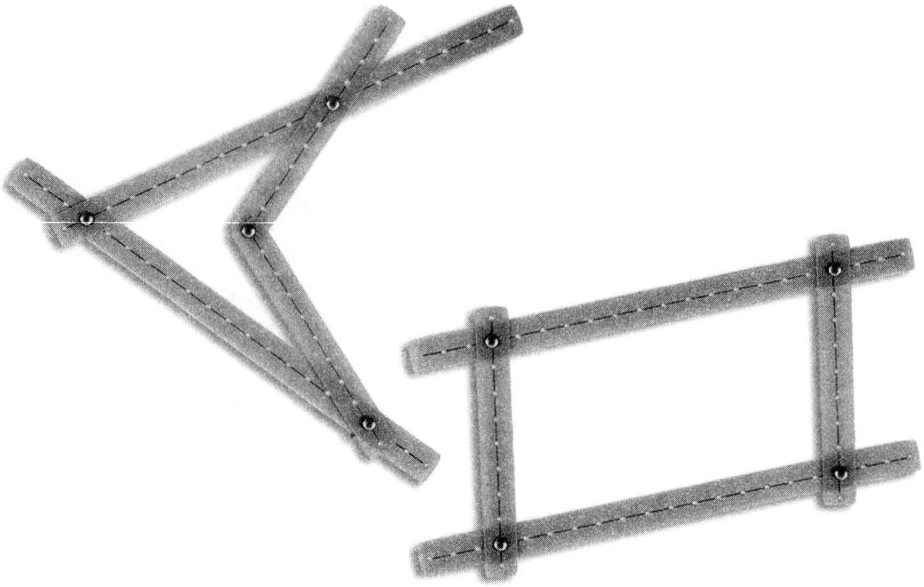

STUDENT PAGE

STUDENT PAGE

Notes ______________________________

4.1 Building Triangles

Bridges, towers, and other structures contain many triangles in their design. *Why are triangles used so frequently in construction?*

Problem 4.1 Building Triangles

Make a triangle using the steps below. Sketch and label your results.

Step 1 Roll three number cubes and record the sum. Do this two more times, so that you have three sums.

Step 2 Using polystrips, try to make a triangle with the three sums as side lengths. If you can build one triangle, try to build a different triangle with the same side lengths.

Repeat Steps 1 and 2 to make several triangles.

A. **1.** List each set of side lengths that did make a triangle.

2. List each set of side lengths that did not make a triangle.

3. What pattern do you see in each set that explains why some sets of numbers make a triangle and some do not?

4. Use your pattern to find two new sets of side lengths that will make a triangle. Then find two new sets of side lengths that will not make a triangle.

B. Can you make two different triangles from the same three side lengths?

C. Why do you think triangles are so useful in construction?

ACE **Homework starts on page 76.**

STUDENT PAGE

STUDENT PAGE

Notes

4.2 Building Quadrilaterals

You need four side lengths to make a quadrilateral.

Will any four side lengths work?

Can you make more than one quadrilateral from four side lengths?

Problem 4.2 Building Quadrilaterals

A. 1. Use polystrips to build quadrilaterals with each of the following sets of numbers as side lengths. Try to build two or more different quadrilaterals using the same set of side lengths.

6, 10, 15, 15	3, 5, 10, 20
8, 8, 10, 10	12, 20, 6, 9

Sketch and label your results to share with your classmates. Record any observations you make.

2. Choose your own sets of four numbers and try to build quadrilaterals with those numbers as side lengths.

B. Use your observations from Question A.

1. Is it possible to make a quadrilateral using any four side lengths? If not, how can you tell whether you can make a quadrilateral from four side lengths?

2. Can you make two or more different quadrilaterals from the same four side lengths?

3. What combinations of side lengths are needed to build rectangles? Squares? Parallelograms?

C. 1. Use four polystrips to build a quadrilateral. Press on the sides or corners of your quadrilateral. What happens?

2. Use another polystrip to add a diagonal connecting a pair of opposite vertices. Now, press on the sides or corners of the quadrilateral. What happens? Explain.

D. 1. Describe the similarities and differences between what you learned about building triangles in Problem 4.1 and building quadrilaterals in this problem.

2. Explain why triangles are used in building structures more often than quadrilaterals.

ACE **Homework starts on page 76.**

active math online
For: Linkage Strips Activity
Visit: PHSchool.com
Web Code: amd-3402

Notes

Did You Know?

Mechanical engineers use the fact that quadrilaterals are not rigid to design *linkages*. Below is an example of a quadrilateral linkage.

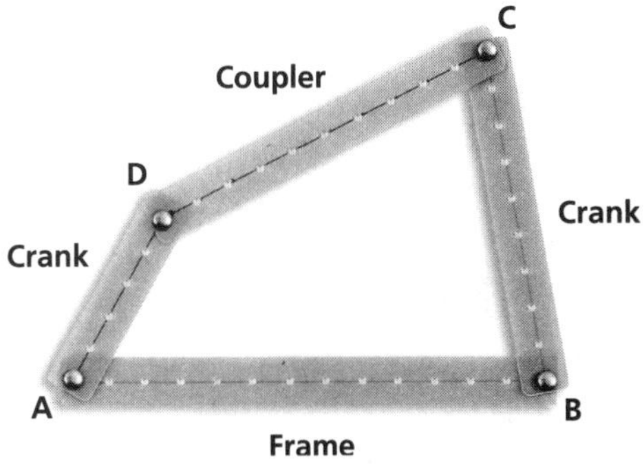

One of the sides is fixed. It is the *frame*. The two sides attached to the frame are the *cranks.* One of the cranks is the driver and the other the follower. The fourth side is called the *coupler*. Quadrilateral linkages are used in windshield wipers, automobile jacks, reclining lawn chairs, and handcars.

In 1883, the German mathematician Franz Grashof suggested an interesting principle for quadrilateral linkages: If the sum of the lengths of the shortest and longest sides is less than or equal to the sum of the lengths of the remaining two sides, then the shortest side can rotate 360°.

Go Online PHSchool.com **For:** Information about linkages **Web Code:** ame-9031

STUDENT PAGE

Notes

4.3 The Quadrilateral Game

The Quadrilateral Game will help you explore the properties of quadrilaterals. The game is played by two teams. To play, you need two number cubes, a game grid, a geoboard, and a rubber band.

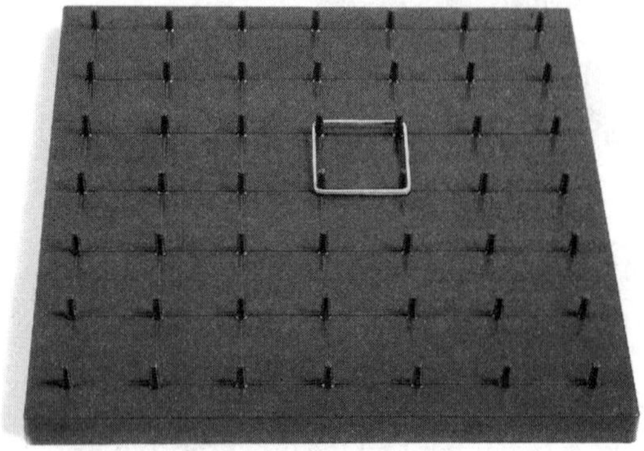

Quadrilateral Game Rules

- Near the center of the geoboard, put the rubber band around a square measuring one unit on each side.
- Team A rolls the number cubes one at a time to locate an entry in the game grid on the next page. The first number locates the row and the second number locates the column. Team A reads the description in this location. Team A then looks at the quadrilateral already on the game board, and forms a new quadrilateral to match the description. They move as few corners of the already existing quadrilateral as possible. Team A receives one point for each corner moved.
- Next, Team B rolls the number cubes and locates the corresponding description on the grid. They make a quadrilateral fitting the new description by moving as few corners of the existing quadrilateral as possible. Team B receives one point for each corner moved.
- Play continues until each team has had five turns. The team with the lowest score at the end is the winner.

STUDENT PAGE

STUDENT PAGE

Notes

Problem 4.3 Properties of Quadrilaterals

A. Play the Quadrilateral Game. Keep a record of interesting strategies and difficult situations. Make notes about when you do not receive a point during a turn. Why did you not need to move any corners on those turns?

B. Write two new descriptions of quadrilaterals that you could include in the game grid.

active math online
For: Quadrilateral Game Activity
Visit: PHSchool.com
Web Code: amd-3403

ACE **Homework starts on page 76.**

Quadrilateral Game Grid

Row 6	A quadrilateral that is a square	**Add 1 point to your score and skip your turn**	A rectangle that is not a square	A quadrilateral with two obtuse angles	A quadrilateral with exactly one pair of parallel sides	A quadrilateral with one pair of opposite side lengths equal
Row 5	**Subtract 2 points from your score and skip your turn**	A quadrilateral that is not a rectangle	A quadrilateral with two pairs of consecutive angles that are equal	A quadrilateral with all four angles the same size	A quadrilateral with four lines of symmetry	A quadrilateral that is a rectangle
Row 4	A quadrilateral with no reflection or rotation symmetry	A quadrilateral with four right angles	**Skip a turn**	A quadrilateral with exactly one pair of consecutive side lengths that are equal	A quadrilateral with exactly one right angle	A quadrilateral with two 45° angles
Row 3	A quadrilateral with no angles equal	A quadrilateral with one pair of equal opposite angles	A quadrilateral with exactly one pair of opposite angles that are equal	**Add 2 points to your score and skip your turn**	A quadrilateral with no sides parallel	A quadrilateral with exactly two right angles
Row 2	A quadrilateral with both pairs of adjacent side lengths equal	A quadrilateral with two pairs of equal opposite angles	A quadrilateral with a diagonal that divides it into two identical shapes	A quadrilateral that is a rhombus	A quadrilateral with 180° rotation symmetry	**Subtract 1 point from your score and skip your turn**
Row 1	A quadrilateral with one diagonal that is a line of symmetry	A quadrilateral with no side lengths equal	A quadrilateral with exactly one angle greater than 180°	A parallelogram that is not a rectangle	**Add 3 points to your score and skip your turn**	A quadrilateral with two pairs of opposite side lengths equal
	Column 1	**Column 2**	**Column 3**	**Column 4**	**Column 5**	**Column 6**

STUDENT PAGE

STUDENT PAGE

Notes ______________________________

Applications

Connections

Extensions

ACE

Applications

Follow these directions for Exercises 1–4.

- If possible, build a triangle with the given set of side lengths. Sketch your triangle.
- Tell whether your triangle is the only one that is possible. Explain.
- If a triangle is not possible, explain why.

1. Side lengths of 5, 5, and 3

2. Side lengths of 8, 8, and 8

3. Side lengths of 7, 8, and 15

4. Side lengths of 5, 6, and 10

5. Which set(s) of side lengths from Exercises 1–4 can make each of the following shapes?

a. an equilateral triangle

b. an isosceles triangle

c. a scalene triangle

d. a triangle with at least two angles of the same measure

For Exercises 6 and 7, draw the polygons described to help you answer the questions.

6. What must be true of the side lengths in order to build a triangle with three angles measuring 60°? What kind of triangle is this?

7. What must be true of the side lengths in order to build a triangle with only two angles the same size? What kind of triangle is this?

8. Giraldo and Maria are building a tent. They have two 3-foot poles. In addition, they have a 5-foot pole, a 6-foot pole, and a 7-foot pole. They want to make a triangular-shaped doorframe for the tent using both 3-foot poles and one of the other poles. Which of the other poles could be used to form the base of the door?

STUDENT PAGE

STUDENT PAGE

Notes

Follow these directions for Exercises 9–12.

- If possible, build a quadrilateral with the given set of side lengths. Sketch your quadrilateral.
- Tell whether your quadrilateral is the only one that is possible. Explain.
- If a quadrilateral is not possible, explain why.

9. Side lengths of 5, 5, 8, and 8

10. Side lengths of 5, 5, 6, and 14

11. Side lengths of 8, 8, 8, and 8

12. Side lengths of 4, 3, 5, and 14

13. Which set(s) of side lengths from Exercises 9–12 can make each of the following shapes?

a. a square

b. a quadrilateral with all angles the same size

c. a parallelogram

d. a quadrilateral that is not a parallelogram

14. A quadrilateral with four equal sides is called a **rhombus.** Which set(s) of side lengths from Exercises 9–12 can make a rhombus?

15. A quadrilateral with at least one pair of parallel sides is called a **trapezoid.** Which set(s) of side lengths from Exercises 9–12 can make a trapezoid?

For Exercises 16 and 17, draw the polygons described to help you answer the questions.

16. What must be true of the side lengths of a polygon to build a square?

17. What must be true of the side lengths of a polygon to build a rectangle that is not a square?

18. Li Mei builds a quadrilateral with sides that are each five inches long. To help stabilize the quadrilateral, she wants to insert a ten-inch diagonal. Is this possible? Explain.

Homework Help Online PHSchool.com
For: Help with Exercise 18
Web Code: ame-3418

19. You are playing the Quadrilateral Game. The shape currently on the geoboard is a square. Your team rolls the number cubes and gets the description "A parallelogram that is not a rectangle." What is the minimum number of vertices your team needs to move to form a shape meeting this description?

Applications

STUDENT PAGE

STUDENT PAGE

Notes

20. You are playing the Quadrilateral Game. The shape currently on the geoboard is a non-rectangular parallelogram. Your team rolls the number cubes and gets the description "A quadrilateral with two obtuse angles." What is the minimum number of vertices your team needs to move to create a shape meeting this description?

Connections

21. Multiple Choice Which one of the following shaded regions is *not* a representation of $\frac{4}{12}$?

A.

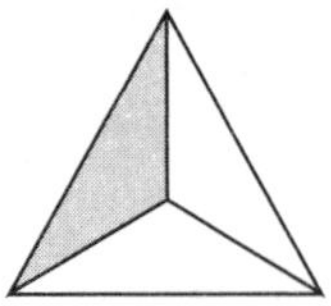

B.

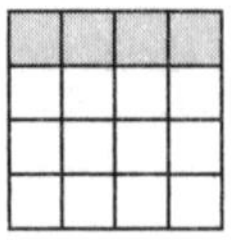

C.

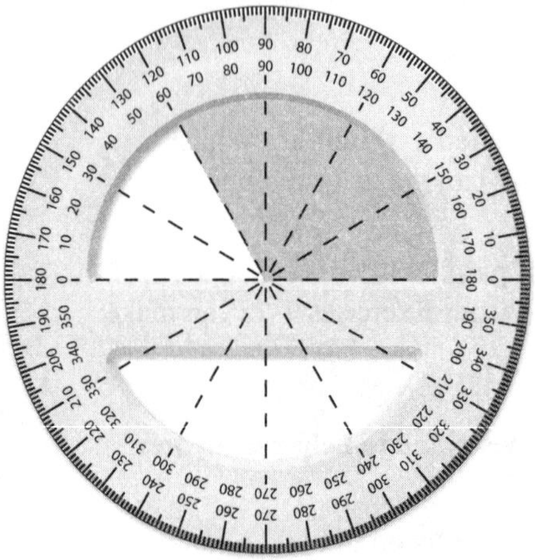

D.

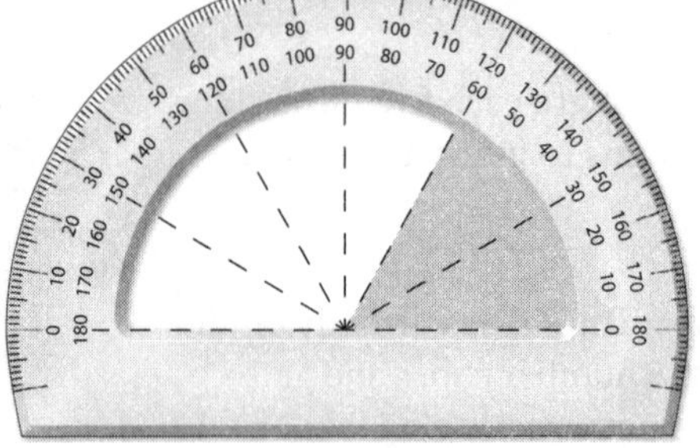

STUDENT PAGE

Notes

22. a. How are all three quadrilaterals below alike?

b. How does each quadrilateral differ from the other two?

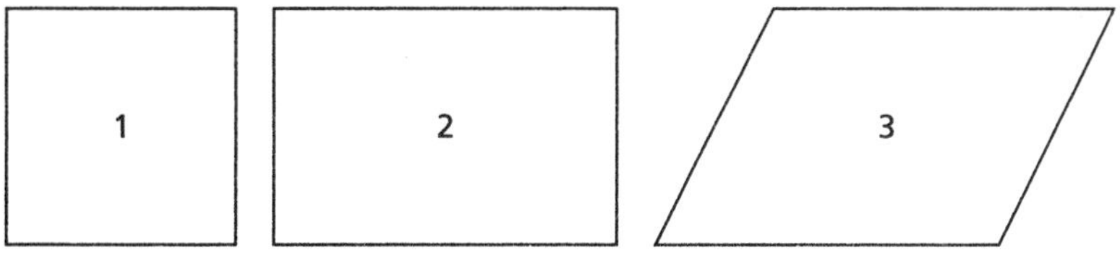

23. In this parallelogram, find the measure of each numbered angle.

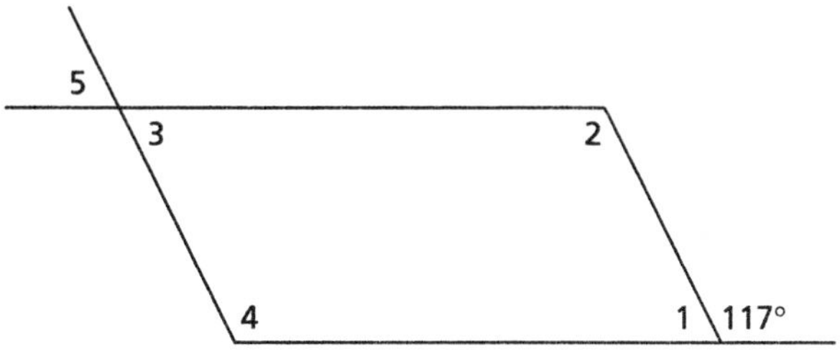

Go Online
PHSchool.com
For: Multiple-Choice Skills Practice
Web Code: ame-3454

24. Think about your polystrip experiments with triangles and quadrilaterals. What explanations can you now give for the common use of triangular shapes in structures like bridges and antenna towers for radio and television?

Notes

Multiple Choice For Questions 25–28, choose the symmetry or symmetries of each shape.

25. rhombus (four equal sides)

F. rotational **G.** reflectional

H. both A and B **J.** none

26. regular pentagon

A. rotational **B.** reflectional

C. both F and G **D.** none

27. square

F. rotational **G.** reflectional

H. both A and B **J.** none

28. a parallelogram that is not a rhombus or a rectangle

A. rotational **B.** reflectional

C. both F and G **D.** none

Extensions

29. In the triangle, a line has been drawn through vertex *A,* parallel to line segment *BC* of the triangle.

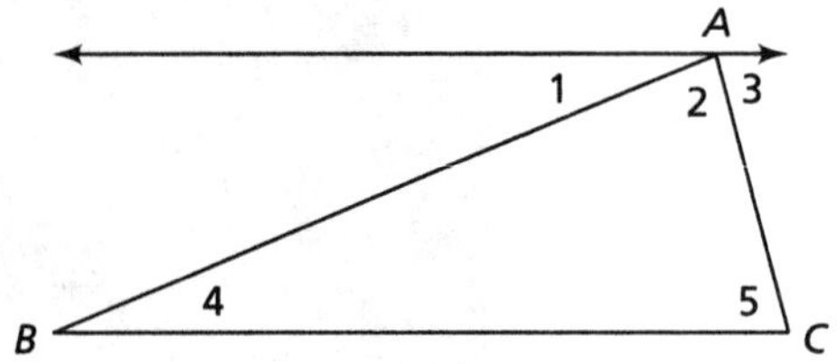

a. What is the sum of the measures of angles 1, 2, and 3?

b. Explain why angle 1 has the same measure as angle 4 and why angle 3 has the same measure as angle 5.

c. How can you use the results of parts (a) and (b) to show that the angle sum of a triangle is 180°?

STUDENT PAGE

STUDENT PAGE

Notes

30. In parts (a)–(b), explore pentagons by using polystrips or by making sketches.

a. If you choose five numbers as side lengths, can you always build a pentagon? Explain.

b. Can you make two or more different pentagons from the same side lengths?

31. Refer to the *Did You Know?* after Problem 4.2.

a. Make a model that illustrates Grashof's principle using polystrips or paper fasteners and cardboard strips. Describe the motion of your model.

b. How can your model be used to make a stirring mechanism? A windshield wiper?

32. Build the figure below from polystrips. Note that the vertical sides are all the same length, the distance from B to C equals the distance from E to D, and the distance from B to C is twice the distance from A to B.

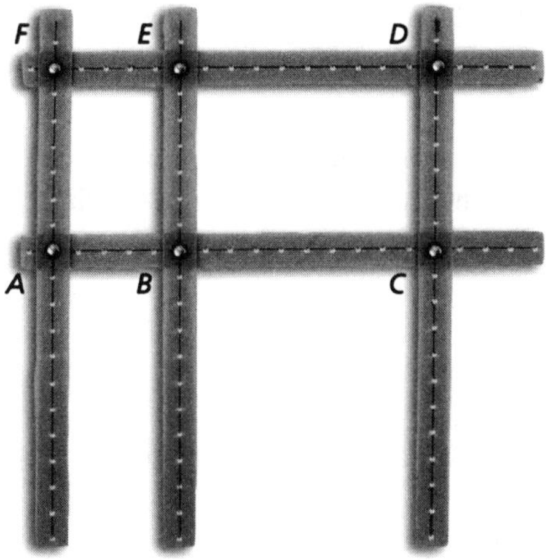

a. Experiment with holding various strips fixed and moving the other strips. In each case, tell which strips you held fixed, and describe the motion of the other strips.

b. Fix a strip between points F and B and then try to move strip CD. What happens? Explain why this occurs.

Connections Extensions

Notes

Mathematical Reflections 4

In this investigation, you experimented with building polygons by choosing lengths for the sides and then connecting those sides to make a polygon. These questions will help you summarize what you have learned.

Think about your answers to these questions. Discuss your ideas with other students and your teacher. Then write a summary of your findings in your notebook.

1. **a.** How can you tell whether three line segments will form a triangle?

   b. If it is possible to build one triangle, is it also possible to build a different triangle with the same three segments? Explain.

2. **a.** How can you tell whether four line segments will form a quadrilateral?

   b. If it is possible to build one quadrilateral, is it also possible to build a different quadrilateral with the same four segments? Explain.

3. Explain why triangles are useful in building structures.

Unit Project What's Next?

What information about shapes can you add to your *Shapes and Designs* project?

Notes

Investigation 4

ACE Assignment Choices

Differentiated Instruction
Solutions for All Learners

Problem 4.1

Core 1–5
Other *Applications* 6–8; *Connections* 21; *Extensions* 29

Problem 4.2

Core 9–13
Other *Applications* 14–18; *Connections* 22–24; *Extensions* 30, 31; unassigned choices from previous problems

Problem 4.3

Core 19–20, 25–28
Other *Extensions* 32; unassigned choices from previous problems

Adapted For suggestions about adapting Exercise 8 and other ACE exercises, see the CMP *Special Needs Handbook*.
Connecting to Prior Units 21: *Bits and Pieces I*

Applications

1. This is the only triangle that can be made with these side lengths.

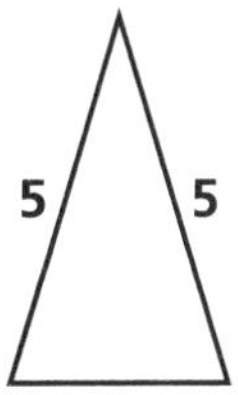

2. This is the only triangle that can be made with these side lengths.

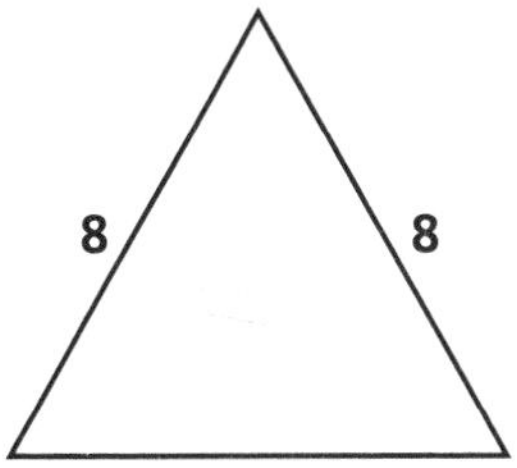

3. It is impossible to form a triangle with side lengths 7, 8, and 15 because $7 + 8 = 15$. The result would be a straight line with the segments on top of each other, not a triangle.

4. This is the only triangle that can be made with these side lengths.

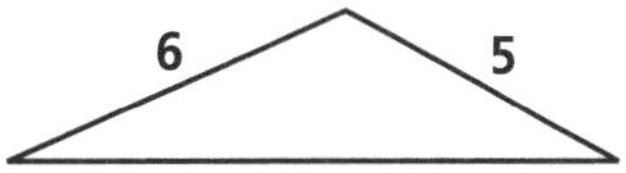

5. a. Exercise 2 is an equilateral triangle because all sides have equal length of 8.

b. Exercise 1 is an isosceles triangle because two sides have equal length of 5.

c. Exercise 4 is a scalene triangle because no sides have equal measure.

d. Exercises 1 and 2 are isosceles triangles because they have two congruent angles and equilateral triangles have three angles with equal measure.

6. The edges must be all the same length. It is an equilateral triangle.

7. The two edges must have the same length. It is an isosceles triangle.

8. The two 3-foot poles and the 5-foot poles will make a tent, but it will be a low tent. The two 3-foot poles and the 6-foot pole, and the two 3-foot poles and the 7-foot pole will not make a tent, because the sum of any two sides is not greater than their third side.

9. This is one quadrilateral that can be formed; a rectangle or an infinite number of other parallelograms can also be formed.

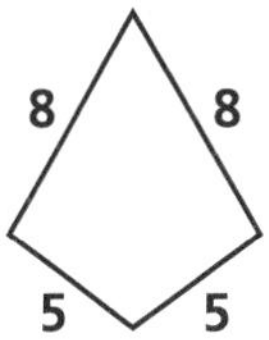

10. This is one quadrilateral that can be formed; many others can be as well. Just change the angles and/or the order of the sides.

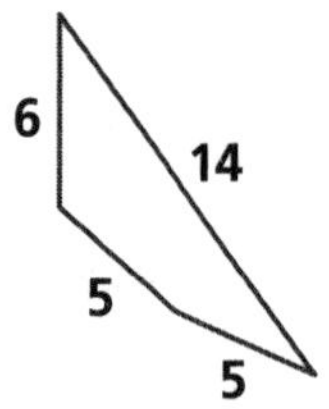

11. A square or an infinite number of other rhombi (parallelograms with 4 equal sides) can be formed.

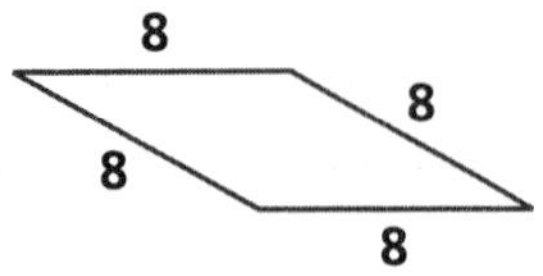

12. These side lengths are impossible to form into a quadrilateral because the sum of 4, 3, and 5 is 12, which is less than 14.

13. **a.** Exercise 11 **b.** Exercises 9 and 11
    c. Exercises 9 and 11
    d. Exercise 10

14. Only side lengths in Exercise 11 can make a rhombus, because all sides are of equal length.

15. The quadrilateral in Exercise 9 with side lengths 5, 5, 8, 8; the quadrilateral in Exercise 10 with side lengths 5, 5, 6, and 14; and the quadrilateral in Exercise 11 with side lengths 8, 8, 8, and 8.

16. The side lengths are equal.

17. Both pairs of opposites sides must be equal, and sides sharing a vertex must be different lengths.

18. No. Since $5 + 5 = 10$, having a diagonal that long would force the quadrilateral to be a straight line.

19. If your team moves two vertices, you can form a parallelogram that is not a rectangle.

20. Your team does not have to move any vertices of the non-rectangular parallelogram, which is probably either a rhombus or parallelogram without 90° angles, because it characteristically has two obtuse angles.

Connections

21. B

22. **a.** They are all parallelograms and they all have two pairs of identical sides.
    b. 1 is different from 2 and 3 because its sides are all the same length. 1 and 2 are different from 3 because they have four right angles.

23. Angles 1, 3, and 5 measure 63°. Angles 2 and 4 measure 117°.

24. They stabilize the structures by making them rigid.

25. H 26. C 27. H 28. A

Extensions

29. **a.** They add up to 180°.
    b. Because they are alternate interior angles formed by parallel lines and a transversal.
    c. The sum of angles 1, 2, and 3 is 180°. Since $m\angle 1 = m\angle 4$, $m\angle 2 = m\angle 2$, and $m\angle 3 = m\angle 5$, then angles 2, 4, and 5 also add up to 180°.

30. **a.** No. The sum of any four needs to be greater than the fifth.
    b. Yes. Simply rearrange them.

31. **a.** As you push on one crank, the driver, the opposite crank, the follower, is pushed outward and shifts the coupler in two ways: down on the side of the driver and up on the side of the follower. The reverse is true when you pull on the crank.
    b. To make a stirring mechanism, attach two spoons to *D* and *C* perpendicular to the plane formed by *A*, *B*, *C*, and *D*. To make a wiping mechanism, attach wipers to *D* and *C* in the same plane as *A*, *B*, *C*, and *D*.

32. **a.** Motion keeps all lines parallel regardless of which strip is held fixed. Angle measures will change, however, angle relationships will not. For example, alternate interior angles formed by the transversal remain congruent. For example: $\angle FEB$ remains congruent to $\angle EBC$.

b. We have a stable shape now made by *A*, *B*, *F*, and *E*. The $\angle FEB$ cannot change now because with the given lengths of *FE*, *FB*, and *ED* there can be only one triangle. Thus $\angle BED$ cannot change either. Since *EDBC* is always a parallelogram, this means that no angle can change. Hence, the whole configuration is stable.

Possible Answers to Mathematical Reflections

1. **a.** The line segments can be used to form a triangle if the sum of any two is greater than the third.

   b. No, any other triangle would be congruent to the original.

2. **a.** The line segments can be used to form a quadrilateral if the sum of any three is greater than the fourth.

   b. An infinite number of quadrilaterals can be built by varying the angles or the order of the side lengths.

3. Triangles are the only rigid shapes. You can only make one triangle out of any three lengths. A quadrilateral is not rigid because out of four side lengths you can make many quadrilaterals. Using triangles will stabilize a construction.

Answers to Looking Back and Looking Ahead

1. **a.** Angle *F*

   b. Angles *B*, *E*, *I*, and *J*

   c. *C* (32.5°), *D* (32.5°), *H* (45°), *F* (90°), *B* (115°), *E* (115°), *J* (120°), *I* (122.5°), *G* (180°), *A* (245°).

2. **a.** 108°

   b. No, it is not possible to tile a floor with regular pentagons. The sum of three interior angles (324°) is less than 360° and the sum of four interior angles (432°) is more than 360°. Also the measure of an interior angle of a regular pentagon is not a factor of 360.

   c. 120° **d.** $360° \div 6 = 60°$

   e. Yes it is possible to tile a floor with a regular hexagon. Three hexagons will fill the space around a point, since the sum of three interior angles is 360°.

   f. Both polygons have reflectional and rotational symmetries. A regular pentagon has five lines of symmetry and five places where the polygon will look exactly the same. A regular hexagon has six lines of symmetry and six places where the polygon will look exactly the same.

   g. A regular hexagon does have parallel sides. If you walk from one side to the side directly across from it, you turn through three 60° exterior angles. So you turn through 180°. That means that you're facing exactly opposite of your start, and the sides must be parallel.

3. **a.** Yes.

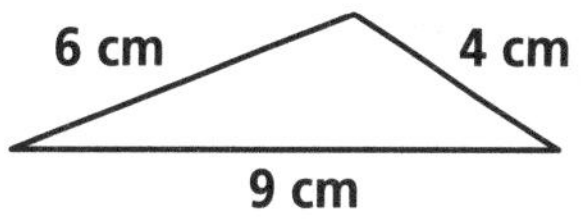

   It is not possible to make another triangle, since three side lengths determine a triangle.

   b. No, since the sum of the lengths of two sides is not greater than the third side. $4 + 2 < 7$

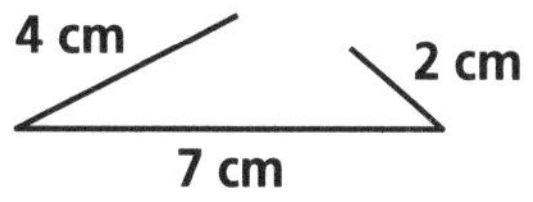

   c. Yes. Sketches may vary. It is possible to make other rectangles.

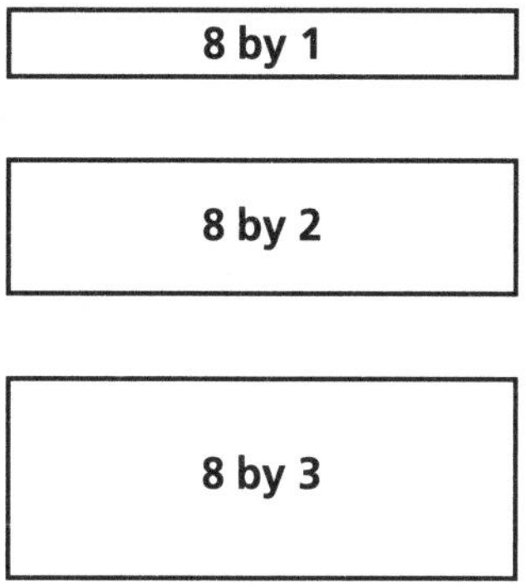

d. Yes. Sketches may vary. It is possible to make other parallelograms.

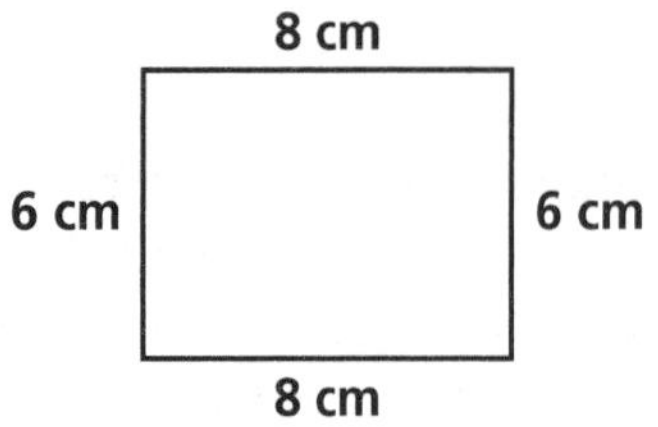

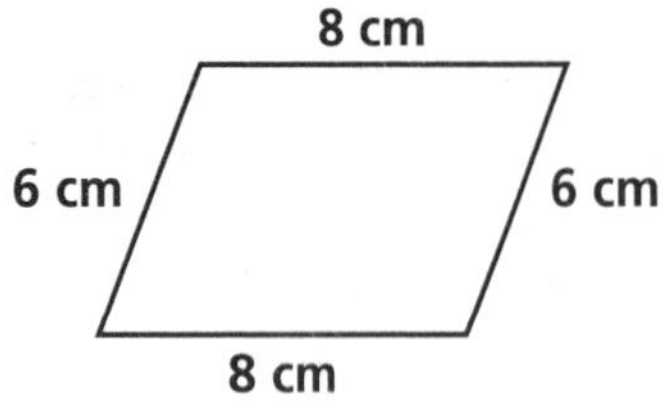

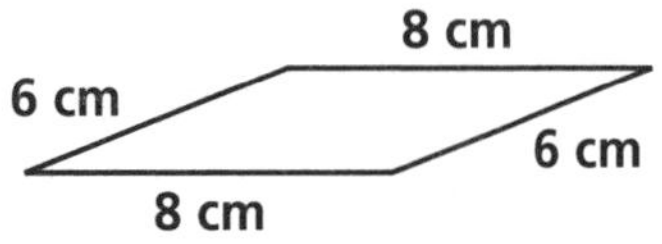

4. Angles can occur as:

- A rotation such as the angle a person covers when turning a corner.
- A wedge such as in the angle formed in a wedge of a pie.
- Two sides with a common vertex as in the lines in the building in Exercise 1 or the corner angles of a polygon in Exercise 2.

Angle measures can be estimated by comparing them to angle measures such as 0°, 60°, 90°, 120°, 180°, 270°, or 360°. They can be measured with a protractor or an angle ruler. The measure of angles can be compared also by tracing one angle onto tracing paper and placing it on top of another angle.

Have students share their strategies for determining angle measures in Exercise 1 and in Exercise 2. For example, in Exercise 2 the angles of a pentagon can be found exactly by noting that the pentagon can be subdivided into three triangles by drawing the diagonals from a vertex to the remaining two vertices. The sum of the interior angles, or angle sum, of the pentagon is 540° and since there are five equal angles, each one is $\frac{540}{5}$, or 108°.

A similar argument is also true for a hexagon. Only there will be four triangles. So the angle sum is $180° \times 4 = 720°$. Thus each of the six interior angles is 120°.

5. a. It is not always possible to draw a triangle given any three lengths. The lengths of any two sides of a triangle must be greater than the length of the third side.

b. No.

c. Since there is only one triangle for any set of sides that meet the criteria in part (a), triangles are rigid and hence very useful in building structures. In Exercise 3a the given lengths of 4 cm, 6 cm, and 9 cm meet the criterion, but the lengths, 4 cm, 7 cm, and 2 cm in Exercise 3b do not meet the criteria.

d. In order to have both types of symmetry, a triangle must be equilateral.

e. Isosceles triangles only have reflectional symmetry.

f. A scalene triangle like Shape I or Shape T has no symmetries.

6. a. It is not always possible to draw a quadrilateral given four side lengths or four angle measures. The sum of any three side lengths of a quadrilateral must be greater than the length of the fourth side. You can reorder the sides or change the angle measures to make another quadrilateral.

b. A quadrilateral is a square if it has four 90° angles and four equal-length sides. A quadrilateral is a rectangle if it has four 90° angles. A quadrilateral is a parallelogram if it has opposite sides that are the same length and parallel.

Guide to the Unit Project

Assigning the Unit Project

The unit project, What I Know About Shapes and Designs, is an integral part of the assessment in *Shapes and Designs.* The project asks students to synthesize and summarize their learning from the unit. It is introduced prior to Investigation 1.

As you near the end of the unit, you will want to discuss the project with the students in detail. Their collection of information should be close to complete, and they should begin thinking about how to present it.

Encourage students to consider a wide variety of formats for presenting their ideas. Each student should decide what form his or her project will take—such as a story, a report, a book, a movie, a slide show, a poster or set of posters, or a mobile. They may even choose a combination of formats. You might suggest that students locate books about architecture and design to help stimulate ideas. Stress that you expect them to use the vocabulary and concepts from the unit. Although students should be encouraged to be creative, the emphasis of the project should be on mathematical content.

Grading the Unit Project

Suggested Scoring Rubric

This rubric for scoring the unit employs a scale that runs from 0 to 4, with a 4+ for work that goes beyond what has been asked for in some unique way. You may use this rubric as presented here or modify it to fit your district's requirements for evaluating and reporting students' work and understanding.

4+ EXEMPLARY RESPONSE

- Complete, with clear, coherent explanations
- Shows understanding of the mathematical concepts and procedures
- Satisfies all essential conditions of the problem and goes beyond what is asked for in some unique way

4 COMPLETE RESPONSE

- Complete, with clear, coherent explanations
- Shows understanding of the mathematical concepts and procedures
- Satisfies all essential conditions of the problem

3 REASONABLY COMPLETE RESPONSE

- Reasonably complete; may lack detail in explanations
- Shows understanding of most of the mathematical concepts and procedures
- Satisfies most of the essential conditions of the problem

2 PARTIAL RESPONSE

- Gives response; explanation may be unclear or lack detail
- Shows some understanding of some of the mathematical concepts and procedures
- Satisfies some essential conditions of the problem

1 INADEQUATE RESPONSE

- Incomplete; explanation is insufficient or not understandable
- Shows little understanding of the mathematical concepts and procedures
- Fails to address essential conditions of problem

0 NO ATTEMPT

- Irrelevant response
- Does not attempt a solution
- Does not address conditions of the problem

Sample of Student Work

As her project, one student chose to make a book about shapes. Here are some excerpts from her project.

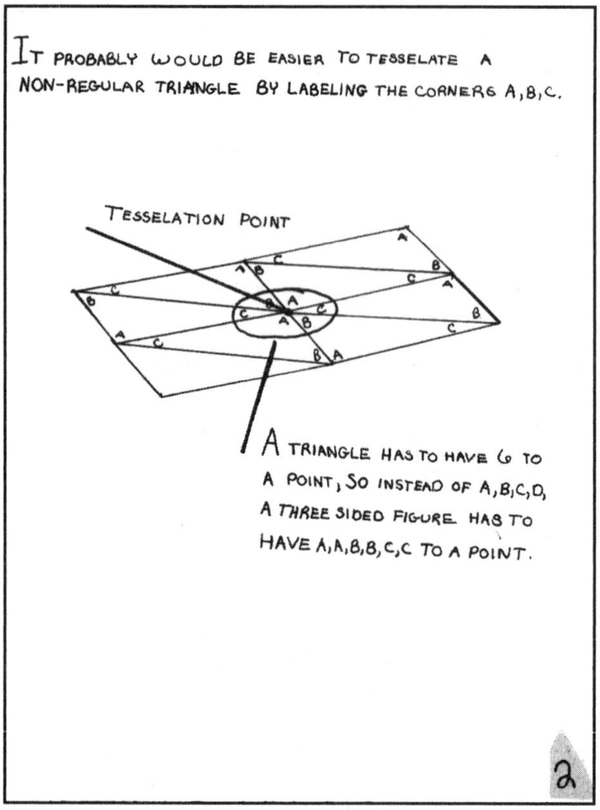
IT PROBABLY WOULD BE EASIER TO TESSELATE A NON-REGULAR TRIANGLE BY LABELING THE CORNERS A, B, C.
TESSELATION POINT
A TRIANGLE HAS TO HAVE 6 TO A POINT, SO INSTEAD OF A, B, C, D, A THREE SIDED FIGURE HAS TO HAVE A, A, B, B, C, C TO A POINT.
2

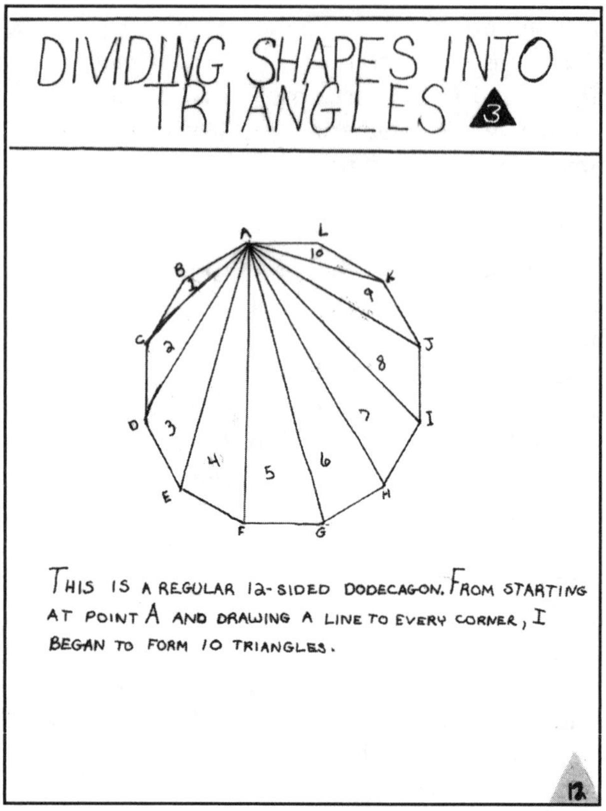
DIVIDING SHAPES INTO TRIANGLES 3
THIS IS A REGULAR 12-SIDED DODECAGON. FROM STARTING AT POINT A AND DRAWING A LINE TO EVERY CORNER, I BEGAN TO FORM 10 TRIANGLES.
12

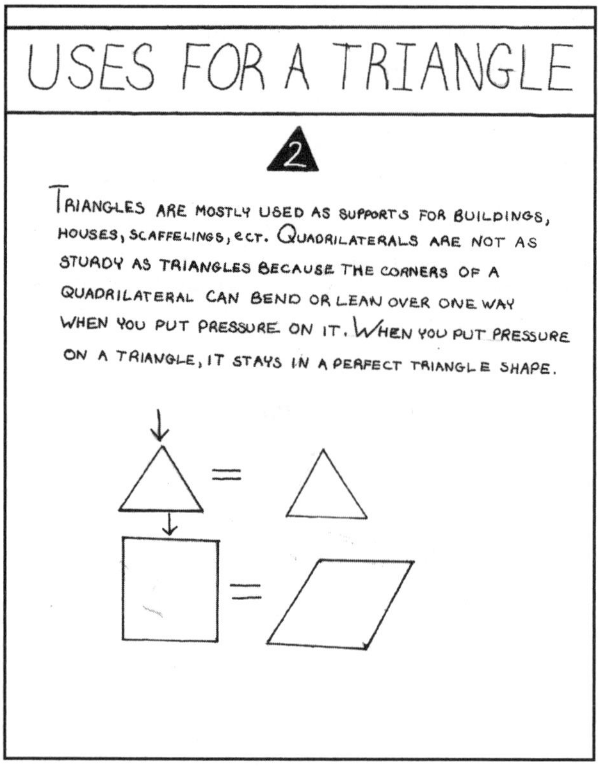
USES FOR A TRIANGLE
2
TRIANGLES ARE MOSTLY USED AS SUPPORTS FOR BUILDINGS, HOUSES, SCAFFELINGS, ECT. QUADRILATERALS ARE NOT AS STURDY AS TRIANGLES BECAUSE THE CORNERS OF A QUADRILATERAL CAN BEND OR LEAN OVER ONE WAY WHEN YOU PUT PRESSURE ON IT. WHEN YOU PUT PRESSURE ON A TRIANGLE, IT STAYS IN A PERFECT TRIANGLE SHAPE.

FAMILIAR TRIANGLES YOU USUALLY SEE
1. A ROOFTOP
2. KITCHEN KNIFE
3. CLOCKHANDS
4. ICE-CREAM CONE
5

Looking Back and Looking Ahead

Unit Review

As you worked on the problems of this unit, you have extended your knowledge of two-dimensional geometry—the study of shapes that fit on a flat surface. You have

- Explored properties of geometric shapes
- Learned how *side lengths* and *angle measures* determine the shapes of *triangles*, *rectangles*, *parallelograms*, and other *polygons*
- Looked at *regular polygons* and discovered why some can fit together to cover a flat surface, while others cannot
- Learned that polygons and angles have important practical uses in the design of buildings, beehives, road signs, and flight paths

Go Online
PHSchool.com

For: Vocabulary Review Puzzle
Web Code: amj-3051

STUDENT PAGE

STUDENT PAGE

Notes

STUDENT PAGE

Use Your Understanding: Shapes

Test your understanding of shapes by solving the following exercises.

1. This drawing of a building contains many angles.

a. Which labeled angles appear to measure 90°?

b. Which labeled angles appear to have measures greater than 90° and less than 180°?

c. List the labeled angles from smallest to largest, and estimate the degree measure of each. Then use an angle ruler or protractor to measure each as accurately as possible.

STUDENT PAGE

Notes

2. A designer is experimenting with new shapes for floor tiles. She is considering regular pentagons and regular hexagons.

   a. What is the measure of each interior angle in a regular pentagon?

   b. Is it possible to tile a floor with copies of a regular pentagon? Explain.

   c. What is the measure of each interior angle in a regular hexagon?

   d. What is the measure of each exterior angle in a regular hexagon?

   e. Is it possible to tile a floor with copies of a regular hexagon? Explain.

   f. Describe the symmetries of these two polygons.

   g. Do either of these regular polygons have parallel sides? Explain your reasoning.

3. Complete the following for parts (a)–(d).

   - Tell whether it is possible to draw a shape meeting the given conditions. If it is, make a sketch of the shape.
   - If it is possible to make a shape meeting the given conditions, tell whether it is possible to make a different shape that also meets the conditions. If it is, make a sketch of one or more of these different shapes.

   a. A triangle with side lengths of 4 cm, 6 cm, and 9 cm

   b. A triangle with side lengths of 4 cm, 7 cm, and 2 cm

   c. A rectangle with a pair of opposite sides whose lengths are 8 cm

   d. A parallelogram with side lengths of 8 cm, 8 cm, 6 cm, and 6 cm

Explain Your Reasoning

To solve Exercises 1–3, you used basic facts about the ways angle measures and side lengths determine the shapes of polygons.

4. Describe three ways to think about an angle. Discuss some methods for *estimating* angle measures and for accurately *measuring* angles.

Notes

5. Suppose you are asked to draw a triangle with three given side lengths.
   a. How can you tell if it is possible to draw a triangle with those side lengths?
   b. If one such triangle is possible, are there other triangles with the same side lengths but different shapes possible?
   c. Why are triangles so useful in building structures?
   d. Sketch a triangle that has both rotation and reflection symmetries.
   e. Sketch a triangle that has only one line of symmetry.
   f. Sketch a triangle that has no symmetries.
6. a. How can you tell if it is possible to draw a quadrilateral given four side lengths? If you can draw one such quadrilateral, can you always draw a different one?
   b. How can you decide whether a given quadrilateral is a square? A rectangle? A parallelogram?

Look Ahead

You will use the properties of angles and polygons you studied in this unit in many future units of *Connected Mathematics*, especially those that deal with perimeter, area, and volume of figures. The side and angle relationships in triangles and quadrilaterals are also applied in many construction and design tasks.

Notes

English / Spanish Glossary

A

acute angle An angle whose measure is less than 90°.

ángulo agudo Ángulo que mide menos de 90°

angle The figure formed by two rays or line segments that have a common vertex. Angles are measured in degrees. The angle at point *A* on the triangle below is identified as angle *BAC* or $\angle BAC$. The sides of an angle are rays that have the vertex as a starting point. Each of the three angles below is formed by the joining of two rays.

ángulo Figura que forman dos rayos o segmentos que tienen en un vértice común. Los ángulos se miden en grados. El ángulo del punto *A* del triángulo representado a continuación se identifica como el ángulo *BAC* o $\angle BAC$. Los lados de un ángulo son rayos que tienen el vértice como punto de partida. Cada uno de los tres ángulos de abajo está formado por la unión de dos rayos.

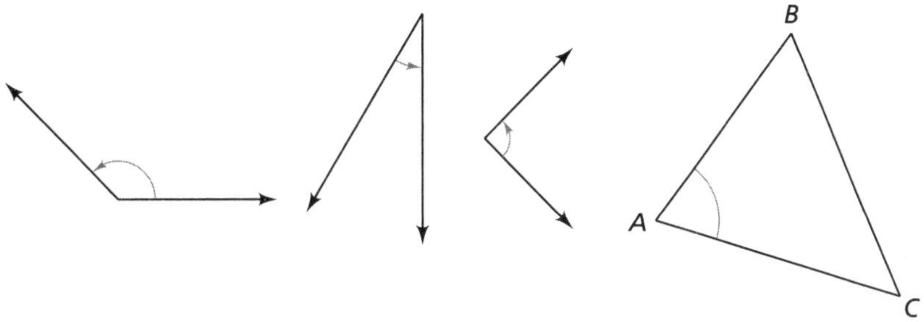

angle sum The sum of all the measures of the interior angles of a polygon.

suma de ángulos Suma de todas las medidas de los ángulos interiores de un polígono.

C

central angle An angle with a vertex at the center of a circle and whose sides are radii of the circle.

ángulo central Ángulo que tiene un vértice en el centro de un círculo y cuyos lados son radios del círculo.

D

degree A unit of measure of angles is also equal to $\frac{1}{360}$ of a complete circle. The angle below measures about 1 degree (1°); 360 of these would just fit around a point and fill in a complete circle; 90 of them make a right angle.

grado Una unidad de medida de ángulos que equivale a $\frac{1}{360}$ de un círculo completo. El ángulo representado a continuación mide aproximadamente un grado (1°); 360 de estos ángulos encajarían alrededor de un punto y llenarían completamente un círculo, mientras que 90 formarían un ángulo recto.

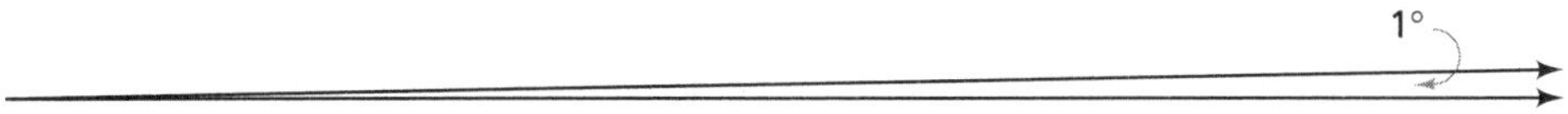

Notes

diagonal A line segment connecting two non-adjacent vertices of a polygon. All quadrilaterals have two diagonals, as shown below. The two diagonals of a square are equal in length, and the two diagonals of a rectangle are equal in length. A pentagon has five diagonals. A hexagon has nine diagonals.

diagonal Un segmento de recta que conecta dos vértices no adyacentes de un polígono. Todos los cuadriláteros tienen dos diagonales, como se representa a continuación. Las dos diagonales de un cuadrado tienen longitudes iguales y las dos diagonales de un rectángulo tienen longitudes iguales. Un pentágono tiene cinco diagonales y un hexágono tiene nueve diagonales.

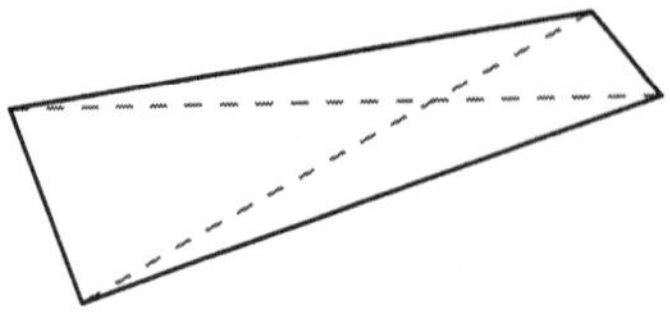

E

equilateral triangle A triangle with all three sides the same length.

triángulo equilátero Un triángulo que tiene tres lados de la misma longitud.

exterior angle An angle at a vertex of a polygon where the sides of the angle are one side of the polygon and the extension of the other side meeting at that vertex.

ángulo exterior Ángulo en el vértice de un polígono donde los lados del ángulo son un lado del polígono y la extensión del otro lado se une en ese vértice.

I

interior angle The angle inside a polygon formed by two adjacent sides of the polygon's sides.

ángulo interior Ángulo dentro de un polígono formado por dos lados adyacentes del polígono.

irregular polygon A polygon which has at least two sides with different lengths or two angles with different measures.

polígono irregular Polígono que tiene al menos dos lados de diferentes longitudes o dos ángulos con diferentes medidas.

isosceles triangle A triangle with two sides the same length.

triángulo isósceles Un triángulo que tiene dos lados de la misma longitud.

L

line of symmetry A line such that if a shape is folded over this line the two halves of the shape match exactly.

eje de simetría Recta por la que si una figura se dobla por ella, sus dos mitades coinciden exactamente.

line segment A line segment consists of two points of a line and all the points between these two points.

segmento de recta Un segmento de recta tiene dos puntos de una recta y todos los puntos entre estos dos puntos.

M

midpoint The point that divides a line segment into two segments of equal length.

punto medio Punto que divide un segmento de recta en dos segmentos de igual longitud.

Notes

O

obtuse angle An angle whose measure is greater than 90° and less than 180°.

ángulo obtuso Ángulo cuya medida es mayor de 90° y menor de 180°.

P

parallel lines Lines in a plane that never meet. The opposite sides of a regular hexagon are parallel.

rectas paralelas Rectas en un plano, que nunca se encuentran. Los lados opuestos de un hexágono regular son paralelos. Los polígonos A y B tienen un par de lados opuestos paralelos. Los polígonos C, D y E tienen dos pares de lados opuestos paralelos.

Polygons A and B each have one pair of opposite sides parallel.

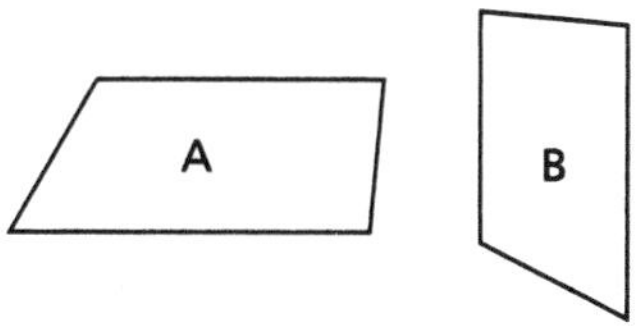

Polygons C, D, and E each have two pairs of opposite sides parallel

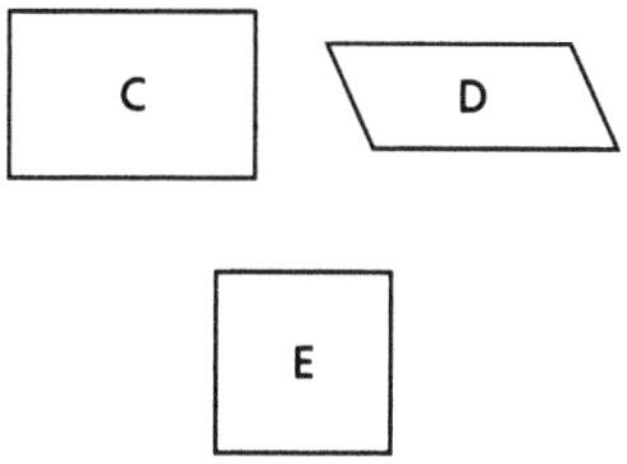

parallelogram A quadrilateral with opposite sides parallel. Both pairs of opposite angles are also equal. In the definition of parallel lines, figure D, rectangle C, and square E are all parallelograms.

paralelogramo Cuadrilátero cuyos lados opuestos son paralelos. Ambos pares de ángulos opuestos también son iguales. En la definición de rectas paralelas, la figura D, el rectángulo C y el cuadrado E son paralelogramos.

perpendicular lines Two lines that intersect to form right angles.

rectas perpendiculares Dos rectas que se intersecan para formar ángulos rectos.

Notes ______________________________

polygon A shape formed by line segments, called *sides*, so that each of the segments meets exactly two other segments, and all of the points where the segments meet are endpoints of the segments.

polígono Figura formada por segmentos de recta, llamados *lados*, de modo que cada uno de los segmentos se junta exactamente con otros dos segmentos, y todos los puntos donde se encuentran los segmentos son extremos de los segmentos.

Polygons

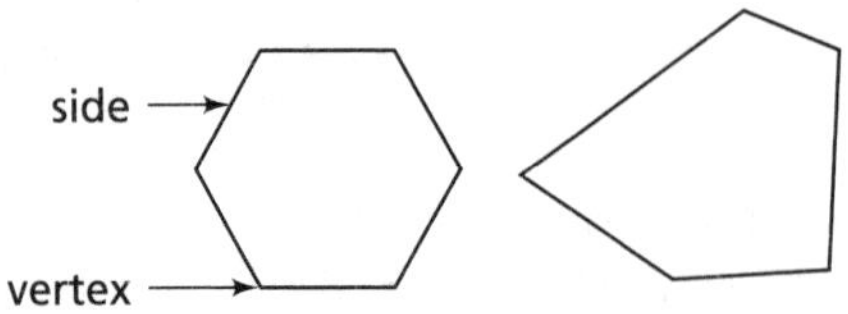

Special polygon names use Greek prefixes that tell the number of sides or the number of angles in the polygon.

- triangle: A polygon with 3 sides and angles
- quadrilateral: A polygon with 4 sides and angles
- pentagon: A polygon with 5 sides and angles
- hexagon: A polygon with 6 sides and angles
- heptagon: A polygon with 7 sides and angles
- octagon: A polygon with 8 sides and angles
- nonagon (also called enneagon): A polygon with 9 sides and angles
- decagon: A polygon with 10 sides and angles
- dodecagon: A polygon with 12 sides and angles

Los nombres especiales con que se designan los polígonos provienen de prefijos griegos que indican el número de lados o el número de ángulos del polígono.

- triángulo: polígono con 3 lados y ángulos
- cuadrilátero: polígono con 4 lados y ángulos
- pentágono: polígono con 5 lados y ángulos
- hexágono: polígono con 6 lados y ángulos
- heptágono: polígono con 7 lados y ángulos
- octágono: polígono con 8 lados y ángulos
- nonágono (también llamado eneágono): polígono con 9 lados y ángulos
- decágono: polígono con 10 lados y ángulos
- dodecágono: polígono con 12 lados y ángulos

Q

quadrilateral A polygon with four sides.

cuadrilátero Un polígono de cuatro lados como los que se muestran a continuación.

Quadrilaterals

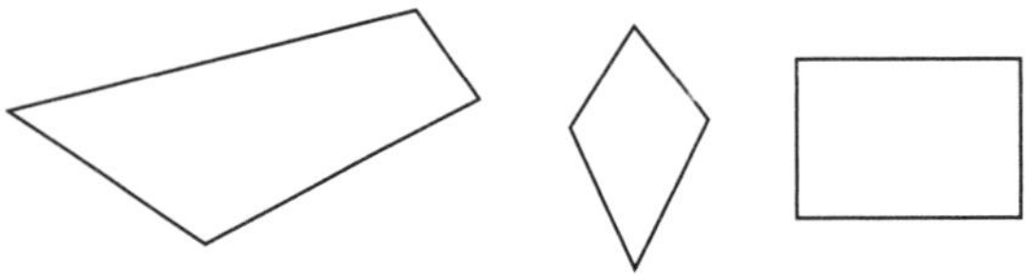

STUDENT PAGE

STUDENT PAGE

Notes

ray A part of a line consisting of a point, called an endpoint, and all the points on the line on one side of the endpoint.

ray Parte de una recta que tiene un punto, llamado extremo, y todos los puntos de la recta están a un lado del extremo.

rectangle A parallelogram with all right angles. Squares are a special type of rectangle.

rectángulo Un paralelogramo con todos los ángulos rectos. Los cuadrados son un tipo especial de rectángulo.

Rectangles

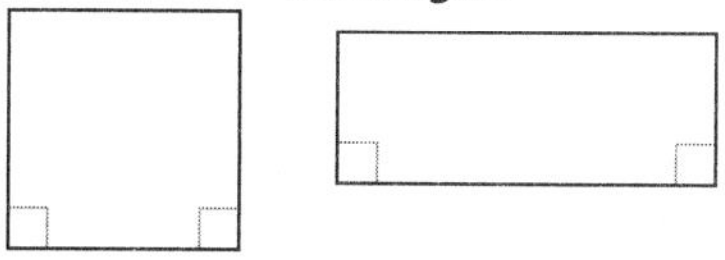

reflection symmetry A shape with reflection symmetry has two halves that are mirror images of each other.

simetría por reflexión Una figura con simetría por reflexión tiene dos mitades que son imágenes reflejas la una de la otra.

regular polygon A polygon that has all of its sides equal and all of its angles equal. The hexagon below is regular, but the pentagon is not regular, because its sides and its angles are not equal.

polígono regular Un polígono que tiene todos los lados y todos los ángulos iguales. El hexágono representado a continuación es regular, pero el pentágono no lo es porque sus lados y sus ángulos no son iguales.

Regular **Not Regular**

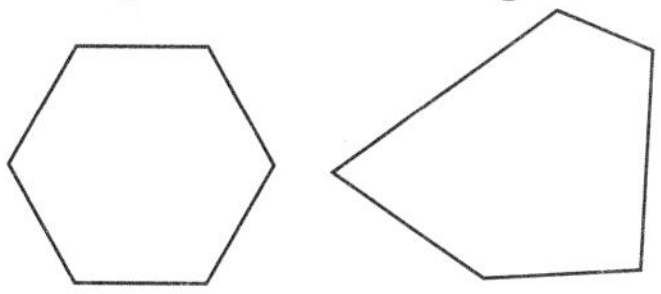

rhombus A quadrilateral that has all sides the same length.

rombo Un cuadrilátero que tiene todos los lados de la misma longitud.

right angle An angle that measures 90°. A rectangle has four right angles.

ángulo recto Un ángulo que mide 90°. Un rectángulo tiene los cuatro ángulos rectos.

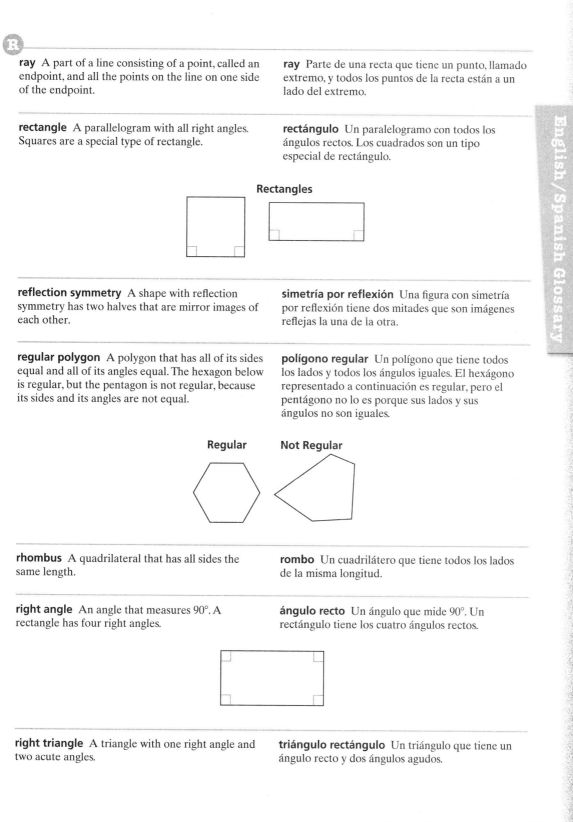

right triangle A triangle with one right angle and two acute angles.

triángulo rectángulo Un triángulo que tiene un ángulo recto y dos ángulos agudos.

Notes

rotation symmetry A shape has rotation symmetry if it can be rotated less than a full turn about its center point to a position where it looks exactly as it did before it was rotated.

simetría por rotación Una figura tiene simetría por rotación si puede girarse menos de una vuelta completa sobre su centro hasta una posición en la que se vería exactamente igual que antes de girarse.

S

scalene triangle A triangle with no side lengths equal.

triángulo escaleno Triángulo en el cual ninguno de sus lados tiene la misma longitud.

side See *polygon.*

lado Ver *polígono.*

square A rectangle with all sides equal. Squares have four right angles and four equal sides.

cuadrado Rectángulo cuyos lados son iguales. Los cuadrados tienen cuatro ángulos rectos y cuatro lados iguales.

straight angle An angle that measures 180°.

ángulo llano Ángulo que mide 180°.

T

tiling Also called a *tessellation.* The filling of a plane surface with geometric shapes without gaps or overlaps. These shapes are usually regular polygons or other common polygons. The tiling below is made of triangles. You could remove some of the line segments to create a tiling of parallelograms, or remove still more to create a tiling of hexagons. In a tiling, a vertex is a point where the corners of the polygons fit together.

embaldosamiento También llamado *teselado.* Embaldosar es llenar una superficie plana con figuras geométricas sin dejar espacios o superponer figuras. Estas figuras suelen ser polígonos regulares u otros polígonos comunes. El embaldosamiento representado a continuación está formado por triángulos. Se podrían quitar algunos de los segmentos de recta para crear un teselado de paralelogramos y hasta eliminar otros más para crear un teselado de hexágonos. En un embaldosamiento, un vértice es un punto donde se unen las esquinas de los polígonos.

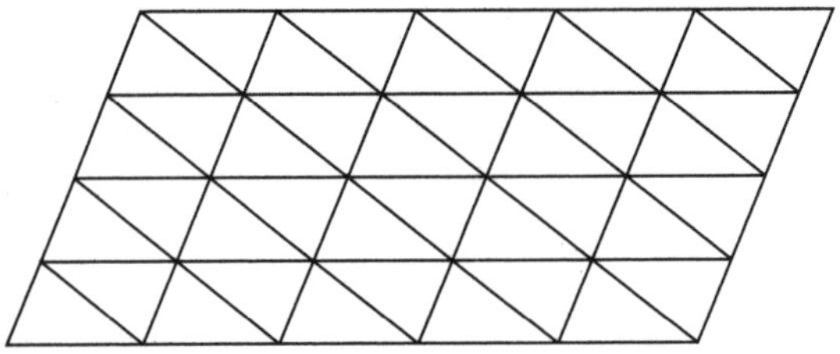

STUDENT PAGE

Notes

transversal A line that intersects two or more lines. Lines *s* and *t* are transversals.

transversal Recta que interseca dos o más rectas. Las rectas *s* y *t* son transversales.

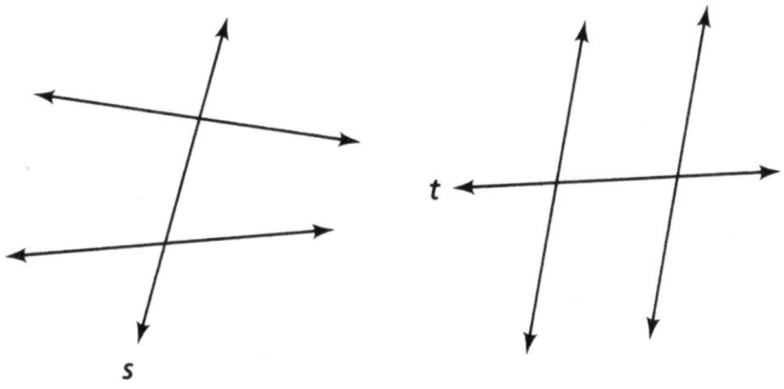

trapezoid A quadrilateral with at least one pair of opposite sides parallel. This definition means that parallelograms are trapezoids.

trapecio Un cuadrilátero que tiene, al menos, un par de lados opuestos paralelos. Esta definición significa que los paralelogramos son trapecios.

Trapezoids

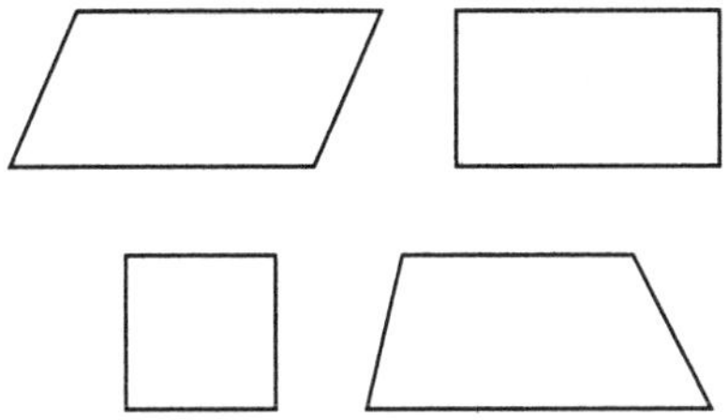

V

vertex A corner of a polygon. For example, *G*, *H*, *I*, *J*, and *K* are all vertices in the pentagon below. All angles have vertices; for example, in the hexagon below, angle *AFE* has a vertex at *F*.

vértice Las esquinas de un polígono. Por ejemplo, *G*, *H*, *I*, *J* y *K* son vértices del pentágono dibujado a continuación. Todos los ángulos tienen vértices. Por ejemplo, en el hexágono representado a continuación, el ángulo *AFE* tiene el vértice en *F*.

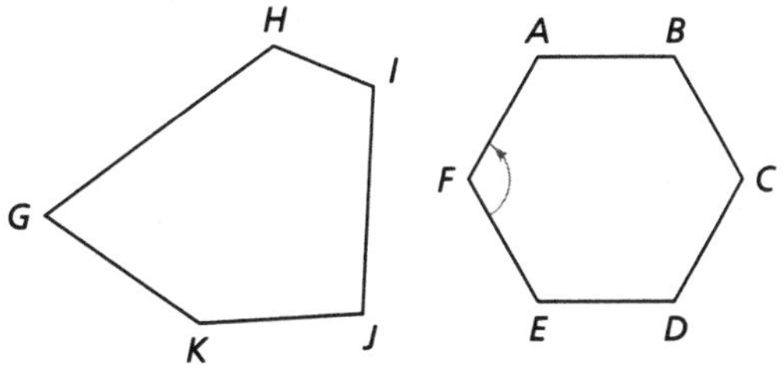

Notes

Academic Vocabulary

The following terms are important to your understanding of the mathematics in this unit. Knowing and using these words will help you in thinking, reasoning, representing, communicating your ideas, and making connections across ideas. When these words make sense to you, the investigations and problems will make more sense as well.

I

illustrate To show or present information usually as a drawing or a diagram. You can also illustrate a point using a written explanation.
related terms: present, display

Sample: **The needle of a compass is pointing 90 degrees from North. In which direction can the needle be pointing? Make a sketch to illustrate this situation.**

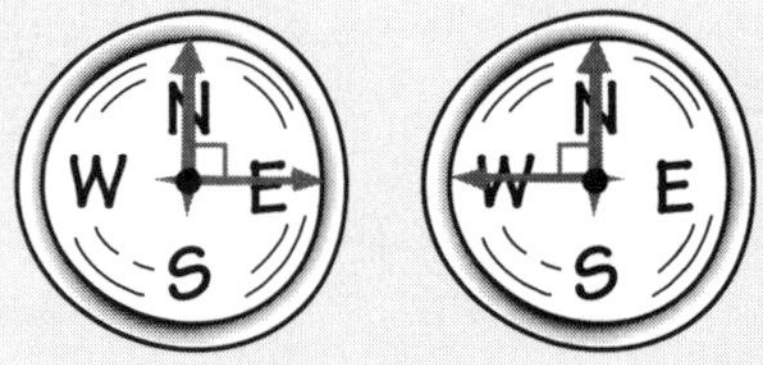

The needle could be pointing East, since a needle pointing east would form a 90° angle with North on the compass. The needle can also be pointing West because it also would form a 90° angle with North.

ilustrar Mostrar o presentar información por lo general como un dibujo o un diagrama. También puedes ilustrar un punto usando una explicación escrita.
términos relacionados: presentar, exhibir

Ejemplo: **La aguja de una brújula apunta 90 grados desde el Norte. ¿En qué dirección puede estar apuntando la aguja? Haz un bosquejo para ilustrar esta situación.**

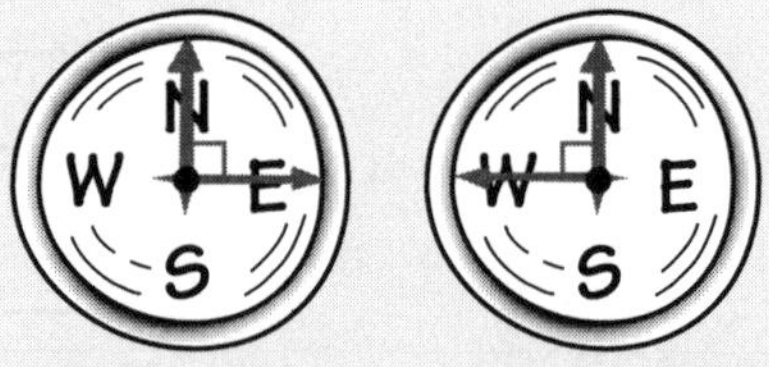

La aguja podría estar apuntando hacia el Este, puesto que una aguja que apunte al este formaría un ángulo de 90° con el Norte en la brújula. La aguja también puede estar apuntando al Oeste porque también formaría un ángulo de 90° con el Norte.

indicate To point out or show.
related terms: demonstrate, show, identify

Sample: **Indicate which symbol is used to represent rotation.**

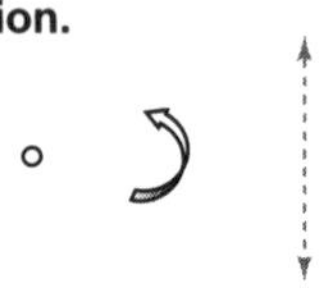

The curved arrow is the symbol used to represent rotation. The small circle indicates the degrees of an angle. The dashed line is used to show symmetry.

indicar Apuntar o mostrar.
términos relacionados: demostrar, mostrar, identificar

Ejemplo: **Indica cuál símbolo se usa para representar la rotación.**

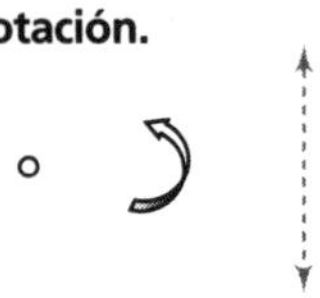

La flecha curvada es el símbolo que se usa para representar la rotación. El círculo pequeño indica los grados de un ángulo. La línea punteada se usa para mostrar simetría.

Notes

J

justify To support your answers with reasons or examples. A justification may include a written response, diagrams, charts, tables, or a combination of these.
related terms: validate, explain, defend, reason

Sample: Tell whether the following statement is true or false. Justify your answer.

All squares are parallelograms.

> The statement is true. All squares are parallelograms because all squares have two pairs of parallel sides.

justificar Apoyar tus respuestas con razones o ejemplos. Una justificación puede incluir una respuesta escrita, diagramas, gráficas, tablas o una combinación de éstos.
términos relacionados: validar, explicar, defender, razonar

Ejemplo: Di si la siguiente afirmación es cierta o falsa. Justifica tu respuesta.

Todos los cuadrados son paralelogramos.

> La afirmación es cierta. Todos los cuadrados son paralelogramos porque todos los cuadrados tienen dos pares de lados paralelos.

R

relate To find a connection between two different things
related terms: connect, match

Sample: Tell how the exterior angles of a quadrilateral relate to the interior angles.

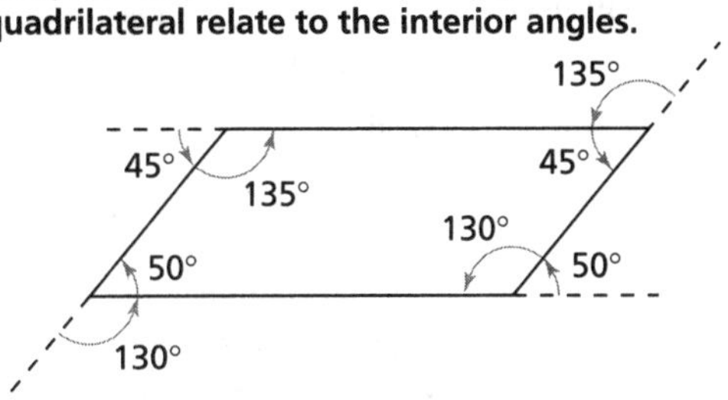

> Each pair of interior and exterior angles of the quadrilateral has a sum of 180° because each pair of angles forms a straight angle.

relacionar Hallar una conexión entre dos cosas diferentes.
términos relacionados: conectar, corresponder

Ejemplo: Indica cómo se relacionan los ángulos exteriores de un cuadrilátero con los ángulos interiores.

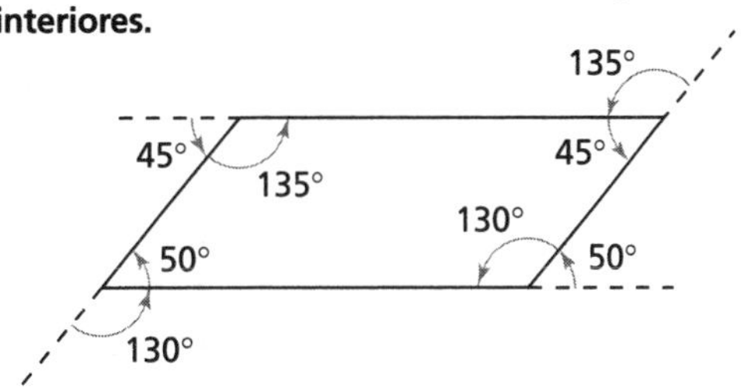

> Cada par de ángulos interiores y exteriores del cuadrilátero tiene una suma de 180° porque cada par de ángulos forma un ángulo recto.

S

sketch To draw a rough outline of something. When a sketch is asked for, it means that a drawing needs to be included in your response.
related terms: draw, illustrate

Sample: Sketch a 30° angle.

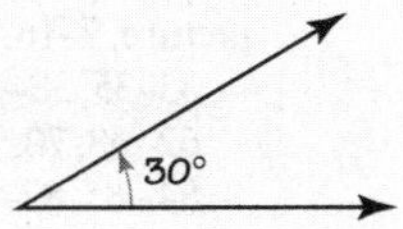

hacer un bosquejo Dibujar un esbozo de algo. Cuando se pide un bosquejo, significa que necesitas incluir un dibujo en tu respuesta.
términos relacionados: dibujar, ilustrar

Ejemplo: Haz un bosquejo de un ángulo de 30°.

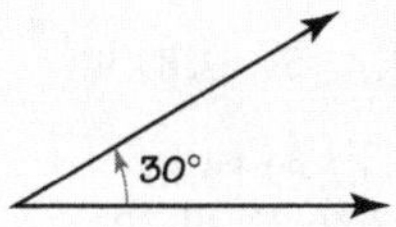

Notes

Index

STUDENT PAGE

STUDENT PAGE

Notes

Notes

STUDENT PAGE

STUDENT PAGE

Notes

Acknowledgments

Team Credits

The people who made up the **Connected Mathematics2** team—representing editorial, editorial services, design services, and production services—are listed below. Bold type denotes core team members.

Leora Adler, Judith Buice, Kerry Cashman, Patrick Culleton, Sheila DeFazio, Richard Heater, **Barbara Hollingdale, Jayne Holman,** Karen Holtzman, **Etta Jacobs,** Christine Lee, Carolyn Lock, Catherine Maglio, **Dotti Marshall,** Rich McMahon, Eve Melnechuk, Kristin Mingrone, Terri Mitchell, **Marsha Novak,** Irene Rubin, Donna Russo, Robin Samper, Siri Schwartzman, **Nancy Smith,** Emily Soltanoff, **Mark Tricca,** Paula Vergith, Roberta Warshaw, Helen Young

Additional Credits

Diana Bonfilio, Mairead Reddin, Michael Torocsik, nSight, Inc.

Illustration

Michelle Barbera: 25, 26, 41, 45, 46, 49, 63

Technical Illustration

WestWords, Inc.

Cover Design

tom white.images

Photos

2 t, Dorling Kindersley; **2 m,** Bonnie Kamin/PhotoEdit; **2 b,** Kelly-Mooney Photography/Corbis; **3,** AP Photo/Bizuayehu Tesfaye; **5,** Richard Haynes; **7 t,** Dorling Kindersley; **7 b,** Musee National d'Art Moderne, CentreGeorges Pompidou, Paris/SuperStock; **14,** Mark Chappell/Animals Animals/Earth Scenes; **16 t,** Kevin Schafer/Corbis; **16 b,** M.C. Escher's "Symmetry Drawing E59" © 2004 The M.C. Escher Company - Baarn - Holland. All rights reserved.; **18,** Christie's Images/Corbis; **19 l,** Judith Miller Archive/Dorling Kindersley; **19 r,** Bonnie Kamin/PhotoEdit; **30,** Richard Haynes; **32,** NOAA Photo Library, NOAA Central Library; OAR/ERL/National Severe Storms Laboratory (NSSL); **35,** Spencer Grant/PhotoEdit; **37,** Bettmann/Corbis; **38,** Royalty-Free/Corbis; **40,** Mark Gibson/Index Stock Imagery, Inc.; **49,** Duomo/Corbis; **59,** Jim Cummins/Getty Images, Inc.; **59 inset,** Russ Lappa; **64,** Michelle D. Bridwell/Photo Edit; **66,** Richard Haynes; **70 all,** Russ Lappa; **71,** Kelly-Mooney Photography/Corbis; **73 all,** Russ Lappa; **74,** Russ Lappa; **76,** Pearson Learning; **79,** Raymond Forbes/SuperStock; **81,** Russ Lappa; **83 all,** Getty Images, Inc.

Note: Every effort has been made to locate the copyright owner of the material reprinted in this book. Omissions brought to our attention will be corrected in subsequent editions.

STUDENT PAGE

STUDENT PAGE

Notes

Name ______________________ Date ____________ Class ____________

Labsheet

Shapes Set

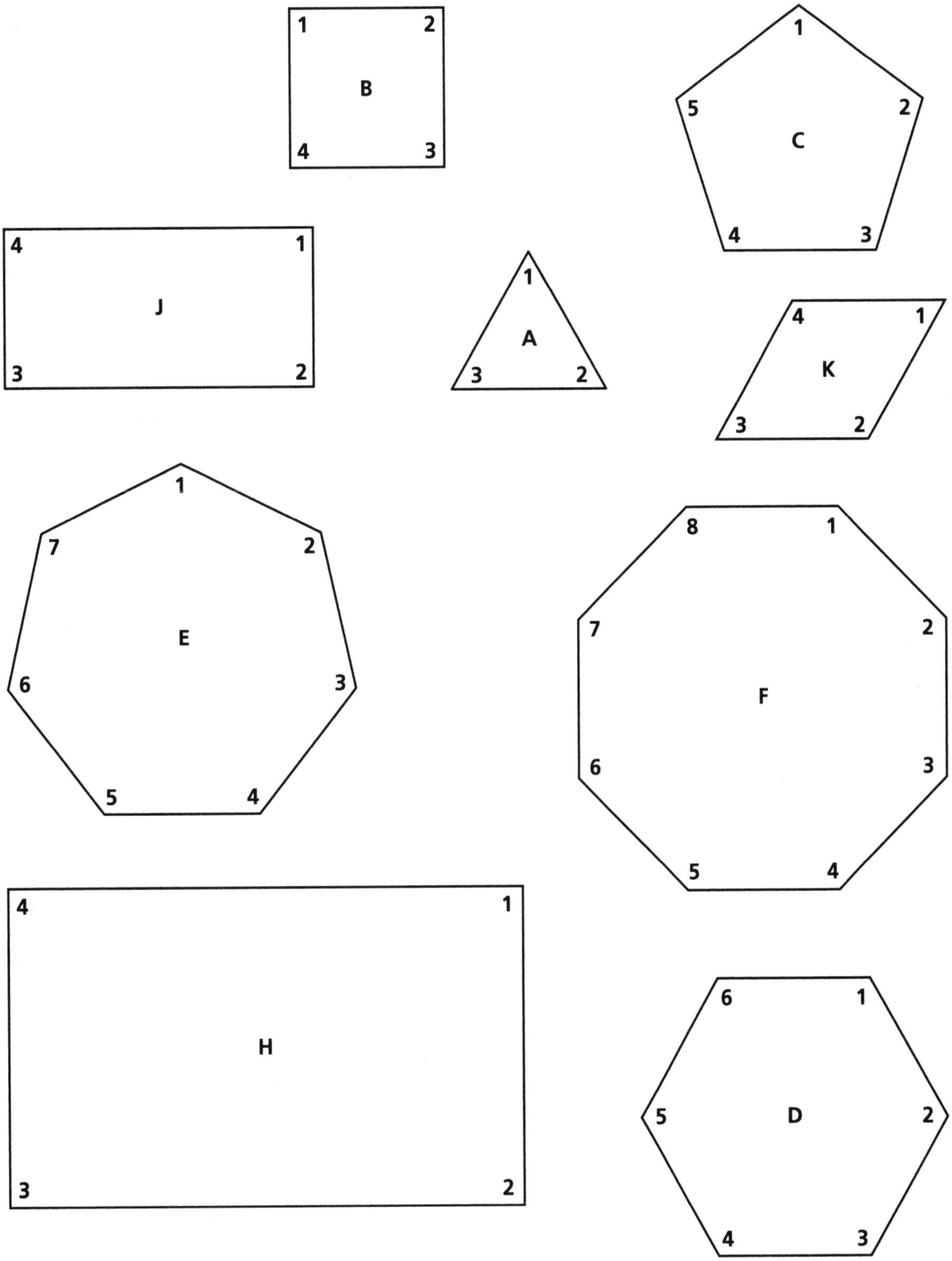

Name ______________________ Date ____________ Class ____________

Labsheet

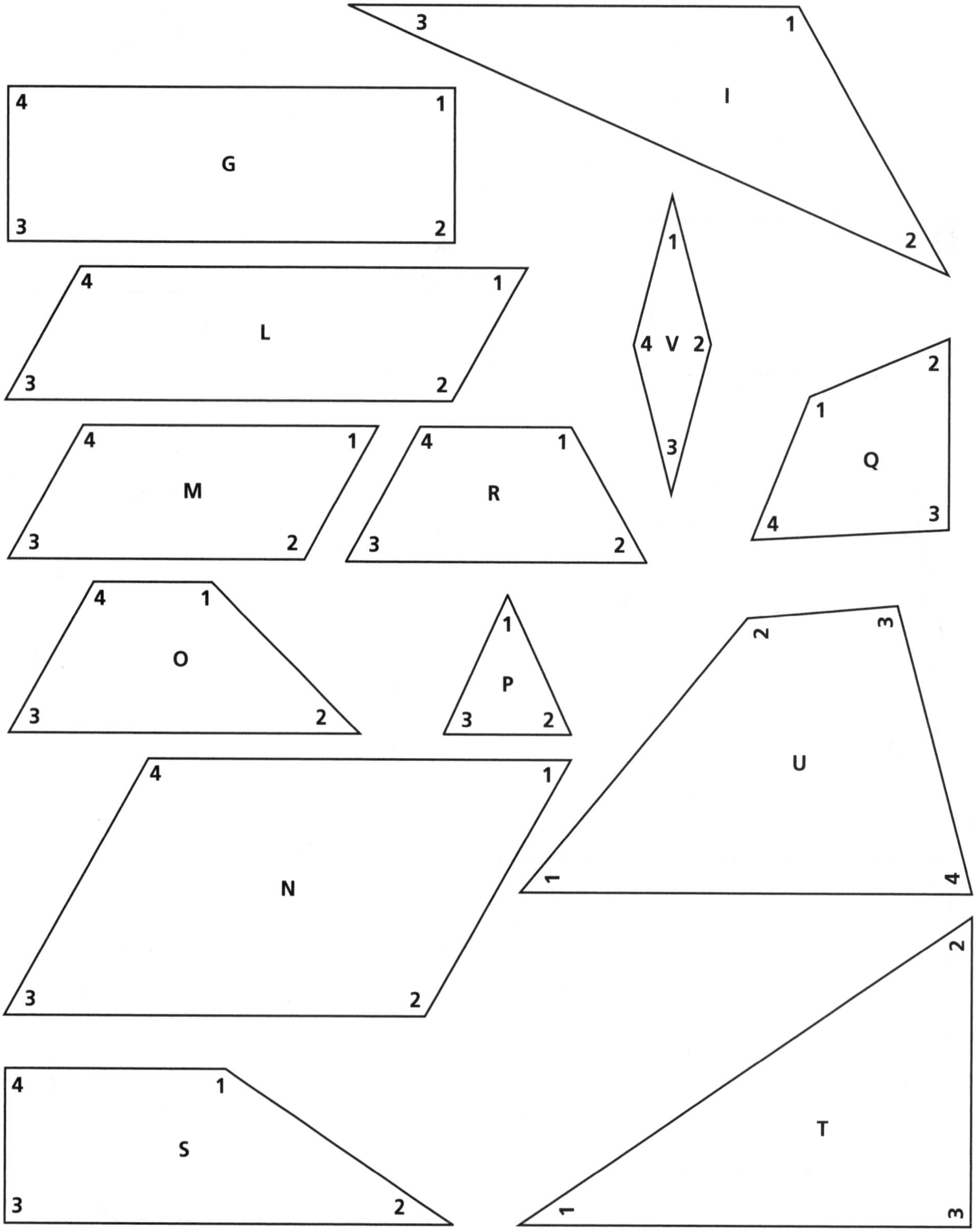

Name ______________________ Date __________ Class __________

Labsheet 1ACE Exercises 3 and 4

Exercise 3

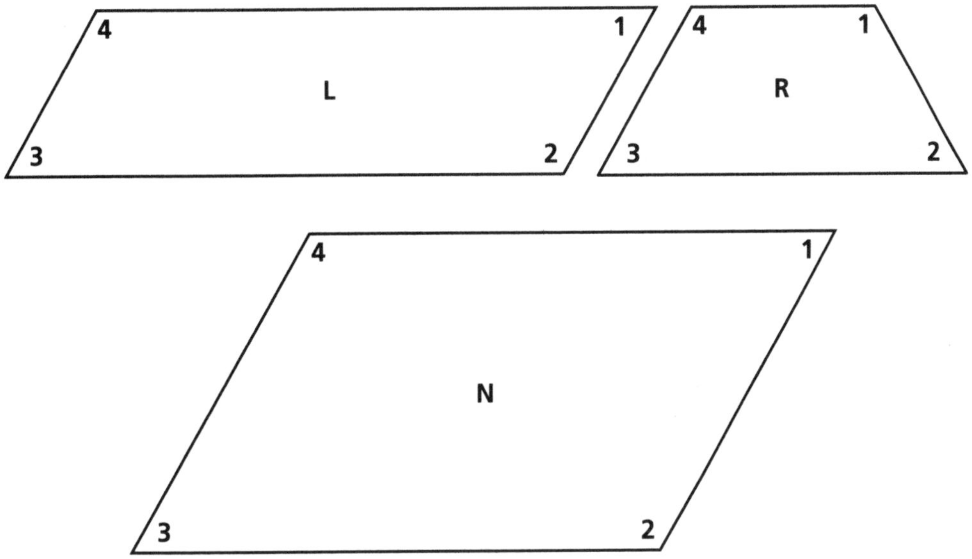

Exercise 4

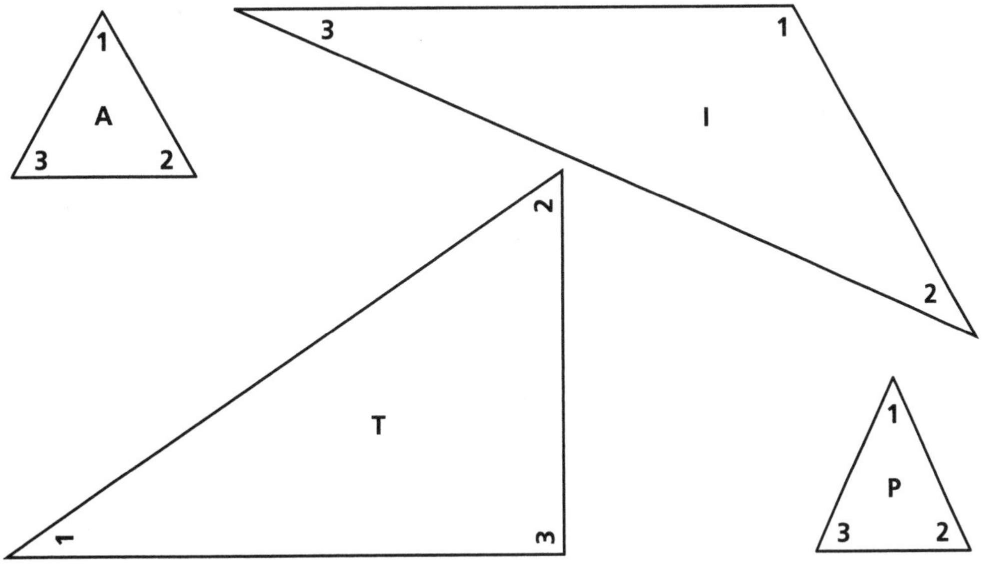

Name ______________________________ Date ____________ Class ____________

Labsheet 2.2

Four in a Row

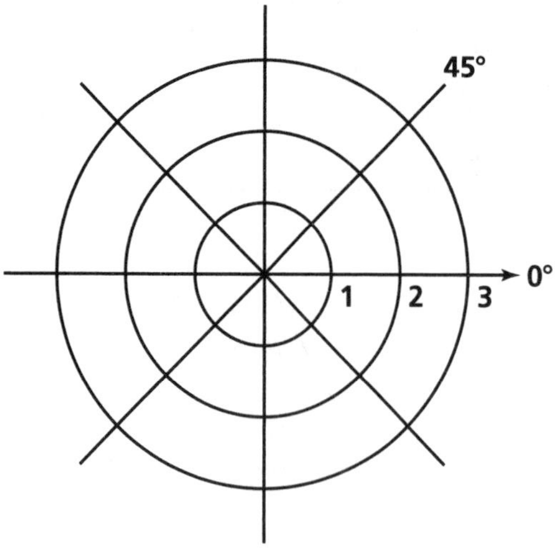

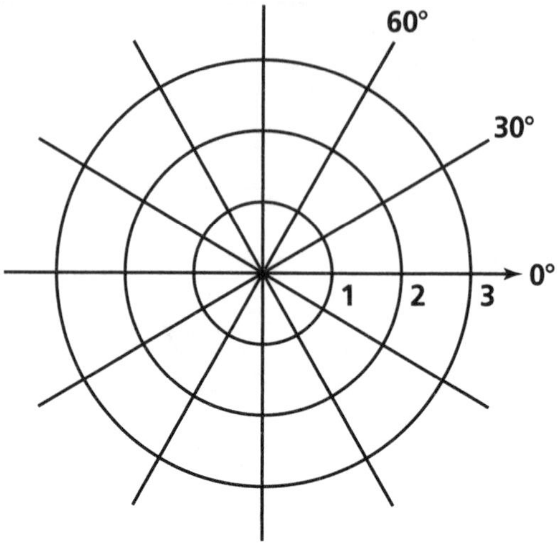

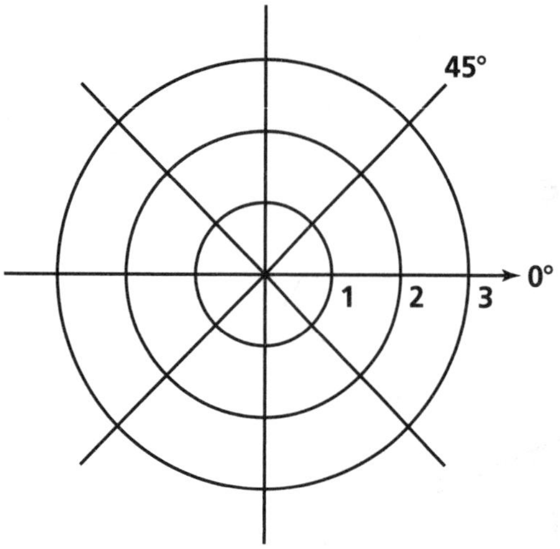

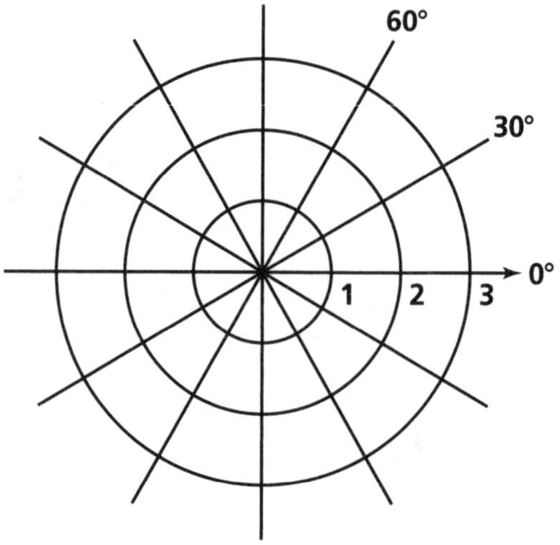

Name ______________________ Date __________ Class __________

Labsheet 2.4

Earhart Map

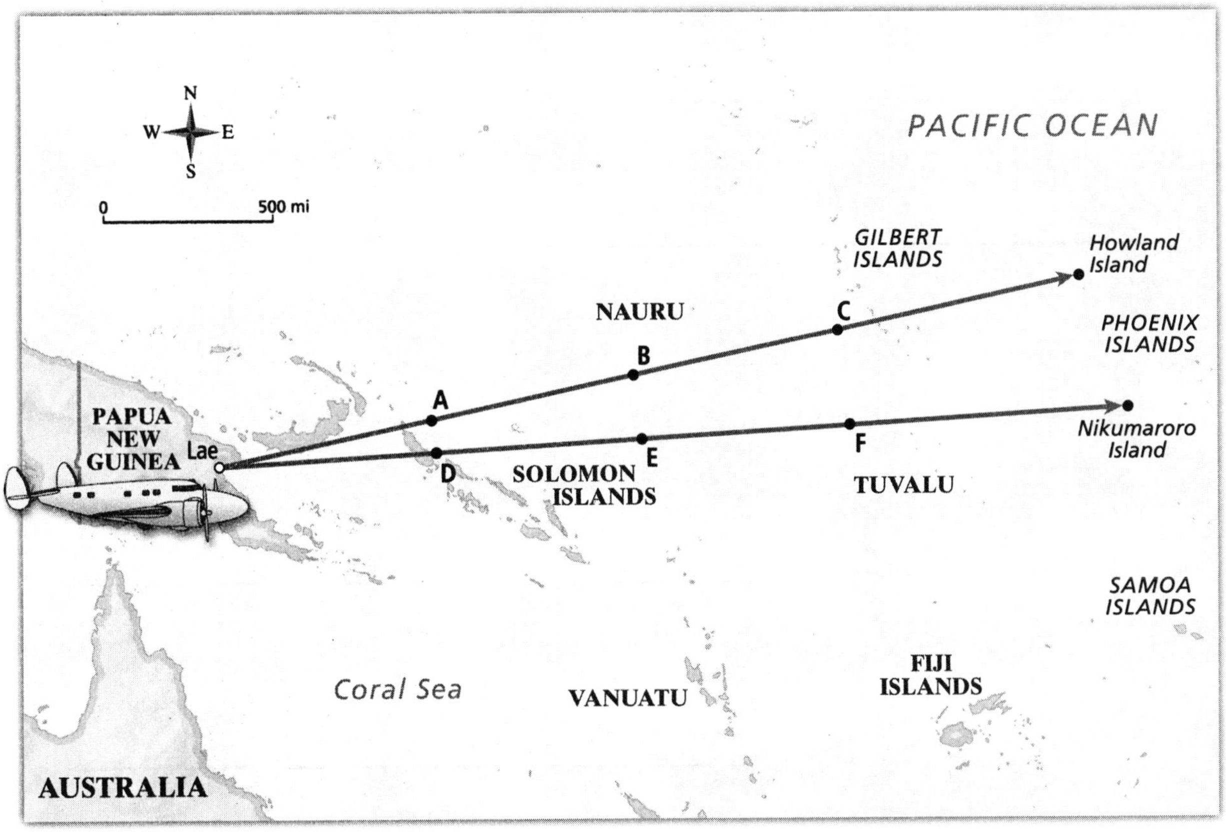

Name ______________________ Date ____________ Class ____________

Labsheet 2.5

Angles and Parallel Lines

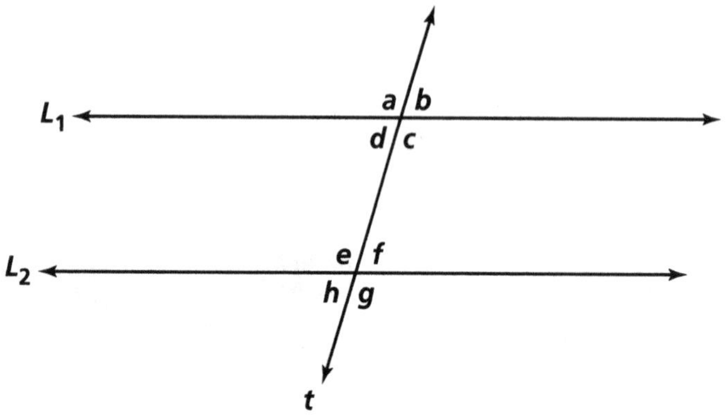

Figure 1

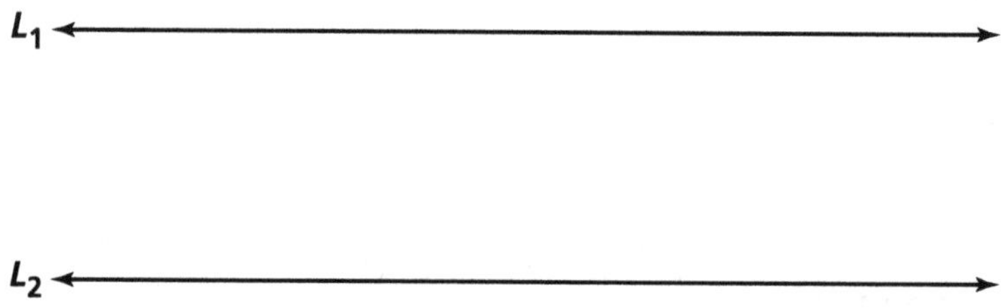

Figure 2

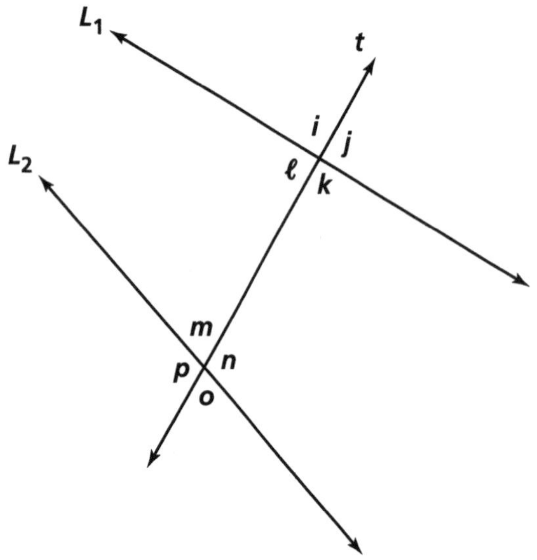

Figure 3

Name ______________________ Date ____________ Class ____________

Labsheet 3.2

Angle Sums

Polygon	Number of Sides	Angle Sum Using Tia's Method	Angle Sum Using Cody's Method	Angle Sum
Triangle	3			
Quadrilateral	4			
Pentagon	5			
Hexagon	6			
Heptagon	7			
Octagon	8			
Nonagon	9			
Decagon	10			

Polystrips

A Polystrip set contains six strips of each length.

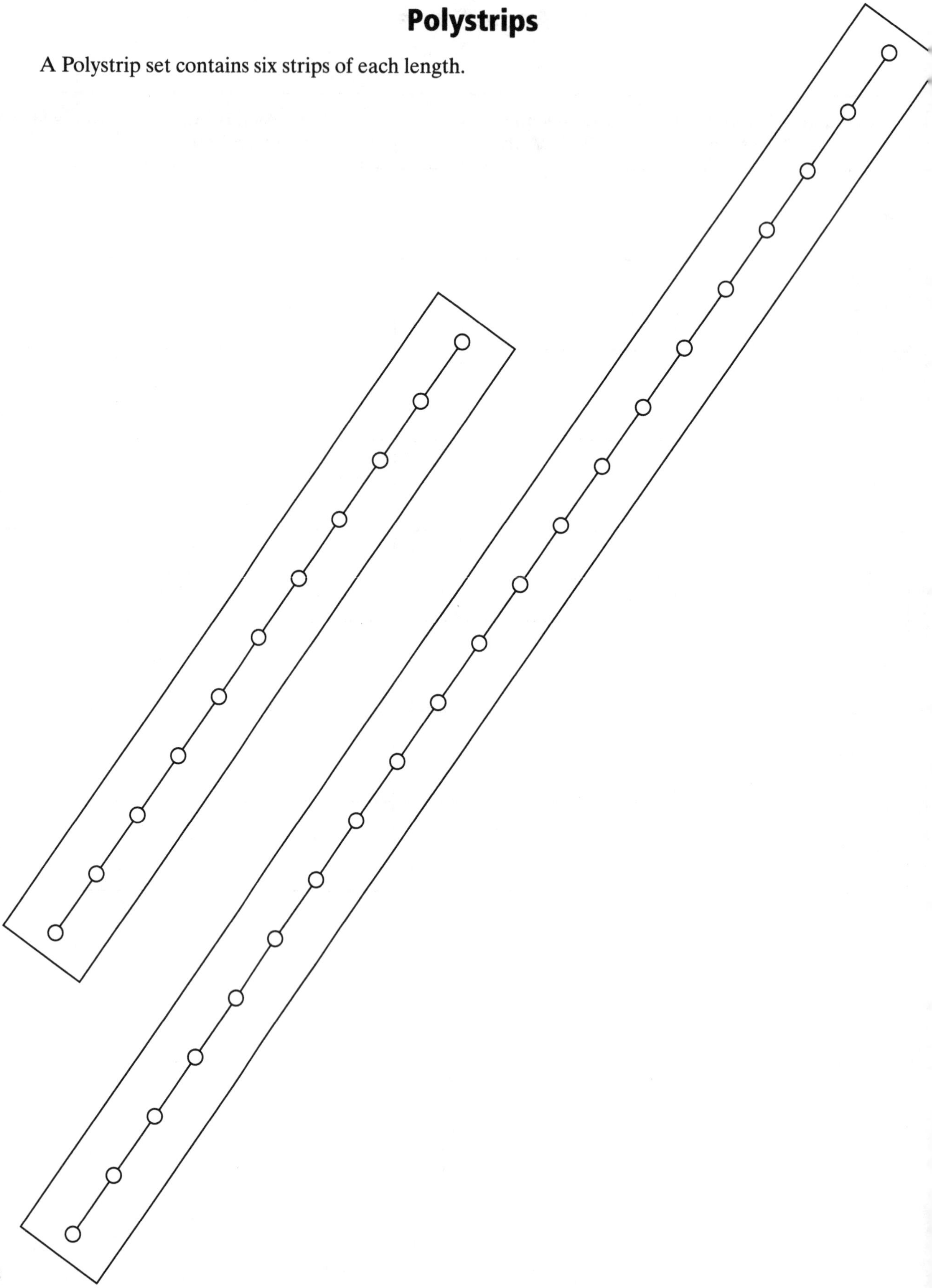

Name ______________________ Date __________ Class __________

Labsheet 4.1B

Building Triangles

Side 1	Side 2	Side 3	Triangle? (yes or no)	Sketch

Name ______________________________ Date ____________ Class ____________

Labsheet 4.2

Building Quadrilaterals

Side 1	Side 2	Side 3	Side 4	Quadrilateral? (yes or no)	Sketch

Name ______________________ Date __________ Class __________

Labsheet 4.3

The Quadrilateral Game

Row 6	A quadrilateral that is a square	**Add 1 point to your score and skip your turn**	A rectangle that is not a square	A quadrilateral with two obtuse angles	A quadrilateral with exactly one pair of parallel sides	A quadrilateral with one pair of opposite side lengths equal
Row 5	**Subtract 2 points from your score and skip your turn**	A quadrilateral that is not a rectangle	A quadrilateral with two pairs of consecutive angles that are equal	A quadrilateral with all four angles the same size	A quadrilateral with four lines of symmetry	A quadrilateral that is a rectangle
Row 4	A quadrilateral with no reflection or rotation symmetry	A quadrilateral with four right angles	**Skip a turn**	A quadrilateral with exactly one pair of consecutive side lengths that are equal	A quadrilateral with exactly one right angle	A quadrilateral with two 45° angles
Row 3	A quadrilateral with no angles equal	A quadrilateral with one pair of equal opposite angles	A quadrilateral with exactly one pair of opposite angles that are equal	**Add 2 points to your score and skip your turn**	A quadrilateral with no sides parallel	A quadrilateral with exactly two right angles
Row 2	A quadrilateral with both pairs of adjacent side lengths equal	A quadrilateral with two pairs of equal opposite angles	A quadrilateral with a diagonal that divides it into two identical shapes	A quadrilateral that is a rhombus	A quadrilateral with 180° rotation symmetry	**Subtract 1 point from your score and skip your turn**
Row 1	A quadrilateral with one diagonal that is a line of symmetry	A quadrilateral with no side lengths equal	A quadrilateral with exactly one angle greater than 180°	A parallelogram that is not a rectangle	**Add 3 points to your score and skip your turn**	A quadrilateral with two pairs of opposite side lengths equal
	Column 1	Column 2	Column 3	Column 4	Column 5	Column 6

At a Glance

PACING: ________

Mathematical Goals

Launch

Materials

Explore

Materials

Summarize

Materials

Glossary

A

acute angle An angle whose measure is less than 90°.

angle The figure formed by two rays or line segments that have a common vertex. Angles are measured in degrees. The angle at point A on the triangle below is identified as angle BAC or $\angle BAC$. The sides of an angle are rays that have the vertex as a starting point. Each of the three angles below is formed by the joining of two rays.

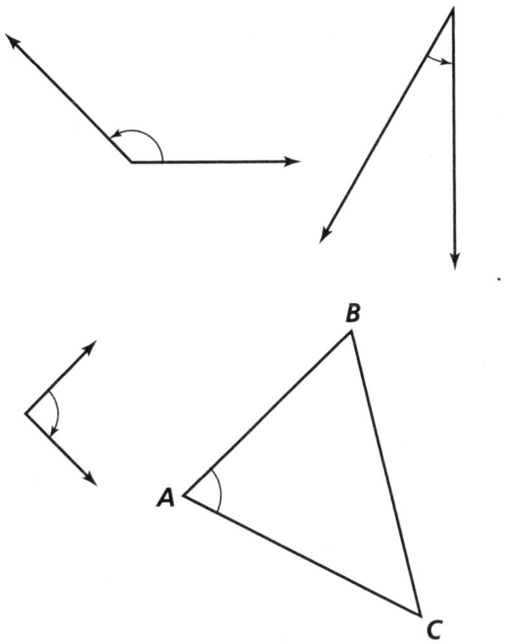

angle sum The sum of all the measures of the interior angles of a polygon.

C

central angle An angle with a vertex at the center of a circle and whose sides are radii of the circle.

D

degree A unit of measure of angles is also equal to $\frac{1}{360}$ of a complete circle. The angle in Figure 1 measures about 1 degree (1°); 360 of these would just fit around a point and fill in a complete circle; 90 of them make a right angle.

diagonal A line segment connecting two non-adjacent vertices of a polygon. All quadrilaterals have two diagonals, as shown below. The two diagonals of a square are equal in length, and the two diagonals of a rectangle are equal in length. A pentagon has five diagonals. A hexagon has six diagonals.

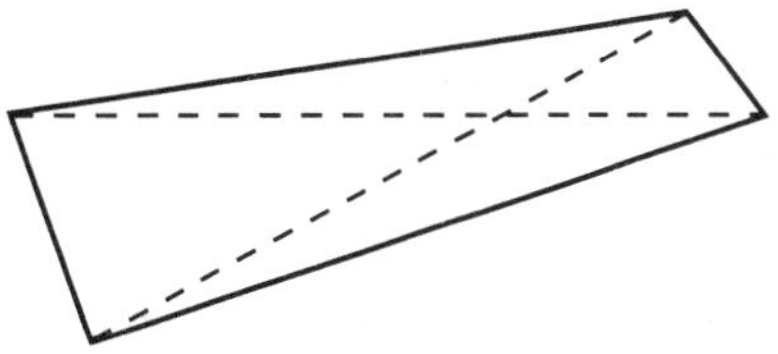

E

equilateral triangle A triangle with all three sides the same length.

exterior angle An angle at a vertex of a polygon where the sides of the angle are one side of the polygon and the extension of the other side meeting at that vertex.

I

interior angle The angle inside a polygon formed by the polygon's sides.

isosceles triangle A triangle with two sides the same length.

irregular polygon A polygon which has at least two sides with different lengths or two angles with different measures.

L

line of symmetry A line such that if a shape is folded over this line the two halves of the shape match exactly.

line segment A line segment consists of two points of a line and all the points between these two points.

M

midpoint The point that divides a line segment into two segments of equal length.

O

obtuse angle An angle whose measure is greater than 90° and less than 180°.

Figure 1

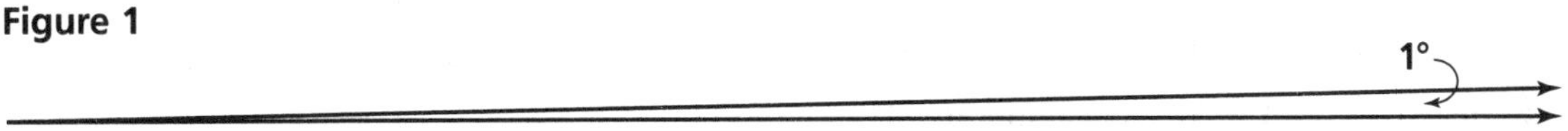

P

parallel lines Lines in a plane that never meet. The opposite sides of a regular hexagon are parallel.

Polygons A and B each have one pair of opposite sides parallel.

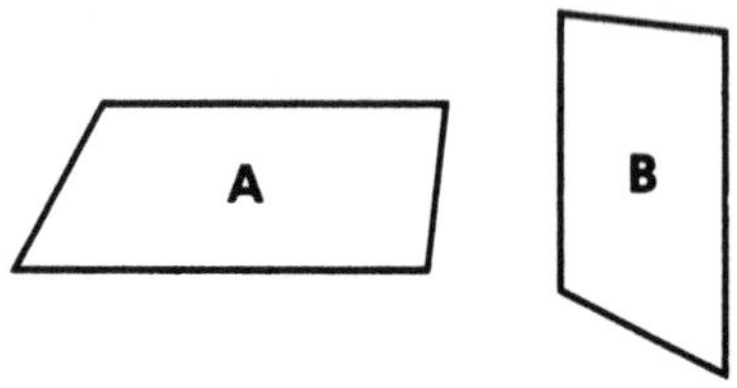

Polygons C, D, and E each have two pairs of opposite sides parallel.

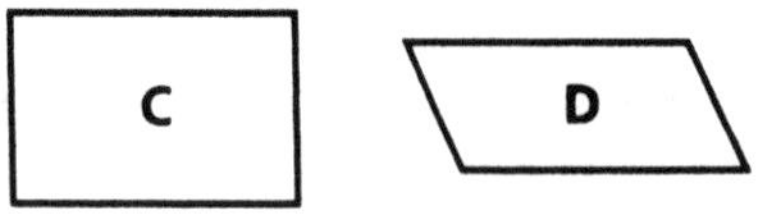

parallelogram A quadrilateral with opposite sides parallel. Both pairs of opposite angles are also equal. In the definition of parallel lines, figure D, rectangle C, and square E are all parallelograms.

perpendicular lines Two lines that intersect to form right angles.

polygon A shape formed by line segments so that each of the segments meets exactly two other segments, and all of the points where the segments meet are endpoints of the segments.

Polygons

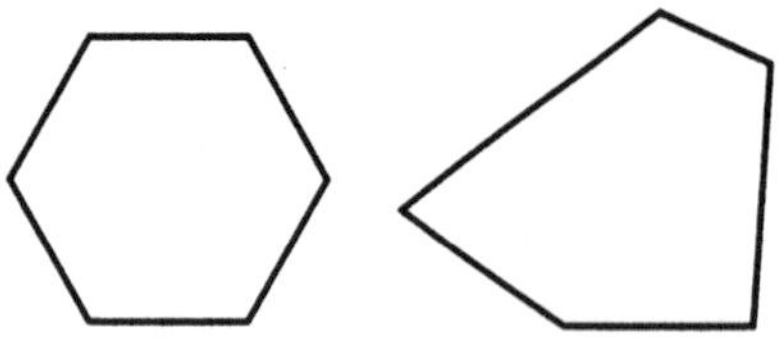

Special polygon names use Greek prefixes that tell the number of sides or the number of angles in the polygon.

- triangle: A polygon with 3 sides and angles
- quadrilateral: A polygon with 4 sides and angles
- pentagon: A polygon with 5 sides and angles
- hexagon: A polygon with 6 sides and angles
- heptagon: A polygon with 7 sides and angles
- octagon: A polygon with 8 sides and angles
- nonagon (also called enneagon): A polygon with 9 sides and angles
- decagon: A polygon with 10 sides and angles
- dodecagon: A polygon with 12 sides and angles

Q

quadrilateral A polygon with four sides.

Quadrilaterals

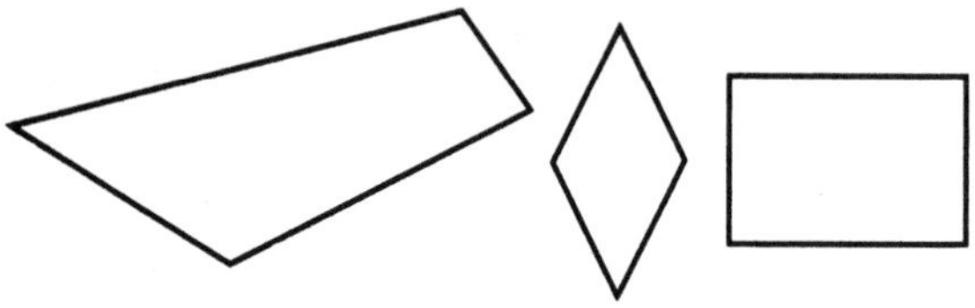

R

ray A part of a line consisting of a point, called an endpoint, and all the points on the line on one side of the endpoint.

rectangle A parallelogram with all right angles. Squares are a special type of rectangle.

Rectangles

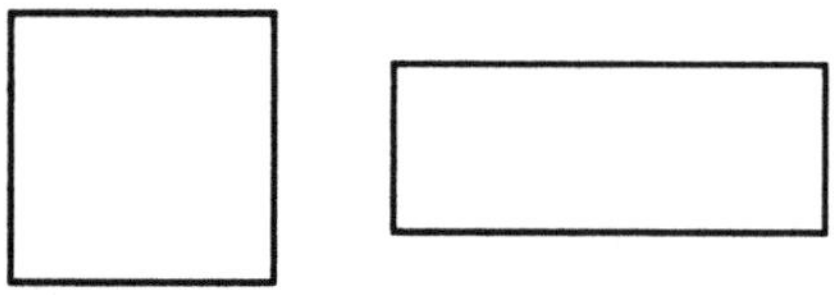

reflectional symmetry A shape with reflectional symmetry has two halves that are mirror images of each other.

regular polygon A polygon that has all of its sides equal and all of its angles equal. The hexagon below is regular, but the pentagon is not regular, because its sides and its angles are not equal.

Regular **Not Regular**

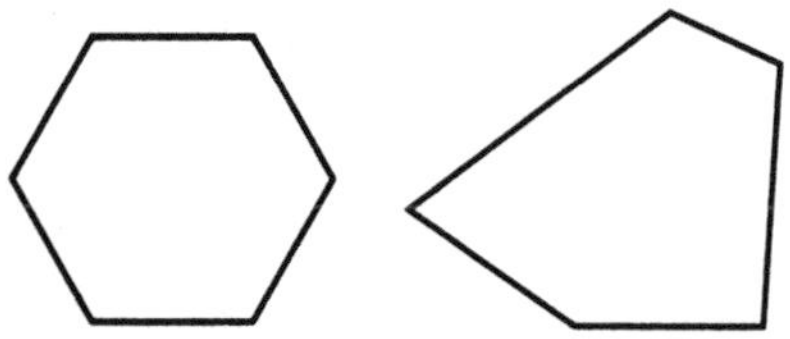

rhombus A quadrilateral that has all sides the same length.

right angle An angle that measures 90°. A rectangle has four right angles.

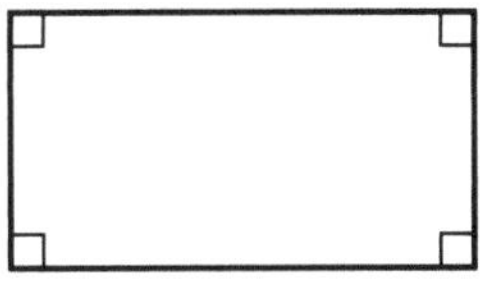

rotational symmetry A shape has rotational symmetry if it can be rotated less than a full turn about its center point to a position where it looks exactly as it did before it was rotated.

S

scalene triangle A triangle with no side lengths equal.

square A rectangle with all side lengths equal. Squares have four right angles and four equal sides.

straight angle An angle that measures 180°.

T

tiling Also called a tessellation. The filling of a plane surface with geometric shapes without gaps or overlaps. These shapes are usually regular polygons or other common polygons. The tiling below is made of triangles. You could remove some of the line segments to create a tiling of parallelograms, or remove still more to create a tiling of hexagons. In a tiling, a vertex is a point where the corners of the polygons fit together.

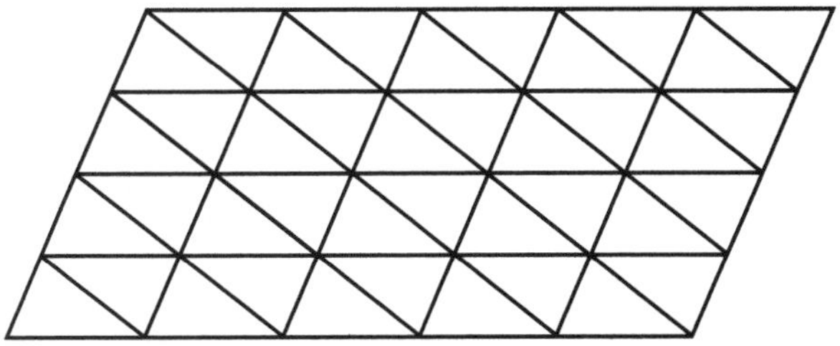

transversal A line that intersects two or more lines. Lines *s* and *t* are transversals.

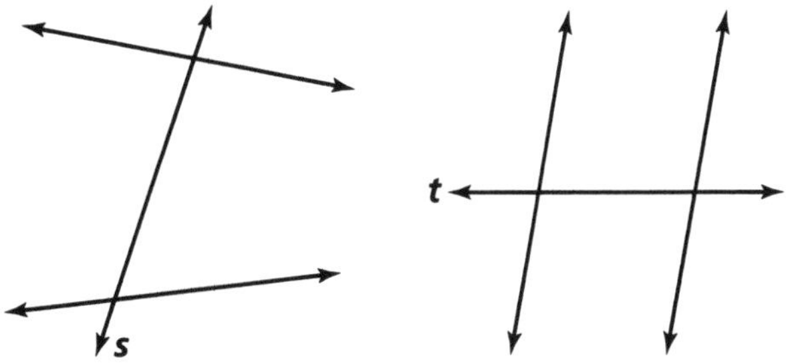

trapezoid A quadrilateral with at least one pair of opposite sides parallel. This definition means that parallelograms are trapezoids.

Trapezoids

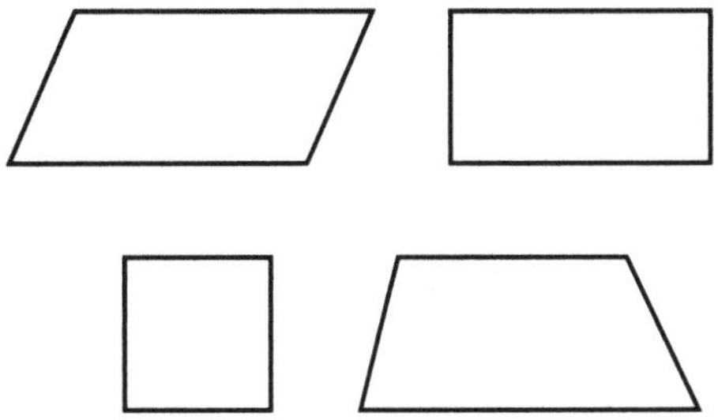

V

vertex A corner of a polygon. For example, *G, H, I, J,* and *K* are all vertices in the pentagon below. All angles have vertices; for example, in the hexagon below, angle *AFE* has a vertex at *F.*

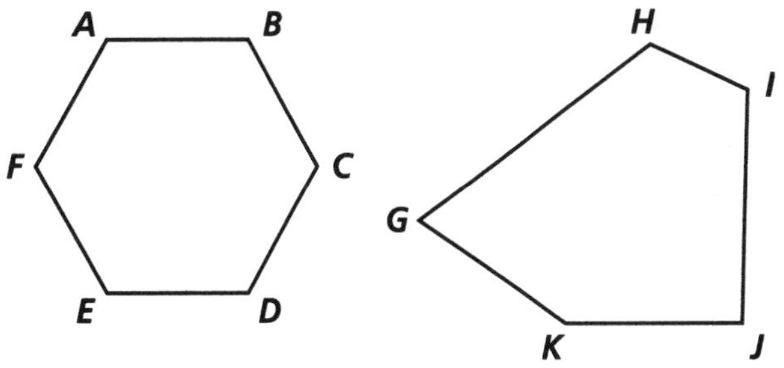

GLOSSARY

Index

Acknowledgments

Team Credits

The people who made up the **Connected Mathematics 2** team—representing editorial, editorial services, design services, and production services—are listed below. Bold type denotes core team members.

Leora Adler, Judith Buice, Kerry Cashman, Patrick Culleton, Sheila DeFazio, Richard Heater, **Barbara Hollingdale, Jayne Holman,** Karen Holtzman, **Etta Jacobs,** Christine Lee, Carolyn Lock, Catherine Maglio, **Dotti Marshall,** Rich McMahon, Eve Melnechuk, Kristin Mingrone, Terri Mitchell, **Marsha Novak,** Irene Rubin, Donna Russo, Robin Samper, Siri Schwartzman, **Nancy Smith,** Emily Soltanoff, **Mark Tricca,** Paula Vergith, Roberta Warshaw, Helen Young

Additional Credits

Diana Bonfilio, Mairead Reddin, Michael Torocsik, nSight, Inc.

Technical Illustration

Seven Worldwide

Cover Design

tom white.images